Who should know what ?

J. A. Barnes

Who Should Know What?

**Social Science,
Privacy and Ethics**

Cambridge University Press

Cambridge
London   New York   New Rochelle
Melbourne   Sydney

Published by the Press Syndicate of the University of Cambridge
The Pitt Building, Trumpington Street, Cambridge CB2 1RP
32 East 57th Street, New York NY 10022 USA
296 Beaconsfield Parade, Middle Park, Melbourne 3206, Australia

Originally published in a paperback edition in Great Britain by
Penguin Books, Ltd., 1979.
United States hardcover and paperback editions first published by
the Cambridge University Press, 1980 with corrections.

Printed in the United States of America

Typeset by Richard Clay (The Chaucer Press) Ltd., Bungay, Suffolk
Printed and bound by the Murray Printing Company, Westford,
Massachusetts
Library of Congress Catalog Number: 79-9656
ISBN 0 521 23359 3 hard covers
ISBN 0 521 29934 9 paperback

... the only safe way to avoid violating principles of professional ethics is to refrain from doing social research altogether' (Bronfenbrenner 1952: 453)

'And in a society of power and wealth, knowledge is valued as an instrument of power and wealth, and also, of course, as an ornament in conversation, a tid-bit in a quiz program' (Mills 1963: 606)

Contents

Preface

Every book, unless it is carefully controlled in the making, tends to grow into a prolegomenon to a complete history of the universe. This book has been delimited as much by the fortuitous range of my competence as by the existence of any natural breaks in the subjects I try to tackle. I am concerned with empirical inquiries made by social scientists but do not provide a handbook on how to conduct research; many good textbooks are readily available. I concentrate on the ethical problems that arise in connexion with social inquiry. These cannot be isolated from the politics of social research, and I discuss the distribution of power in the conduct of research in connexion with ethical issues, rather than in its own right. My discussion is intended to be analytic rather than normative, for I try to provide not a cookery book for answering ethical queries but an historically-based framework within which the resolution of ethical questions may be considered and debated. My own views on the ethical implications of social research are, however, inevitably disseminated throughout the book, and I well realize that my preference for presenting ethical questions in an historical and political framework is itself part of my own ethical stance. I realize also that my effort to write about social science in general will be regarded as subversive by those of my colleagues to whom disciplinary boundaries are barricades to be defended.

The book deals with practice or praxis, in two respects. I discuss the development of empirical social inquiry rather than of the philosophical and epistemological bases of social understanding. For purposes of this book I simply make the gigantic assumption that some kind of social science is possible. Likewise I try to deal with ethical issues as they have arisen in

Preface

the actual practice of social research, with what we might call pastoral ethics, and say nothing about more fundamental and general problems in moral and political philosophy. My examples, too, are drawn largely from those disciplines and parts of the world about which I know a little: from sociology, social anthropology and psychology rather than from political science and economics; from Britain, Australia, India, north America and Scandinavia, thus neglecting much of the world and the communist countries in particular. I concentrate on issues that are distinctive of research in social science and neglect those ethical questions that social scientists share with scholars in other disciplines, for example in their relations with colleagues, students and administrators. The book is thus more limited in scope than some might have preferred; but it would have been impracticable to extend it to include these other important topics.

Throughout the book I use a masculine pronoun when referring to a social scientist. I do not intend to imply that all social scientists are male. Unfortunately the compound pronouns *he or she*, *hers/his*, *s/he* etc., still seem clumsy, and the other expedient I tried out, of shifting from one sex to the other at random, seemed unduly distracting. The English language greatly needs a common gender pronoun, more human than *it*.

My title is adapted from Robert S. Lynd's *Knowledge for what?*, a book I was given to read by I. Schapera while I was a graduate student in the University of Cape Town. In writing this book I have been helped by many friends and colleagues. I wish to mention particularly the assistance given by Martin Barnes, Leonard Berkowitz, Gerald D. Berreman, Kjeld Brœkhus, David Donnison, Paula Glick, R. A. Gould, L. R. Hiatt, Cathie Marsh, John Mulvaney, D. M. Thompson, J. P. S. Uberoi and Gehan Wijeyewardene. Frances Barnes commented in detail on an early draft. Shortly after beginning work on the book I gave three lectures in Bangalore, at the Institute for Social and Economic Change, on some of the ethical issues in social research that seemed relevant in an Indian context during the Emergency. These lectures have now been published as *The ethics of inquiry*

10

Preface

in social science. I am much indebted to M. N. Srinivas for getting me started on this theme.

My own practical experience of social inquiry has been confined to central Africa and Norway. I have however been most fortunate in supervising the work of students carrying out inquiries of various kinds in Britain, Australia and several parts of Asia, Oceania and Latin America. Any merit this book may have stems from what I have learnt from them.

J. A. B.
Churchill College
22 April 1977

1 Social research in an ethical context

This book is about some of the ethical problems that arise in connexion with social research. At first glance, these problems seem rather mixed: what questions ought a government to include on its census forms, what information about individuals ought to be published openly or in disguised form, what constraints on a social inquiry ought to be placed by the sponsor who pays for it, what practical use ought to be made of scientific knowledge about how societies operate, and so on. Do individuals have an absolute right to privacy, or is this right overridden by the needs of the search for knowledge? Yet despite their apparent heterogeneity, these problems all arise out of a fairly simple social process, a process that may be thought of as a structured interaction between various kinds of people. Social research is systematic inquiry into the ways in which people, and the social institutions that they create and operate, behave in relation to one another and to their environment. This research takes many forms, ranging from asking simple questions about preferences among brands of breakfast cereals to observing over many years how a newly established parliament establishes its customary modes of procedure. In this book our attention will be focused on part of this range of inquiries, mainly on those carried out by sociologists, social anthropologists and psychologists, both in the real world and within the artificially contrived environment of the laboratory. These are the kinds of social inquiry where ethical issues have been most clearly seen and most often discussed. Nevertheless many of the comments that arise from discussing these inquiries are relevant to other areas of social research where so far ethical matters have been ignored.

Whatever form the inquiry may take, whether it lasts for

13

minutes or years, and whether it occurs in the back of beyond or in a laboratory on the university campus, there are normally four groups or individuals in the process. First there are the people whose preferences for cereals or propensities for parliamentary innovation form the focus of the inquiry. These people are usually referred to as the 'subjects' of the inquiry, or the 'objects' of the research. Neither term is satisfactory and I shall call them 'citizens', for it is their rights and duties as fellow human beings, and as members of organized societies, with which we shall be mainly concerned. Then there are the people who carry out the inquiry and who analyse the findings; these are the 'scientists', though we shall not forget that they too are citizens and that they do not escape from their commitments as members of society by putting on the white coat, blue overalls or safari jacket of the social scientist. Most of the problems we shall consider impinge on the relation between the scientist and the citizens he (or she) studies. But there are two other parties to the process of inquiry who have interests and obligations that have to be taken into account. In most instances of social inquiry there is a sponsor, some philanthropic patron, charitable foundation, commercial organization or government department which provides the financial and material resources for the inquiry to be made and which may, in many cases, want some tangible return for the investment it has made. Sometimes scientists are able to sponsor their own inquiries, and sometimes a group of citizens may sponsor an inquiry into some aspect of its own affairs. But in general there is a separate sponsor whose interest in the inquiry differs from those of the scientist and the citizens. Lastly, in many instances but not in all, there are the individuals and institutions who are known sometimes as facilitators but whom we shall call gatekeepers, who control access to the citizens. For example, in a country like Britain, anyone with a clipboard or tape recorder in his, or more often her, hand can stop citizens in the street and ask their opinion about who is going to win the next election; no gatekeeper intervenes. But to be able to ask the same question of a sample of workers in a factory, the scientist may first have to negotiate with managements and trade unions, even though these

14

bodies are not themselves the focus of his inquiry. Likewise a scientist who is interested in, say, the inheritance of property may be able to carry out his inquiries in his own country without needing to obtain permission from any authority; but if he tries to make the same inquiry in another country he may first have to satisfy the foreign government that the inquiry is in the national interest, as it sees it, and that the investigation will be carried out in a way acceptable to it. Gatekeepers may control access not only to citizens but also to archives and other records, and sometimes to reports on other scientific inquiries. Indeed, after a scientist has completed his research he may need permission from somebody not directly connected with the inquiry before he is free to publish or act on what he has found out.

Social inquiry may thus be seen as a process of interaction and negotiation between scientist, sponsor, gatekeeper and citizens. These four parties to the process do not, of course, exist in isolation from the rest of the world. The wider community is involved in the process in several ways. The sponsor is often some branch of government and thus ostensibly the embodiment of some aspect of public interest, however this may be defined. The output of the process of inquiry is often publication, i.e. transmission to the world at large, and this may be followed by action taken by the community or by some part of it.

If the scientists and others directly concerned with a particular inquiry all belong to the same national or cultural community, there is likely to be some amount of consensus among them about basic social values, though, so I shall argue, social research as we know it depends on the acceptance of a plurality of interests and views within the community. In the special case of what I call the 'colonial situation', there is minimal consensus of views between the citizens and the scientists; inquiries and publications then take a distinctive form. But whether or not they share a common set of cultural values, each of the parties in the process of inquiry is certain to have its own interests and values, its own expectations or lack of them, about what may or should emerge from the inquiry, and maybe its own ideas about what is morally right or wrong in making inquiries into social phenomena. It may have

15

its own perception of the nature of social science. These ideas and expectations constrain the range of possibilities in social research, and impinge not only on the ethical issues with which we are concerned but on other aspects of the process of inquiry as well. A great deal has been written about how to conduct empirical inquiries in social science, but most of the topics in handbooks on scientific method do not concern us here. We are not primarily concerned with questions of internal validity and reliability and the like, but only with those aspects of the negotiations between the parties, or of the lack of negotiation, that raise ethical issues.

By ethical problems I mean those that arise when we try to decide between one course of action and another not in terms of expediency or efficiency but by reference to standards of what is morally right or wrong. We all face, and solve, problems of this kind in everyday life. For example, most people probably have views one way or the other on whether to facilitate the procurement of abortion, to boycott fruit from South Africa, to encourage separate schools for Pakistani girls in Britain, and to oppose demands for euthanasia. For most of us, our views on these and similar matters are determined mainly by reference to ends which we hold to be good or bad in themselves; we may believe, for instance, that the institutionalized inequality entailed by apartheid is wrong in itself, and that to buy South African fruit would be to condone or support this wrong. Likewise, in social science, we may believe that if, as scientists, we are told something in confidence by a citizen we cannot betray that confidence by passing on the information without the citizen's permission, because betrayal is wrong in itself. But just as we may weigh our moral dislike of apartheid against the likely effectiveness of our boycott in contributing to its disappearance (or to its perpetuation), so likewise as scientists we may weigh our obligation to the citizen against the likely harm (or good) to him and to mankind in general that our betrayal of his confidence may entail. In other words, ethical considerations do not necessarily always override considerations of other kinds. Hence, in discussing social research, we must look at practical and pragmatic considerations whenever these bear on ethical issues as they arise in practice.

Honesty may sometimes pay but there are other times when a price has to be paid for being honest, and we should know what the price is before we decide to buy.

Ethical problems are not confined to everyday life and social inquiry. They arise in the natural sciences and in medicine as well. But just as the social sciences differ from the natural sciences in certain structural features, and in their intellectual achievements so far, so do the ethical issues that arise in the two branches of science. Indeed, it is partly because of these differences in achievement that the ethical issues differ. In recent years there has been a good deal of discussion about ethical issues raised by research on nuclear weapons and other means of mass destruction, by the use of high technology on a planet with limited resources, by the possibilities of embryo transfer and genetic engineering. But the ethical problems encountered in natural sciences and, to a lesser extent, in medicine relate to the application of scientific knowledge in the real world rather than to the process of scientific discovery in the laboratory. Though in the future the balance may shift, in social science at the present time ethical problems are posed by the process of social inquiry itself at least as much as by the application of the scientific findings of these inquiries. We are certainly deeply concerned about the use made of information collected from individual citizens, and groups of citizens, in the course of social inquiry, but this use is, more often than not, little more than the application of common sense principles or traditional ways of behaving rather than of some newly discovered law of social interaction. For example, during the Vietnam war, social scientists asked peasants in Indochina questions designed to elicit the state of their morale and political allegiance; the ethical issue that arose was the alleged use of the banner of scientific inquiry to gain information for the old-fashioned selection of bombing targets, not the devilish application of some scientifically validated principle of morale formation.

Although most of medicine cannot be considered as a branch of social science, ethical issues are salient in both medical research and ordinary medical practice. In some contexts, there is close similarity between medicine and social science in the ethical

17

problems they have to face, and I shall mention some of these. But medical ethics is a well-discussed topic (Barber et al. 1973), and there is no need for me to expand the scope of this book to deal adequately with it.

If we confine ourselves to a simple contrast between natural science and social science, ignoring the middle ground of medicine, then we might argue that ethical issues feature differently in the two branches of science because social science is comparatively immature. Indeed, some of its critics condemn social science to a state of permanent adolescence. In social science there is certainly as yet no corpus of interdependent propositions, tested against reality, that can match the formidable body of systematic discovery in natural science. Whether or not there ever will be is open to debate, but there is no doubt that at present there are perilously few tested generalizations in social science that might provide a reliable basis for a programme of social engineering, whether for good or ill. In other words, social science is still largely at an ideographic stage, whereas natural science has long ago moved on to nomothetic knowledge. Consequently, whereas ethical issues in natural science arise mainly in connexion with the practical application of the validated results of laboratory research, in social science they tend to arise at the stage of data collection as well.

But in my view there is a more fundamental difference than this between the two kinds of science. The four-part model of social inquiry that I sketched cannot be applied unchanged to natural science. There are certainly scientists and sponsors, and for certain kinds of research in natural science there are gate-keepers too, who, for example, may control access to expensive or scarce materials. But there are in nature no citizens, no fellow human beings with whom the natural scientist has to negotiate. There is no society for the prevention of cruelty to atoms, and although Heisenberg's principle of uncertainty may perhaps be understood to entail some kind of feedback relation between the atomic physicist and the particles he studies, the principle does not permit negotiation between them. Only when transmutated atoms and particles impinge on citizens do ethical problems arise.

18

Hence the discussion of ethical problems in natural science turns much more on the application of, rather than the discovery of, scientific knowledge not only because there is so much that can be applied but also because only in its application does natural science impinge on the interests of citizens. Genetic engineering is an exception to the general rule, for here there are grounds for doubting whether scientists will have the technical capacity for controlling how artificial genes, the material by-products of intellectual inquiry, may apply themselves to citizens and to the environment. The exceptional status of genetic engineering is shown by the virtually unprecedented agreement among scientists not to pursue at all certain specified lines of research.

In general, ethical issues in natural science have arisen during the last thirty years because of our greatly increased ability, by utilizing recent scientific discoveries, to modify, deliberately and intentionally, the environment in which we live. The shift in the distribution of power that has occurred in natural science is, in the first instance, between man and nature, rather than between man and man, though it is only because man depends on nature that man's increased power to control or destroy nature raises ethical issues. Men have controlled and destroyed one another long before the emergence of social science, and as yet the contribution that social science can make to techniques of control and destruction is quite modest. The dangers inherent in social science inquiry lie in its potential contribution towards improving old forms of tyranny and oppression rather than its capacity to provide new ones. Yet because the subject matter of social science is people and their relations with one another, these dangers are inherent at all stages in the process of inquiry and not merely in the applications of the results of research.

Social science is younger than natural science and the discussion of ethical issues in social science is younger still. Serious and sustained consideration of ethical questions began in earnest only about twenty-five years ago. Some commentators write about these questions as if they are eternal, not bound by time and space and historical circumstance, and treat it as a fortunate accident that within the last few years social scientists have belatedly begun

19

to think about them. The burst of interest in ethics during the last ten years does indeed give the appearance of being caused in part by a sense of guilt that these questions have been neglected for so long; we must try to make up for lost time. Handbooks on research methods, which previously had nothing to say on ethical matters, now often devote a section explicitly to discussions of ethics (e.g. Sjoberg and Nett 1968: 120–28, 327–32). One recent textbook (Smith 1975) even begins with a chapter on ethics, with the expressed intention of putting first things first. Ethical issues are now set out didactically in professional journals. Professional associations of sociologists, anthropologists and other social scientists have drawn up their own codes of ethics or have involved themselves in many acrimonious debates before coming to the conclusion that their ethical issues are far too complicated to be handled by a professional code. Elections to ethics committees of professional bodies have been contested by scientists who hold divergent views about the policy their association should adopt on ethical issues, and ethical considerations have influenced the choice of members to fill ordinary administrative positions (Berreman 1973a: 8). Sessions on ethics are held at annual professional conferences on the same footing as those on such familiar topics as stratification, kinship and deviance. A new label, 'ethicist', has appeared to identify a social scientist who concerns himself with the ethical implications of social inquiry. Ethical interest has become one more variable to be correlated with others; experiments show that psychologists express more stringent views on ethics than do most other people (Sullivan and Deiker 1973).

This activity among scientists has been matched by the major sponsors of social science research, some of whom have now codified the ethical terms and conditions on which they are prepared to provide financial support. In those countries where social inquiry has become a regular feature of the social scene even citizens, either individually or collectively, have begun to state explicitly the increasingly stringent conditions that must be met before they are prepared to cooperate in the process of social inquiry.

Ethical issues may be only extrinsic to natural science but nevertheless, ever since the explosion of the first atomic bomb, many natural scientists have taken a lively professional interest in ethical questions that arise out of pure research as well as from its practical application. We might therefore interpret the growth of interest in ethics among some social scientists as merely another example of the immature, unsuccessful social science trying to emulate its more successful co-disciplines in the natural and medical sciences. The natural sciences have provided social scientists with models of inquiry in the past; why not also borrow from them their recently acquired social concern?

This diffusion effect exists but can account for only part of the increase of ethical awareness among social scientists. Nowadays there is a good deal more self-consciousness than there used to be among social scientists about the desirability or appropriateness of borrowing methods of procedure from the natural sciences. Although some continue to aim at building social science to a plan that matches that of natural science, others stress the irreconcilable differences between them. Very roughly speaking, the first group acclaims the actual or potential propositional or nomothetic characteristics of social science while the second sees social science as qualitative and interpretative. If a concern with ethics was due mainly to diffusion from natural science we would expect this concern to be more marked among members of the first moiety, who are much closer to natural science in most of their thinking, and less prominent among the second, whose orientation is closer to the humanities than to the so-called hard sciences. This is not so. Thus the fact that both branches of science have become aware of the ethical implications of their research activities at about the same time, immediately following the end of the Second World War, should not be attributed mainly to intellectual contagion. Certainly the actions of bodies such as the various national societies for social responsibility in (natural) science and the Association of Atomic Scientists have had some impact on social scientists. But a better analysis of what has happened in social science in this respect during the last thirty years must be based on changes in the wider social structure within which social scientists

21

operate, changes which have had an effect also on the thinking and responses of natural scientists.

Increased awareness in ethical matters has its dangers. Before long lecture courses will be announced on 'Introductory ethics for social scientists' and 'Advanced ethics'. Proposals for a course on 'anthropological ethics' have already been made (Appell 1976). But then the fashion will pass, and the next trendy subject will take its place. My fear will prove to be misplaced if social scientists, and the public at large, come to see that the current accentuation of interest in the ethics of social inquiry is not just a transient fad that will soon disappear but is rather the outcome of an historical process whose effects are likely to be with us for a long time to come. My thesis is that the recent increase in concern about what topics shall be investigated, where support for the inquiry shall come from, how the data shall be collected and aggregated, and how the results of the inquiry shall be published has not come about accidentally. It springs from an historical shift in the balance of power between the four parties to the research process, and from the institutionalization of social inquiry in the ambient culture of industrialized societies. It is one outcome of a movement away from positivism towards a hermeneutic view of knowledge, and from an evaluation of knowledge as a source of enlightenment to an evaluation in terms of power and property. The basis of ethical concern in social science is therefore significantly different from that of the growth of ethical awareness among natural scientists and among those who see themselves threatened by the application of natural science.

Social research entails the possibility of destroying the privacy and autonomy of the individual, of providing more ammunition to those already in power, of laying the groundwork for an invincibly oppressive state. Yet we would be fatally misled if we inferred that to avoid these objectionable consequences we should stop making social inquiries, or that the main threat to our liberties as citizens comes from the activities of social scientists. Douglas (1976:xiv) may create too rosy an impression when he says that 'We know of no single instance in which our research has injured anyone'; he cannot be referring to all of social

22

inquiry (cf. Reynolds 1972 : 695). Nevertheless he is right to assert the relative innocuousness of social inquiry. The main dangers lie elsewhere, in the insensitive or malign application of traditional techniques of social control, in the unsophisticated utilization of existing information carelessly or with evil intent, and in the unmonitored working-out of social processes of concentration and homogenization. In a recent survey of *The technology of political control* (Ackroyd et al. 1977), almost no reference is made to any contribution by social science. In this book we are then concerned with an activity which is a threat, but only a minor threat, to liberty but which also constitutes the only technique whereby liberty and diversity may be preserved for the future and enhanced.

We can begin then by looking at the way in which this process of inquiry has altered during the last one hundred and fifty years or so, from the beginnings of organized social inquiry in the early nineteenth century up to the present time when, as so often in the past, social science is said to be in a state of crisis. I shall argue that initially empirical inquiries in social science conformed to a natural science paradigm, in which citizens and scientists were not only socially but also analytically and epistemologically unequal; the new knowledge which was expected to emerge was perceived as a source of enlightenment for the elite. With the passage of years, citizens have come much closer to scientists not only socially but, with the decline in positivist theories of knowledge, epistemologically as well. At the same time the power of sponsors and gatekeepers vis-à-vis the scientists has increased and, partly by analogy with natural science, the knowledge gained by social science inquiry has been seen by sponsors as a source of power. Gatekeepers and citizens, however, have in some instances come to perceive knowledge as a kind of private property, whether or not it may also be a source of power, for which there is only a restricted market. This new perception challenges the validity of the goal of a unified universalistic social science analogous, in the world of social relations, to natural science in the world of nature.

Empirical inquiry in sociology began with the poor, in social

23

anthropology with natives, and in psychology, after an early period when highly trained respondents were used (Schultz 1969), with students. In all three contexts, scientists were powerful and the objects of their inquiries were weak (cf. Kelman 1972: 990). Hence the natural science paradigm could be applied and ethical issues did not arise. Nowadays the balance of power has changed and the foci of attention have been enlarged (Berreman 1973b: 58). I suggest that any worthwhile practical attempt to resolve ethical issues in social inquiry has to take into account the distribution of power between scientists, citizens, sponsors and gatekeepers, and will often involve negotiation between the parties rather than the inflexible application of operationalized rules of procedure. These negotiations will be facilitated if the parties take into account not only their diverse interests and their powers over one another but also their diverse perceptions of the objectives and likely outcome of the inquiry. This assumption of legitimate diversity or, in other words, of pluralism in culture and society is, in my view, a necessary condition for social science to flourish. By the same token, pluralism is also a necessary condition for the recognition of a right to privacy, for the need to balance the scientist's and sponsor's interests in finding out against the citizen's interest in preventing them from doing so; privacy may also include the citizen's right to remain in ignorance about himself. But nowadays the existence of pluralism is continually threatened by concentrations of power, and the future of social science is thus continually in jeopardy.

The following chapters fall into three groups. In Chapters 2, 3 and 4, I discuss the historical development of social inquiry from the early nineteenth century until now. In Chapters 5, 6 and 7 I talk about various aspects of the process of inquiry: why people want to make inquiries or to prevent them from being made, the different settings in which they are made, and the ways in which the results of the inquiries can be made public or kept hidden. In the last two chapters I look at social scientists as a specialist group, and at their relation to the wider society.

2. The natural science paradigm

Little attention was paid to ethical problems by the pioneer social scientists who began to make systematic inquiries into various aspects of social life during the nineteenth century. Although many imperfections in their methods of social inquiry may be explained by the fact that, to a large extent, they were starting from scratch, it would be wrong to imagine that the absence of interest in ethics was due to the lack of any developed tradition of empirical research on which they might have drawn. A concern with ethics is not a methodological feature, like for example path analysis and one-way screens, that appears only as the result of many decades of trial and error in techniques of social inquiry. Ethical questions in other contexts had been under continual discussion for more than two and a half thousand years by the time the first social scientists got to work collecting data. The lack of ethical concern in the context of social inquiry springs not from lack of experience in handling ethical questions but from the particular perception of the process of inquiry held by the scientists and those who supported or tolerated their activities.

A convenient label for the model of social inquiry that characterized data collection and analysis during the nineteenth century is the natural science paradigm. By this I mean a process of inquiry in which the scientist treats the citizens as far as possible as he would treat natural or inanimate objects. The paradigm has the following features: (1) the participation of the citizens in the process of inquiry is limited to being observed or responding to questions and other stimuli supplied by the scientist; they have no part to play in deciding what shall be investigated, how the inquiry shall be carried out, how the data shall be interpreted and analysed, and how the results shall be disseminated; (2) the scientist tries to minimize the extent to which the citizens' behaviour is altered by the observations he makes on them, and assumes that the disturbances can be kept significantly small; (3) the raw data collected in the inquiry are regarded as objective, in the sense that any competent scientist would obtain the same data from any given event and do not in any way depend for their validity on whether or not the citizens are aware of them; (4) while sponsors may legitimately exercise their discretion in choosing what inquiries to support, decisions about how an inquiry shall be carried out shall be made by the scientist alone; and (5) gatekeepers are obstacles to be overcome. This paradigm is, of course, an ideal type, though many actual inquiries conformed very closely to it and many still do. In this paradigm there is no room for ethical considerations, or, more precisely, for ethical considerations that are specific to the process of inquiry. This aspect of the paradigm is expressed, with characteristic forthrightness, in a remark by Homans (1949:330): 'People who write about methodology often forget that it is a matter of strategy, not of morals.'

Nineteenth-century scientists recognized the rights and duties they had towards other human beings, and did not suspend recognition when certain of these human beings came to be the objects of scientific scrutiny; to this extent the citizen was never completely assimilated to the plant under the microscope or the chemical in the crucible. Nevertheless the natural science paradigm remained an ideal, not only in Weber's special sense but also as a model to which the aspiring social scientists should approximate as closely as possible if he was to be truly scientific (cf. Filstead 1970).

Here there is space only to sketch very briefly the historical context in which the natural science paradigm appeared as the initial model for social inquiry. Although social science has established itself as a major branch of higher learning only during the twentieth century, it has a long and complex intellectual heritage which enthusiastic historians of ideas have traced back, with varying degrees of plausibility, to the philosophers and theologians of

26

classical Greece and ancient India (Becker and Barnes 1952; Gouldner 1965a). But these intellectual roots, though they are still important for an understanding of some of today's theoretical debates, do not directly concern us. The practice of social inquiry, as distinct from the corpus of social theory on which it is explicitly or implicitly based, is much more recent (cf. Oberschall 1972). Throughout the centuries thinkers and writers have pronounced on the characteristics of social life as they saw them, and models of society have always been a standard component of every traditional culture. But these models, and the departures from them advocated from time to time by innovating thinkers and prophets, were until recent times not at all based on systematic data collection from the real world. Yet data collection, usually for administrative and fiscal purposes, has almost as long a history, going back to the early empires of the Mediterranean and Middle East. What was missing was any link between aggregated information about trade and taxation and discussions about the nature of society. For example, the Norman Domesday book, for which the data were collected in England in 1086, was 'perhaps the most remarkable administrative accomplishment of the Middle Ages'; unfortunately there were no social scientists ready to analyse its findings until many centuries later.

Continuous data collection may be said to have begun in Europe with the inception of ecclesiastical registration of baptisms, weddings and burials in France in 1308 (Cox 1976:22). Sir William Petty's *Political anatomy of Ireland*, described by Zeisel (1971:100) as 'the first sociographic study', was published in 1691. National censuses began in the eighteenth century, and the first regular official census in Britain was taken in 1801. At the beginning of the nineteenth century, social theorizing and systematic data collection came together significantly for the first time. Abrams argues that, at least so far as Britain is concerned, this union sprang from the model of society held by the followers of Adam Smith, applying his views of political economy to the contemporary problems of a developing industrial society. As he puts it, 'In the face of conflict, since the social order was axiomatically rational, the political economist resorted to information' (Abrams 1968:9). The economists, in the modern restricted sense of the term, were largely able to make use of data collected by the State, but the sociologists and their forerunners, interested then as now in many matters lying outside the regular concern of the state, had to begin to collect their own social data. The first *Statistical account of Scotland* appeared from 1791 to 1799, based on the replies to a questionnaire with 160 items sent to ministers of religion by Sir John Sinclair. In England, Eden used a similar procedure to collect data for his *State of the poor* (1797). Particularly after the passing of the Reform Bill of 1832 the state went beyond its decennial censuses in promoting the Parliamentary Select Committee reports which have become classic studies in the harshness of early industrialization, and private individuals and newly founded associations arose to collect information on topics which were perceived as being of public concern. The Manchester Statistical Society was founded in 1833, and the Statistical Society of London followed in 1834. The London society soon began to implement a programme of surveys, aimed at discovering by the administration of questionnaires information about crime, strikes, rents, and other aspects of the condition of the poor. A few years later, the society began a series of intensive inquiries, using paid agents, into particular communities, again with a focus on the social concomitants of poverty. Indeed, the emphasis on the bad effects of industrialization was derived from the doctrine that the state could function efficiently, and provide the right conditions for a capitalist market economy, only when it was fed with facts so that it could apply the principles of political economy appropriately. The 'statisticians' took it upon themselves to collect information that nowadays might be collected by a government agency or by a university social science department, in the expectation that this information would be taken into account by an essentially rational government in deciding its policies. The initial enthusiasm of the societies for sponsoring their own empirical inquiries soon faded (Elesh 1972) but they continued to flourish, while the data collection undertaken by the state more than made up for the decline. From this point of view, we may say that social theorizing and data collection became linked not so much from an effort to make theorizing scientific as from the adoption of a model of the state and of the economy that required a continual generation of centrally available social data to function efficiently (cf. Wax 1971:23–8).

In Gouldner's scheme for the periodization of the history of sociology, the first half of the nineteenth century is the period of sociological positivism, when one of the tasks of sociology was to map the social world in a cognitive, rational and scientific effort (Gouldner 1970:99). It was also a time when geology constituted the shining exemplar of a successful natural science, and when it was tempting to believe that the separation of fact from opinion would be as easy to maintain in the social world as it was with rocks. Abrams outlines how the difficulties of maintaining a division between fact and opinion soon beset the early British statisticians, many of whom were in 'the front rank of public servants' and not in the least disposed to retreat to an academic ivory tower of pure science. But even if by the end of the century the notion of hard social facts pointing unambiguously to determinate rational social policies had been abandoned, the concept of objective fact remained. The facts of poverty, slums, drunkenness and wages remained waiting to be discovered, even if members of the elite disagreed among themselves about what public response should be made to them. As we might expect, the 'facts' about the condition of the poor were in practice what was said or written about them by their social superiors – employers, landlords, policemen, ministers of religion, factory inspectors, workhouse masters and the like – rather than what they had to say themselves. The words of the poor do appear in abundance in Henry Mayhew's *London labour and the London poor: a cyclopaedia of the condition and earnings of those that* will *work,* cannot *work, and* will not *work* (1851), but his inquiries lay in the field of journalism, outside the mainstream of contemporary social science. Even Mayhew distinguished between 'facts', which were official statistics, and 'opinions', which were the oral testimony of the poor (Humpherys 1971: x: cf. Thompson, E. P., 1967).

It was not until the end of the century that the importance of listening directly to the citizens began to be recognized by social scientists. Thus for example, in 1884 the secretary of the Workman's Association for Defence of British Industry complained, at a session on the condition of the working classes at the annual conference of the National Association for the promotion of social science, that

The writers of the papers had been talking of the working classes as though they were some new-found race, or extinct animal. The best way to have dealt with the question, and to have arrived at the truth, would have been to have called a meeting in the town-hall, where the working man could have spoken for himself. (Pettifer 1885:635)

But the working man, even if he had been allowed to speak, would not have had the resources to produce statistical 'facts' but only 'opinions'. Pettifer also complained, quite rightly according to any modern textbook on scientific method, that statistics, 'figures', could give a distorted picture of the condition of the working class. The next speaker in the discussion disagreed with him; 'on the contrary, it was the most difficult thing to make them express anything else than what they obviously meant'. The main speaker responded to the discussion with the bland comment that 'Statistics were rather the parents of one's views than the sequence of one's own opinions' (Levi 1885:640).

During the same formative period of the nineteenth century there were many other significant parallelisms between the theories advanced to explain social and natural phenomena, notably in the theories of social evolution and natural selection. But at that time, as now, there was considerable diversity in the rival theories put forward to explain history, society and culture, and none of them approximated to the mathematical precision that had already been achieved in the ruling theories of physics and chemistry. On the other hand, there were fewer fundamental controversies about how to conduct social inquiry, and the dominant mode, at least as an ideal, remained close to natural science. Pettifer spoke only for the future; for the moment the natural science paradigm remained supreme, and indeed was to remain so well into the twentieth century. A concern for ethical

30

questions had to wait. Even Mayhew, despite his atypical interest in listening to what the poor had to say, took the natural science paradigm as his ideal. He wrote in 1850

I made up my mind to deal with human nature as a natural philosopher or a chemist deals with any material object. (Humpherys 1971: xiv)

The methodological assumptions of nineteenth-century anthropology were much the same as those of sociology. If sociology may be regarded as an applied intellectual response to the social problems of developing capitalism in metropolitan countries, then nineteenth-century anthropology was an analogous response to the problems of imperialism in undeveloped countries overseas (cf. Easthope 1974: 16). Firth (1972: 200) may be right to insist, against some Marxist critics, that 'anthropology is not the bastard of colonialism but the legitimate offspring of the Enlightenment', but however far back we choose to trace the intellectual roots of the discipline, we cannot deny that its praxis became established under colonialism. Gouldner (1970: 126–32) argues that whereas sociology in the early nineteenth century was in harmony with the interests of the bourgeois middle class, anthropology was closer to the interest of the aristocracy. But despite this difference, both branches of learning were fostered by the elite for purposes defined by the elite. The earliest detailed accounts of the social life of tribal peoples were provided by missionaries and travellers in the seventeenth century, and in the latter half of the eighteenth century colonial administrators began to add their contributions to the ethnographic corpus. Only in the nineteenth century were learned societies formed to promote the study of tribal peoples as a delimited intellectual endeavour, and it was not until the very end of the century that anything like academic anthropologists conducting empirical inquiries on their own account began to appear on the scene. Yet throughout the nineteenth century the mode for ethnographic inquiry and anthropological analysis was the natural science paradigm. The natives were the objects being scrutinized. Official statistics were few and far between, so that there was not the contrast between 'facts' and 'opinions' that characterized nineteenth-century

31

sociology. Nevertheless the natives spoke only from a distance, often through interpreters who translated into a lingua franca, and even if missionaries and travellers did not all confine their inquiries to chiefs and headmen, their main function in the scientific division of labour was to supply information for savants sitting in their studies in Europe and north America, the so-called armchair anthropologists. Sir James Frazer's well-known surprise at the suggestion that he might investigate at first hand some of the peoples about whom he had written at such length in *The golden bough* accurately indicates his nineteenth-century affiliation. With a few significant exceptions the deliberations of the anthropological learned societies were not directly linked to programmes of social action. When they were, as for example in connexion with the abolition of slavery, the action envisaged was to be taken by the colonial governments, as guardians of the natives, rather than by the natives themselves. The publications of the learned societies, and of the armchair savants, were aimed at the intelligent and cultivated reading public of the metropolitan countries, not at the peoples whose beliefs and behaviour were described in them.

In the 1880s scientists themselves, with a specialized interest in the lives of tribal peoples, began to make expeditions to distant lands specifically for the purpose of studying these peoples at first hand. Thus the tradition of anthropological fieldwork began. But the shift towards specialized data collection did not at first entail any substantial move away from the model of natural science. The first academically-affiliated field ethnographers, men such as Boas, Seligman, Haddon and Rivers, were all grounded in natural science, and although they modified their mode of inquiry to fit their new subject matter, the model remained essentially unchanged. At one level the scientists had to interact with the natives, unenfranchized citizens, as fellow human beings. They had to secure for themselves somewhere to live, a supply of food, and the like; they also had to encourage the natives to cooperate in the inquiry. For example, Haddon describes how, while leading the Cambridge anthropological expedition to Torres Straits in 1898, he and his colleagues gave an evening entertainment for the islanders at which he explained the purpose of the expedition. The scientists also played gramophone records and showed magic lantern slides (Haddon 1901:37). This kind of interaction was not, however, perceived as forming part of the objectives of the investigation, which was 'to recover the past life of the islanders' (Haddon 1935:xiv). The reports of the inquiry, which appeared up to thirty-six years after the expedition had returned to Britain, were published in Cambridge, not in Australia, and clearly were not intended to have any practical consequences at all for the islanders or for the Queensland administration which controlled them.

Haddon, like other anthropological fieldworkers of his period, was certainly aware that his presence disturbed to some extent the social field he was trying to investigate. But like a good natural scientist he and his fellows tried to minimize this disturbing effect by aiming at 'recovering' the past and by concentrating on the collection of types of data, such as reminiscences of the past, myths and legends, and accounts of customary behaviour rather than the observation of contemporary acts and of formal ceremonials rather than of the ephemera of ordinary-day life. More recent studies suggest that this emphasis was misguided; these kinds of social data are not necessarily more invariant than others. For example, even so careful an observer and scientist as Charles Darwin was misled in 1832 by the replies given by certain kidnapped Yahgans from Tierra del Fuego into stating that they were cannibals. Better evidence suggests that the Yahgans invented fantastic stories about themselves merely for the amusement of seeing them believed by their English captors (Lienhardt 1964:12–14; Darwin 1959:204; Bridges 1948:33–4). Such fabrication of evidence may seem likely enough to us but, at the time, scientists, whether or not they had begun to specialize in social inquiries, thought that they could collect data from members of other social groups as if they were at home in the laboratory studying some natural object. In this respect there was no essential difference between the anthropologists working overseas and the sociologists studying the poor in the metropolis (cf. Leclerc 1972).

For both sociology and anthropology the intellectual dominance of the natural science paradigm was complemented by the political context in which the paradigm was applied in practice. The focus of scientific attention in both disciplines was the powerless rather than the powerful, the poor working class at home and the conquered tribal peoples overseas. The positivistic ontology whereby social facts were held to exist in their own right was matched by a real world in which the initiative for social action was held by a ruling minority. The two were linked by an investigative praxis whereby these independently existing unbiased facts were assumed to be known to the guardians of the poor rather than the poor themselves. With this version of the process of social inquiry dominant throughout the nineteenth century it is not surprising that ethical considerations went unnoticed. The same perceptions lasted far into the present century. For example Lurie (1972 : 159) describes the view taken by an early twentieth-century anthropologist by saying that 'He felt that the few old people who possessed special knowledge should be exploited by any means, no matter how they might feel about it, before their precious knowledge died with them.' But she goes on to note that since that time, 'the followers of the old ways were more determined than ever to keep their secrets'.

Although in the twentieth century psychologists began to concern themselves professionally with ethical problems ahead of their colleagues in sociology and anthropology, in the nineteenth century they were no more alerted to these problems than were the others. The standard history of the discipline makes no mention at all of ethical problems (Murphy and Kovach 1972). This is scarcely surprising in a branch of learning which adopted the natural science paradigm wholeheartedly. As Flugel says of the beginnings of nineteenth-century psychology, 'the very essence of the new psychology that was shortly to arise lay in separation from metaphysics and adoption of the point of view common to the physical sciences' (Flugel and West 1964:14).

In this period, scientists and citizens were characteristically unequal; the citizens of our model were not yet fellow citizens. The disparity of status was not always as extreme as when Darwin wrote of the Yahgans that 'Viewing such men, one can hardly

make oneself believe that they are fellow-creatures, and inhabitants of the same world' (Darwin 1959: 203), but there was seldom
any approximation to equality. By contrast the interests of
sponsors did often approximate to those of the scientists, for members of the learned societies and associations provided their own
funds for the research they sponsored, scientists were themselves
often men of means, and the state administration itself was largely
manned by members of the same elite group. There were no large
philanthropic institutions concerned to promote social research,
corresponding to the foundations of the mid twentieth century
There were gatekeepers such as colonial administrators, factory
managers and custodians of archives, but they seem rarely to have
obstructed the pursuit of scientific knowledge. For example,
the Cambridge anthropological expedition to Torres Straits was
greeted on arrival by a telegram from the Premier of Queensland
on behalf of the government expressing its hope that the expedition would be successful (Haddon 1901: x). In general, scientists
were the social equals of gatekeepers, and could be trusted not to
rock the boat.

3 The institutionalization of social inquiry

The social sciences became institutionalized in north America, Britain and other Western countries during the first forty years of the twentieth century. Although the timing, extent and emphasis with which the various sciences were accepted as part of the academic and professional structure differed greatly, an international community of specialists in the several disciplines began to be formed during this period. Governments recruited social scientists on a regular basis and government officials received formal instruction in social science as part of their training. Social anthropology was taught to colonial administrators from Britain and other metropolitan countries, while in the Netherlands East Indies the administration provided virtually the whole support for a special academic sub-discipline, Indology (Held 1953). From the First World War onwards, military organizations began to use psychologists in the screening of recruits, as did civilian firms in personnel selection and in the planning of production and marketing (Baritz 1960). Vocational guidance, based on psychological tests, became publicly accepted and the intelligence quotient became a folk concept. By the late 1930s the social survey, usually conducted as in the nineteenth century with some perceived 'problem' of poverty, crime or overcrowding in mind, had become in the United States a standardized procedure carried out by professionally qualified social scientists (Oberschall 1972:218). In many countries professional associations were formed to articulate the collective interests of social scientists.

By and large, during this period the natural science paradigm remained unchallenged as the model of inquiry to which social scientists should approximate as closely as possible. The first inkling of a change to come may be seen in the use of pseudo-

36

nyms. Here was a recognition that citizens who had been the objects of scientific scrutiny might perhaps suffer if the reports of this scrutiny were published in undisguised form. The use of pseudonyms and other disguises to protect the identity of citizens is still a lively issue and we shall have more to say about it later on. Apart from this concession to common humanity, there was little change prior to the Second World War in the way social scientists went about their inquiries, at least in their own metropolitan countries.

The main challenge to existing modes of inquiry appeared overseas. In the colonies, particularly in those British territories committed to a policy of Indirect Rule, anthropologists began to find themselves in an increasingly equivocal position. In a very few instances, the colonial government hired its own anthropologist, who became a specialist civil servant working within the constraints of a bureaucracy, and who, like any other bureaucrat, had to wrestle in private with his conscience if he found himself at odds with official policies. Most of the anthropologists who went to British colonies to carry out empirical inquiries were not members of the local administration, which for them was a gatekeeper rather than a sponsor. Most of the financial support for overseas fieldwork came in this period from private foundations, so that the field anthropologist appeared as an autonomous scientist, seeking to be allowed access to groups of colonial citizens and, if at all possible, to government files and records. The doctrine of Indirect Rule called for a thorough analysis of indigenous social institutions, in order that these might be modified constructively to match the requirements of a developing colonialism. The visiting anthropologist was a potential, or at least a self-proclaimed, expert on these institutions, and hence the colonial administration had an interest in furthering his work, even if many old hands in the administration were confident that they knew best (Firth 1956:202–10). Conversely, the anthropologist was heavily dependent on the goodwill of the administration, which in many places had a monopoly of means of communication and logistic facilities.

Yet if this convergence of interest induced a kind of elitist

37

coalition between anthropologist and high-level colonial servant, in the field the situation was quite different. Natives were notably absent from the Secretariat, save as peons, but in the village even the low-level administrator was at best an occasional visitor. Away from district headquarters the anthropologist was entirely dependent on the goodwill of the citizens he had come to study, whose language he had to learn and whose culture he had to comprehend. Hence, at least in day-to-day affairs, he had to identify himself much more closely with the viewpoint of the citizens than had, for example, his sociological colleague studying the poor in the slums of the metropolis. The divergence between the current interests and future aspirations of the citizens and their rulers was much greater in the colonies than in the metropolitan slums. Yet the sociologist working in his own country was much freer to take an independent stance in relation to officialdom than was the anthropologist working under colonial conditions. In both contexts the citizens were unlikely to have had any part in bringing the social scientist into their midst, or in choosing what he should inquire into, whereas the colonial government would have given its approval to the planned inquiry and, in some instances, have taken the initiative in suggesting it.

In these colonial settings, loyalty to the natural science paradigm was put under heavy strain. The strain was increased for those anthropologists who adopted, in varying degrees, that mode of intensive fieldwork advocated by Malinowski and others which is now known as participant observation. But even if they clung to the more old-fashioned technique of formal interviewing, as some were still doing even in the fifties (cf. Holleman 1958:34–7; Hilger 1954:26–33), they were forced to grant the citizens some say in how the inquiry was conducted. The more sensitive of them were aware that they could not ignore the conflict of interest between rulers and ruled (cf. Gluckman 1940; Leiris 1950), whether or not they accepted the notion of colonial rule as a form of benevolent despotism. A few anthropologists began to advocate that tribal peoples should be left alone to continue living undisturbed and the exceptional individual, notably

Verrier Elwin in India, fought politically to achieve this (Elwin 1964; Misra 1973). At the other extreme, Godfrey Wilson (1941 & 1942), in what was then Northern Rhodesia (now Zambia), advocated radical changes that would have undermined the colonial system (cf. Brown 1973). In both kinds of response we can see the beginnings of the notion that research that is unrelated to social action is irresponsible and basically repressive.

Most anthropologists kept well clear of these two poles. The most effective way of surviving cross-pressure was to narrow one's area of interest, to concentrate on the local community isolated in time and space. This defence was in any case encouraged by the ruling theoretical paradigm, the functionalist model of society. Turning their backs on the pseudo-history of nineteenth- and early twentieth-century social evolutionalism and diffusionism, the functionalists threw away real history as well. They ignored the problems of imperialism and yet saw themselves as the paternalistic, but not very powerful, protectors of indigenous social institutions, particularly at the domestic and village level. 'While some functional anthropologists conceived it their societal duty to educate colonial administrators, none thought it their duty to tutor native revolutionaries' (Gouldner 1970:132). Thus they tended to be sensitive to the citizens' interests when these were based on traditional tribal values, and less ready to support newly emergent interests. Batalla (1966) claims that the advice given by anthropologists in this period was typically conservative, aimed at avoiding rapid changes.

How anthropologists attempted to take account of the citizens' interests, and also to satisfy their own calling as scientists, while providing support, either reluctantly, unthinkingly or wholeheartedly, to the colonial regime, can be seen in the work of Evans-Pritchard while he was directly employed as an anthropologist by the government of the Sudan. His study of *Witchcraft among the Azande* has become a classic. Various associations of Azande had been formed for the practice of magic in assemblies. The colonial government disapproved of the associations and had banned one of them, the Mani association. Nevertheless Evans-Pritchard joined the association and attended a few of its assemblies. He also collected descriptions of the rites of the association from members. Whereas he published the real names of most of the people who told him about Zande life, his informants on the Mani association remain anonymous. He also collected information about another association but decided not to use it. 'Europeans generally feel so strongly against this association and so fiercely punish its members that I refrain for the present from publishing an account of its rites, for some of them would offend European sentiments' (Evans-Pritchard 1937:511).

Though the natural science paradigm was thus being challenged, but not displaced, overseas, it was hardly being even nibbled at in the metropolitan homelands. Social scientists working in metropolitan countries were much less committed to techniques of participant observation, and continued to collect information by surveys and questionnaires, often employing paid assistants to do the donkeywork. Hence although the cultural distance between scientist and citizen was usually much greater overseas, the social distance between them was often greater at home. The involvement of individual citizens in the inquiry was less, and by aggregating their responses it was easy to provide them with anonymity. In metropolitan countries more social inquiry could be carried out impersonally, from documents and reports already in the public domain, than in the poorly documented colonies. Sociologists tended to accept the status quo, and did not feel themselves subject to cross-pressure except perhaps in such quasi-colonial contexts as studies of Black–White relations in the United States. The initial challenge to the natural science paradigm, such as it was, came from within the process of inquiry itself rather than from a change in the social environment in which research was being carried out.

Studies carried out during 1927 to 1932 at the Western Electric Plant outside Chicago, aimed at discovering ways of improving productivity, led to the identification of what is usually known as the Hawthorne effect, after the name of the factory where the inquiry was made (Roethlisberger and Dickson 1939; Landsberger 1958; Dickson and Roethslisberger 1966:19–36). Probably the evidence from the study fails to support all the conclusions drawn from it (Carey 1967); nevertheless the notion of a Hawthorne effect has influenced the planning of social inquiry, even if the effect was not present in the Hawthorne factory itself. In the inquiry scientists discovered, or thought that they had discovered, that, in certain industrial contexts, the productivity of workers was increased more because they were being studied by a sympathetic and enthusiastic research team than by any of the accepted spurs to greater productivity such as better lighting, rescheduled rest periods, changes in styles of supervision, and rearranged seating. Like most sociological discoveries, this one now seems quite banal. Such is the fate of all sociological discoveries in retrospect, for valid discoveries pass securely and quickly into common knowledge and are soon part of folk wisdom, even if they get distorted along the way. What is surprising is not the alleged discovery itself, but the fact that at the time it was seen as a discovery. Its categorization as something new indicates how firmly the natural science paradigm was accepted by social scientists. The study showed that, contrary to the paradigm, the process of inquiry itself could make a significant difference to the citizens being studied.

Yet apart from this departure from the paradigm, the study conforms to type. The identity of the workers who were studied is concealed in the report and information collected about their lives outside the factory is omitted to protect them further. The citizens did not participate in preparing the report, and although it has been extensively discussed and attacked by many scientists, no one seems to have been interested in discovering what effect, if any, it had locally when it appeared. In most respects the citizens remained segregated under the scientists' microscope.

Following the end of the Second World War the use of the natural science paradigm in social inquiry came under much more serious attack. As we shall see, some scientists advocate that it should be abandoned completely, while others stress that in certain specified contexts it must be modified substantially. But even now most inquiries in social science conform more or less to the natural science paradigm. Confidentiality, anonymity and disguise remain the only widespread concessions to the fact

41

that people, not things, are being studied. By and large, not much harm and often substantial good arises from social inquiries carried out in this way. Nevertheless it seems sounder practice to start, if we can, with a model of the process of inquiry specifically designed to accommodate human beings rather than retain as an ideal a quite inappropriate model. We can then see, in any given context, to what extent the model can be simplified without harming the persons involved. Gropings towards a better model are discussed in the next chapter.

With the institutionalization of social science came a shift in public attitudes towards the knowledge gained from social inquiry. The aphorism that 'knowledge is power' goes back at least to Francis Bacon and, as we have seen, the proto-social-scientists of the early nineteenth century regarded the knowledge they gained from inquiry as the basis for whatever public remedial action might be necessary. But such knowlege was, in a sense, a public commodity; it provided ammunition for the forces of good against the forces of evil, rather than for one legitimately constituted group in society against its competitors. In these circumstances knowledge was seen more as a source of enlightenment to the whole community rather than as a source of private power. In the natural sciences the results of inquiries should be published quickly and widely, so that all mankind might benefit from the special skills and opportunities of the gifted few. The same norm was applied to social research.

As social inquiry became more a regular part of the ongoing activities of industrialized societies and, maybe, as the results of these inquiries became more usable, the notion of knowledge as a source of general enlightenment began to be overshadowed by the idea that it was a potential source of private or sectional power. This shift may have been due partly to the increased reliance on governmental support for inquiries, rather than on private philanthropy or the contributions of members of learned associations. Government agencies were more inclined to look for practical advantages in the expected outcome of the inquiries they sponsored, even if these advantages were in some instances fairly remote. Thus for example, in the less travelled parts of the

42

colonial empire, even the most superficial information about the names of peoples and their leaders might be of potential use to the administration. Ahmed (1973:266–9) shows how in the 1920s the Sudan government used the anthropologists who worked in its territory, and whom it supported financially as well as logistically, to fill in the gaps in its knowledge of the inhabitants so that it might avoid grave administrative errors made 'through ignorance of local beliefs and habits and insufficient understanding of savage ways of thought'. The Anglo-Egyptian Sudan was typical in this respect of most colonial territories (cf. Kuper 1973:123–49; Leclerc 1972; Asad 1973). At the other end of the spectrum, the United States Army, during the First World War, employed psychologists to develop intelligence tests because of its immediate practical interest in building up quickly an efficient and reliable fighting force (cf. Kamin 1977:32–3). We might perhaps argue that the rulers of the Sudan, 'a land of Blacks ruled by Blues', saw themselves as heirs of the Enlightenment and that no change had taken place there from the view of knowledge held by the political economists of the early nineteenth century. Yet if so they were resting on their laurels, for,notwithstanding any use that may have been made of his reports, Evans-Pritchard (1946:97) claims that in fifteen years of working on sociological problems in the Sudan, he was never once asked for advice by the government. At least in our American example it is clear that a change of the use of knowledge had taken place.

Whether seen as a source of universal enlightenment or as a basis for sectional power, the findings of social inquiries were until recently used in what we may call a passive sense. Inquiry revealed that, say, drunkenness among the poor was more. widespread in Manchester than in Birmingham, that prostitution was declining in London but rising in Plymouth, that Smith was more intelligent than Robinson, and thus enabled administrators to take informed decisions about what action was needed. The inquiry provided a map of the present rather than a detailed blue-print for the future. Most social inquiries nowadays are still used in this way. But during the last forty years or so the knowledge gained from social inquiry has begun to be used more actively,

43

so that its potential as power can be exploited consciously. This active use is sometimes referred to as social engineering, the deliberate alteration of the parameters of social life so as to bring about some scientifically predicted end desired by those who are able to make these alterations. The possibility of social engineering, of sociologically informed intervention in social life, was envisaged by Jeremy Bentham and found a prolific advocate in Lester F. Ward, whose *Applied sociology* appeared in 1904 (cf. Barnes, H. E. 1966:126–43). In practice, sociology did not begin to be applied in this sense until after the First World War, and serious issues of principle arose only after 1945. Speaking very broadly, sociology and economics began to be applied scientifically at much the same time, with declarations of the possibility of application before 1914, isolated examples of would-be scientific intervention between the wars, as in the Soviet five-year plans, and widespread application after 1945.

The application of natural science to practical affairs has a much longer history, and it was via natural science that social science began to be applied in what has become one of the major manifestations of the use of the natural science paradigm, in the field of 'development'. Significantly, this linkage between the two branches of science occurred in the colonial setting where, in most respects, the similarity between the modes of inquiry in the two branches was closer than in metropolitan countries. Prior to 1939, the relation of social science to official policy in the colonial world was typified, with many exceptions, by that experienced by Evans-Pritchard in the Sudan. The government expected its subjects to keep the peace, pay their taxes and work as required for expatriate entrepreneurs, but otherwise intervened in their lives only to a limited extent. After 1945 a much greater effort began to be directed throughout the colonial and ex-colonial world towards social and cultural, as well as economic, change. Particularly in economic matters, colonial governments were able to draw upon the results of scientific experiments. In Britain and other Western countries, field trials of crops had reached a high level of scientific and statistical sophistication in the inter-war period. By the late thirties experiments were beginning to be carried out in tropical countries to discover not only the best strains of crops but also the best ways of stimulating tribesmen and peasants to grow them, and to form cooperative societies and other marketing associations.

After the war, spurred on by the wide-flung call to develop or improve the poor countries of the tropics and, so I guess, by the wartime successes of operational research, these research activities were resumed more vigorously and were followed by action programmes designed to reproduce wherever possible the social arrangements which research had shown to be optimal for achieving results. Applied anthropology in the tropics, though it had been argued about and practised during the inter-war years (cf. Brown and Hutt 1935; Held 1953; Hogbin 1957; Foster 1969), came to life as an example of social engineering only in the post-war period of late-colonial development. The task of development was recognized as difficult, calling for experts from developed countries who were to apply their skills to eradicate poverty, malnutrition, illiteracy and other impediments to progress. Social science constituted the core of their expertise. The goals of development were set by the rich nations, and development schemes varied in the extent to which an effort was made to translate these goals into 'felt needs' in the minds of the poor people who were to be developed.

Particularly since the end of the period of classic colonialism the basic assumptions of Western-sponsored development in the Third World have come under serious sustained attack from critics who view it as essentially a means of continuing the economic hegemony of the West in a new political and administrative context (cf. Hayter 1971; Oxaal et al. 1975). I am not here concerned with the force of this criticism; my point is simply that, as it worked out in practice, development was largely an exercise in applied social science following a natural science paradigm. The literature was necessarily aimed at the literate elite of experts, including social scientists (e.g. Mead 1953), while the ends and means alike were, and still are, determined by a political and administrative elite, located partly in the capitals of developed and underdeveloped nations and partly in international agencies.

45

Negotiation with the citizens who were to be encouraged to grow more productive crops, to adopt healthier practices of child care, to shift to more modern forms of administration and political organization and so on took place, if at all, within narrow terms of reference. Anthropologists, acting as advisers rather than as executives, were concerned with the instruction of administrators and other agents of enforced culture change in the best ways of introducing the new elements with the least difficulty. This is the paradigm that leads Manners (1956: 8–9) to comment that 'the anthropologist's professional advice may, if it is used at all, serve to facilitate the manipulation of the local population in violence of their own immediate interests'.

Nevertheless the short-term, local effects of campaigns to stop soil erosion by digging contour ridges, to reduce infant mortality by promoting baby clinics, to form cooperative societies for the purchase of seeds and the marketing of crops and the like were often beneficial to the citizens concerned. It is therefore not surprising that little attention was given at the time to the ethical issues raised by these moderately successful examples of moderately benign social engineering. Although the notion of development, as applied in colonies, came under criticism long before the end of colonialism in its classic guise, it is only in the last ten years or so that discussion of the ethical and political implications of the part they have played in that process has become widespread among anthropologists and other scientists directly involved.

The catalytic stimulus to face up to the ethical problems inherent in social inquiry came from an attempted exercise in the use of power that, unlike campaigns for building contour ridges and baby clinics, could not be categorized unproblematically as benign. This was the now notorious Project Camelot. As Horowitz (1973: 176) puts it, with Project Camelot, 'The age of sociological innocence was at an end.' Even though the project was cancelled in 1965 before any substantial research had been done, its story is complex and still not entirely clear; it raises many issues, though some of them are not relevant here (Lowe 1966; Horowitz 1967; Sjoberg 1967a; Beals 1969; Klare 1972: 92–101;

46

Deitchman 1976). Briefly, it was an inquiry sponsored by the United States Department of the Army. The scientists were mainly American sociologists, political scientists and anthropologists. It was seen as a basic social research project, aimed at identifying the preconditions of internal conflict and at discovering the effects of action taken by local governments in easing, exacerbating or resolving these preconditions. Empirical inquiry was envisaged in various countries in Latin America, and eventually elsewhere in the world as well. The project was based on the assumption that increased knowledge gained from the inquiries would enable the United States Army to cope more effectively with internal revolutions in other countries. The project was attacked by left-wing Chilean politicians when the tentative possibility of research being carried out in Chile came to light. The US Ambassador to Chile had not been told of the possibility and the project was cancelled by McNamara, as Secretary of Defense, partly because of pressure from the State Department, who considered that it endangered the success of the Department's policy in Chile. The cancellation was followed by widespread debate among social scientists and the general public in the United States and stimulated discussions among scientists in other countries including Britain.

The issues raised by the Project, and by the mode of its cancellation, are political as well as ethical, and the two strands are intertwined. The two phases of the proposed enterprise, the inquiry and the eventual utilization of the results by the Army, were likewise closely linked. This is scarcely surprising with a sponsor whose main involvement in research is in natural rather than social science, and whose specialized purpose and justification within the wider society, however we may choose to define this, certainly does not include a commitment to the pursuit of knowledge for its own sake. Almost all of the criticism directed at the Project, and at similar inquiries where social scientists have accepted military sponsorship, is aimed at the scientists rather than at the sponsor. An army that spends its money supporting research to further its own military objectives is acting correctly within its brief. The State Department objected to Project

Camelot partly because the Army, in its view, was spending funds on research aimed neither at military ends nor at pure knowledge but at foreign policy, where the State Department claimed a monopoly of interest. In the United States, the identity of the sponsor, who operated through a Federal Contract Research Center, located at the American University with the macabre name of SORO (Special Operations Research Office), seems not to have been kept secret (Beals 1969:6; Kelman 1968: 93; Deitchman 1976:144; cf. Greer 1977), but in Chile the Army's connexion with the Project was, either deliberately or inadvertently, denied when it was first discussed with leading academics. The aims of the project, and the Army's sponsorship, were brought to the attention of Chilean intellectuals by a Norwegian sociologist who had been invited to join the project but had refused on political and ethical grounds.

Project Camelot was an attempt to use the natural science paradigm to provide the knowledge necessary for social engineering. It differed from other projects in its scale, and in the clear association between the special interests of its sponsor, the methodological assumptions that determined the form of the inquiry, and the purposes for which the results would be used. The Project was based on the assumption that political stability is always desirable, and that revolution is always undesirable. The outcome hoped for from the inquiry was 'a computer-based model that would permit the rapid prediction of various types of outcomes of social change and conflict situations and the assessment of the effectiveness of different action programs in resolving or averting conflict' (Beals 1969: 5–6; cf. Deitchman 1976: 126). In the present state of the world, only governments are likely to be able to mount an inquiry on the scale of Project Camelot, and funds of this magnitude are likely to be available only as part of the pursuit of some major goal of national policy. Therefore large-scale attempts at social engineering are prone to attack from poorer countries who see themselves as assigned a passive role as objects of inquiry, and from citizens anywhere who are opposed to these national goals. But much of the criticism that was directed against Project Camelot, particularly against the scien-

48

tists who participated in it, could equally well be made against more modest projects, where citizens are studied so that their lives may more efficiently be directed along paths chosen by the sponsors of the inquiry, and where often the political interests which the scientists are serving are less salient, though still questionable.

For while political stability at all costs is likely to be rejected by people under oppression, there may be other objectives that everyone seems to want: life rather than death, health rather than illness. It is then easy to approve of action programmes, and the research that lies behind these programmes, aimed at such benign ends, even though they ride roughshod over the sentiments of the citizens whose lives are being improved. If the scientists concerned stress that the best plans in the world cannot succeed without the citizens first coming to realize that participation is in their own best interests, we are inclined to commend their appreciation of the practical limitations of the natural science paradigm in human affairs. Thus for example we may wish to approve of Foster (1953:842) when he writes 'After the most practical public health program for a given country or area is determined the people must be convinced that the program really is good for them, that it is in their interest to adopt the new and abandon the old.' But unfortunately the scientist working within this framework is likely to consider that determining the 'most practical public health program' is a matter for the scientist alone, because the citizens do not know what is in their own best interests. He therefore uses his scientific expertise to determine not only the programme but also the best means of getting the citizens to accept it. For Foster goes on to say that 'popular resistance to public health programs can be scientifically studied, and methods can be developed whereby these resistances can be greatly reduced'. But there is nothing specific to public health programmes in Foster's approach. The same argument can be applied in other contexts. Thus 'Here is the first proposal for systematically analyzing public resistance to new technology . . . Naturally a constantly changing societal value system presents a moving target of public expectations. But recognizing what

49

stage of resistance is being entered should provide some guidance for resolving disagreements and keep the technology producer from escalating the resistance to its activities' (Jopling et al. 1973:53, 65). But whereas Foster is talking about public health programmes, these authors are discussing nuclear power stations. It is in the area of public persuasion that the political implications of scientific inquiry are perhaps made clearest of all.

For example, market research, aimed at discovering what people really want and how existing products and services can be improved, may seem benign and desirable, both in a free-enterprise economy and perhaps even more so in a directed economy. But people do not 'want' in a vacuum; their wants can be created as well as discovered. The recurrent objections to subliminal advertising indicate the dislike and fear most people have of being led unknowingly to want something they would not have thought of spontaneously. Furthermore, products and services are not the only things that can be modified to suit the market. Firms can construct their published financial statements in the light of what social inquiry has indicated about citizens' attitudes to profit. Inquiries designed to elicit information about attitudes towards commercial firms, carried out among employees and potential customers with a view to building up an appropriate 'corporate image', form a recognized branch of market research (Worcester 1972). Likewise propaganda broadcasts can be geared to the results of research into what citizens would be pleased to hear. When political programmes and election platforms are constructed mainly in the light of empirical inquiry into what the electorate says it really wants, it is scarcely surprising that election promises remain unfulfilled. If two parties utilize the same sort of empirical data to construct their public electoral image, the differences between them cease to be differences in advertised aims; they compete instead only as to the efficiency with which they can attain what the modal voter wants. If both parties espouse a theory of political activity based on the assumption that voters and legislators act to maximize their interests rather than to further their principles (Olson 1971), the difference between the two parties becomes minimal; each seeks to be as little different from the other as possible, so as to capture the maximum range of votes. Only the emergence of third parties can break the impasse. Thus opinion polls and a theoretical framework drawn from political science may combine to bring about a transformation of the political scene that no one 'wanted' to occur.

A departure from the natural science paradigm of a different kind, and at the same time a consequence of the institutionalization of social research as a recognized part of social life, occurs when citizens become their own scientists. In Britain, the acceptance of social inquiry as a routine process was heralded in 1937 by the formation of Mass-Observation. This organization was based on the premiss that anyone could make inquiries in social phenomena. As described by its founders, 'Ideally, it is the observation by everyone of everyone, including themselves.' Julian Huxley compared it with birdwatching and natural history observation (Madge and Harrisson 1937:6, 10). The movement did not long survive the war in its original form (Harrisson 1961; Mitchell 1968:210–12), but the idea behind it has survived in what are now usually known as community self-surveys, in which interested citizens make inquiries about various features of the social lives of their neighbours and other citizens. These inquiries are usually carried out to provide evidence for making decisions about local policy, or to provide support for policies that have already been decided upon. Not surprisingly, the citizens who make these inquiries are often unaware of the ethical obligations they should acknowledge in relation to their data. Wolf (1964), with community self-surveys carried out in the Detroit area in mind, claims that ethical standards are constantly violated, and that the activities of amateur social surveyors are likely to bring all social inquiries of this kind into disrepute, including those conducted by qualified professionals. In Britain, this do-it-yourself attitude towards social inquiry seems not to characterize voluntary associations, but somewhat similar effects may arise from inquiries made by students as part of their training in social science unless particular attention is paid to alerting them to the ethical implications of their inquiries. Many students desire to work collectively rather than on their own, so that the difficulties of respecting the confidences of citizens and of honouring any promises of anonymity are increased. On the other hand, collective work may have economies of scale and may raise morale. If research is directly linked to social action, then collective inquiry seems particularly appropriate, and an appreciation of the short-term and long-term consequences of breaches of confidence, and of other aspects of the moral relation between scientist and citizen, becomes just as important as an understanding of sampling errors and other technical sources of uncertainty, if effective action is to emerge from the research.

Social inquiry has thus become an activity which even amateurs can engage in, and for which regular training courses are available for aspiring professionals. The natural science paradigm still usually provides the plan of the investigation even when it is carried out by qualified social scientists. But attempts to use the model for debatable ends have led scientists to question its appropriateness for social science, and to give more attention to the ethical issues that the model tends to conceal.

4 The challenge to universalism

Citizens, both in industrial countries and in tropical jungles, have come to see social research as a regular feature of ordinary life. Yet the institutionalization of social inquiry has not been achieved without comment or evaluation, nor has it been un-challenged, for it is an activity which has impinged on many other aspects of social life. The practice of social inquiry and even the acceptance of specified social theories have become significant elements in relations between nations and other organized social groups. Social science has come to be perceived as one of the contexts in which the imbalance of power between the West and the Third World is expressed and maintained. Scientists in the Third World and their governments have en-deavoured to respond to this imbalance, and in all parts of the world citizens have tried to play a larger part in the process of inquiry, or to prevent the process occurring. These shifts in power have been accompanied and facilitated by a shift in the perception of knowledge. The findings of social inquiry are no longer thought of as a source of enlightenment, nor necessarily as a source of power, but rather as a kind of non-negotiable private property.

In this chapter we discuss some of the ways in which govern-ments and sponsors have reacted to institutionalized social research and how the participation of social scientists in the research process has been influenced by their own ethnic and national identity. We can begin by looking at the response of some of the citizens to the inquiries made about them.

Because social inquiry has become commonplace, it has be-come part of popular culture. Conventional attitudes towards social science are now found not only among scientists and sponsors but also among the citizens at large. The clipboard carried by the market research interviewer is recognized as her badge of office, and she does not have to explain to her respondents what a social survey is. More than twenty years ago Vidich and Bensman (1954:22) noted that 'In an age of psychological tests, public opinion polling and the popularization of social science findings, the respondent is aware in part of the consequences of his response.' In the small country town where they were working, surprisingly many citizens had heard of the Lynds' *Middletown* and were familiar with monographs on the Navaho. One struggling voluntary association in the town was being kept alive partly by the interest taken in its activities by the research team.

Whereas fifty years ago each professional anthropologist had to negotiate for himself a social role that previously was unknown to the community which he had selected for study, the present-day graduate student, sent on a field assignment to a well-documented society as part of his training, is likely to find that his role is already as familiar to the citizens as is that of the market researcher in his own home town. For example Cambridge (1971:96) writes of growing up on an Indian reservation in the United States: 'First of all you recognize the missionary and then you recognize the Bureau of Indian Affairs official. But in the summer time there are twenty million graduate students coming down and saying, "I'm not going to bother you". So, he sits there with his pen, watching you.' Research saturation may perhaps be higher on reservations in the United States than in the Third World, but the sentiments Cambridge expresses would be understood in many areas. Gatekeepers for Aboriginal settlements in Australia claim that these are the attitudes held by many Aborigines, and in Papua New Guinea jokes are common among ex-patriate social scientists about discussions among the citizens on the relative merits of the various people who have studied them. Likewise in industrialized countries citizens have begun to question the part they have been assigned as informants, as respondents to questionnaires and as participants in laboratory experiments. Individually or collectively they ask 'What's in this for me?

Why should I answer your questions? If you can ask me, why shouldn't I ask you?' (cf. Blauner and Wellman 1973:321).

This type of antagonistic response is not entirely new, for from the earliest beginnings of systematic social inquiry in the nineteenth century there have always been some individuals who have refused to cooperate, who have given deliberately misleading answers, remained silent or who have obstructed research in a variety of ways. From its foundation in 1941 the Society for Applied Anthropology stressed the interactive quality of the process of social inquiry and in 1952, in its journal, Wax (1952: 34) advised the scientist to ask himself, 'Why should anybody in this group bother to talk to me? Why should this man take time out from his work, gambling, or pleasant loafing to answer my questions?'

At that time the initiative still usually lay with the scientist. It is, I think, only in the last fifteen years or so that uncooperative citizens have started to challenge significantly the course of inquiry in principle as distinct from merely obstructing it in practice. Thus Blacks in the United States may refuse to give information to interviewers on the ground that the interviewers are White or that, though Black, they are stooges working for Whites (Josephson 1970:122). Similar responses have been made by Australian Aboriginals and North American Indians. There have always been objections to revealing information that was perceived as private or secret, such as scandals, rituals and crimes, but the new objections now being made do not depend on the content of the questions, which may indeed relate to such open and public topics as names and ages and places of residence. The objections are to how the inquiry is carried out, the role assigned to the informant, and the use to which the information will be put. In the extreme case there is simply a blanket objection to social inquiry as such, particularly when the inquiry is being made by a governmental agency, or when the data are to be stored in a computer.

In the United States, refusal to answer questions in social surveys has been seen by citizens as 'a form of protest against some part or all of established society' (American Statistical

Association 1974:32). In Britain similar views were expressed in connexion with the 1971 census and are being foreshadowed for the next census in 1981. Whether or not they would contemplate breaking the law by refusing to participate in a compulsory census, most people see decent obscurity as an important part of their personal freedom (cf. Warner and Stone 1970:114). For some citizens, their notion of privacy has been extended to embrace not only information about oneself but also any conclusions that may be drawn from aggregating this information with similar data from other individuals. If poor people provide information while those who collect it appear to grow rich, there is an added reason for refusing to answer personal questions (cf. Fenton 1972:114–17).

Citizens now behave differently towards the scientists who wish to study them. Yet we should not infer that necessarily their attitudes have changed. As Gould (1973:164) puts it,

It may be that the populations we treated so casually in the past have always hated our arrogance and selfishness. The difference now is that they have the political resources to tell us so, to deny us access, to demand responsibility from us.

The institutionalization of social inquiry has affected not only many of the citizens of Third World countries but also the social scientists who belong to them. For the international relations of social inquiry have not been symmetrical. Scientists have gone from metropolitan countries to the Third World to study there and have then returned home; some traffic has flowed in the opposite direction (Beals 1969:44), but one stream has been a flood and the other only a trickle. Scientists from Third World countries have gone to the West to be trained academically, while very few indeed have gone the other way. The Third World has been a source of data and experience of great value for our general understanding of human society and culture, but for the most part it has been mediated by Western commentators and analysts. In terms of our model of the process of inquiry, Third World intellectuals have functioned more often as citizens than as scientists. A programme on British television a few years ago showing a team of intrepid African social scientists venturing across wildest Lancashire, interviewing the natives, to arrive after many adventures at the sacred centre of England near Fountains Abbey in Yorkshire, provided good entertainment, for such expeditions are in fact unknown in northern England while in parts of Africa they are commonplace.

The similarity between old-style social research in colonial and Third World countries and the economic exploitation of these territories is well brought out in Blair's (1969:24) expression 'intellectual mercantilism', referring to a process in which Guatemalan social scientists were employed as hired hands to gather data, which was then exported as raw material for refining in the United States (Portes 1973:151). Other writers have referred to academic imperialism, and scientific or intellectual colonialism (Saberwal 1968; Singh 1968). In part the debate on this issue is about social theory: to what extent can social science, as an intellectual product of the West, be accommodated to the ideological autonomy necessary for national liberation? (cf. Uberoi 1968). Our interest here is confined to the practice of social inquiry rather than its basis in social theory, though the two aspects of science cannot be treated in isolation from one another. Galtung's (1967:13) definition of scientific colonialism is simply that it is 'that process whereby the center of gravity for the acquisition of knowledge about the nation is located outside the nation itself'. Academic imperialism in Melanesia, says Keesing (1975:33), is based on the assumption 'that Melanesians constitute a scientific resource to be used by Western scholars'. This colonial condition affects the conduct of research in the country concerned and the relations of its own scientists with their colleagues elsewhere. The resources for research available to expatriate scientists are much greater than those available to local scholars, and the criteria used in selecting topics for inquiry are different. Hence there is tension between local and foreign scientists. For example, writing of United States scientists working with colleagues in Latin America, Portes (1975:136) says 'Scholars from the largest sociological establishment in the world cannot sit with those from weak institutions in countries long dependent

57

and pretend that differences are only incidental.' Latin American social scientists see their professional activities as not so much analysing the existing structure of society as providing intellectual leadership in efforts to change it. United States social scientists working in Guatemala, says Blair (1969: 19), see the outcome of their inquiries as contributions to knowledge and, simultaneously, as contributions to their own pay, promotion and prestige Local social scientists, however, tend to see research primarily as a way of attacking immediate problems, and thus of proving the practical utility of the social sciences. In our terms, both groups subscribe to the notion of knowledge as enlightenment, but as a source of power they wish to apply it in different directions.

In Latin America, some social scientists object on principle to participating in any research project supported by a United States sponsor. They see their objection as part of their effort to break the structural dependence of their countries on the United States. The striving for international recognition, they argue, divides an indigenous 'jet-set' elite from the main body of their compatriot social scientists; the disproportionately greater funds available for research projects supported by U S sponsors diverts scarce indigenous intellectual resources away from inquiries crucial for meeting local social needs; and the more social scientists accept substantial grants from wealthy US sponsors, the harder it becomes for them to contemplate organizing research more cheaply with local funds, so that the dependency relation is perpetuated (Portes 1975: 137–8). The same sentiments have been expressed by social scientists in India. One writer on the theme of 'Academic colonialism' advocated in 1968 a five-year moratorium on foreign aid for academic needs in India (Berreman 1969).

Even if a scientist subscribes to the notion of knowledge from social inquiry as a source of enlightenment, he may consider that the advantages to be gained from its pursuit are outweighed by the attendant disadvantages. This seems to be the position adopted by many intellectuals in the Third World who cherish their membership in the world community of scholars while objecting to the way in which the products of scholarship are applied. Thus

Saberwal (1968:13) asks 'how does the stimulus of communication with the international intellectual community balance the hazards resulting from the flow of data concerning our societies into the US war machine?' This flow of data he regards as one aspect of academic colonialism, the other being the dominance exercised by north American academics over their colleagues and students in Third World countries in the practical conduct of inquiries and in the intellectual frameworks they induce them to accept uncritically.

Third World governments lack the resources that would be needed to end scientific colonialism by sponsoring research on any significant scale, and in Third World countries there are few independent sponsors who might do the job for them. But these governments do have significant power as gatekeepers, and some use their power in an effort to change the pattern of social inquiry away from the neo-colonial mode. Foreign social scientists have higher social visibility in the Third World than they have at home, and local governments have become well accustomed to wide-ranging requests for information and facilities from graduate students. In both contexts the questions put by the scientist are not only read at their face value but are also categorized as part of the wider ongoing activity of social research, and evaluated accordingly. Thus for example many Third World governments have responded to 'intellectual mercantilism' by treating information about tribal customs as a national asset that should not be exported freely, to be converted into doctoral dissertations in metropolitan universities. Accordingly some of them have imposed what is in effect an export tax: expatriate research workers must study only topics judged to be in the national interest, must train local assistants so that eventually research may be conducted without reliance on expatriate expertise, must leave their field records in the country, must provide their hosts with copies of all publications arising from the research and so on (Blair 1969:25; Mead, S. M. 1976; Solomon Islands 1976). Some countries require foreign scientists to become affiliated to local universities, and some of these have set up regular procedures for granting affiliation (e.g. University of Papua

59

New Guinea 1975). Some of these requirements provide protection for the citizens and revenue for their countries, but others often pose serious ethical dilemmas for social scientists who are as much concerned to protect the citizens they study from local tyranny as they are to avoid intellectual colonialism.

Some sponsors have become aware of the undesirable effects of scientific colonialism and have endeavoured to counteract them. Portes (1975) makes the important observation that in Latin America, following the debacle of Project Camelot and similar enterprises during the sixties, there was great resistance by governments and by local social scientists towards further research by United States scientists. In this situation, the most constructive steps towards the resumption of research in a more cooperative mode were taken not by universities or professional associations but by sponsors, mainly those in the private sector. He says 'Granting agencies seem to have arrived at a consensus that while the "content" of research can be safely entrusted to academics, the "policy" aspect of research – the topics, sites and human relationships involved – cannot.' Thus for example, the Ford Foundation has backed projects of a collaborative nature, entailing research carried out jointly by academic institutions in the United States and Latin America. It has supported selected academic departments in Latin America, and meetings of local social scientists. The United States Social Science Research Council has insisted, since 1968, that holders of its pre-doctoral fellowships establish institutional affiliation with a university or research centre in the countries where they intend to make their inquiries. Grants given to two or three scholars who wish to work together on a research topic related to Latin America are available only if at least one of the participants is a Latin American. We may, of course, interpret these changes in sponsoring policy as merely an indication that sponsors, even in the private sector, are trying to make social research subservient to national policy. The United States wishes to be friendly with countries in Latin America; therefore sponsors must use their resources to foster that friendliness. Yet private enterprise sponsors in a pluralist society may combine a concern for international relations with a desire to demonstrate that they are not lackeys of government, as we shall see in Chapter 5. Since these changes in policy followed so soon after the Camelot affair, it looks as though the precipitating cause was the realization of the detrimental effect that earlier policies, cast in the mode of intellectual colonialism, had had on international relations, rather than a newly-found desire to treat Latin American scholars as fellow citizens. Indeed, it can be argued that collaborative research arrangements can serve only to perpetuate a relation of structural dependency between relatively impoverished indigenous scholars and relatively affluent overseas sponsors. Even so, the fact that the initiative came from sponsors rather than from scientists, either individually or collectively, reflects poorly on the extent to which social scientists see their research activities in a broader social and political framework. The proposed division of labour between scientists and sponsors, the former to be concerned only with techniques and the latter only with policy, is unsatisfactory for both.

The positivist universalism of the natural science paradigm has been challenged not only by changes in the distribution of power among scientists and others. Its validity has come under attack along with the idea of positivism itself. Scientists and laymen alike, though they express their doubts in different terms, are less ready nowadays to accept that there are social facts that exist in some absolute sense, and that it is purely a technical matter to gain knowledge of them. The division between facts and opinions, which Mayhew and many others in the nineteenth century took for granted, has for many social scientists in mid twentieth century been replaced with a stress on what is usually known as the social construction of reality or, as Pascal put it, that what is truth on one side of the Pyrenees is error on the other (Berger and Luckmann 1966).

In the nineteenth century, despite his fundamental philosophical antipathy to positivism, Marx, in *Capital*, made use of the empirical data collected by Her Majesty's Factory Inspectors and published on behalf of Her Majesty's Stationery Office, for purposes radically different from those that the inspectors, or

Her Majesty, had in mind. Later, in the 1920s, as part of an effort to detach American sociology from its origins in social work and social reform, and to give it academic respectability, leading professors espoused notions such as 'that as a multiplication table should be reliable both for the Tory and the Communist, so the conclusion of social trends should be valid alike for the radical and the conservative' (Odum 1951:151; Oberschall 1972: 242–4). Against such attempts, Lynd's *Knowledge for what?* (1939) was a strong statement of the view that social science neither should nor could be carried on in isolation from the major social and political struggles of the society to which its practitioners belonged. At about the same time Hayek began publishing articles attacking the misapplication, as he saw it, of the methods of the natural sciences for elucidating topics in the social sciences, later reissued as *The counter-revolution in science* (1952). Oberschall could still say in 1972 that the value-free stance of the 1920s was the institutionalized professional ideology of American sociology, with the corollary that the task of the scientist, qua scientist, is to seek knowledge without troubling himself what use might be made of it (Nash 1975). But during the last twenty-five years or so, in the United States as well as in other countries, this view has increasingly come under attack. Some critics focus on the impossibility of separating the professional activities of the scientist from his moral responsibilities as citizen, while others stress the inescapability of the political assumptions that necessarily underlie the analysis and even the collection of empirical data.

At the same time as scientists have explored the philosophical implications of rejecting positivism and the practical difficulties of achieving inter-subjectivity, in understanding how the world is perceived by others, many laymen have begun to assert that inter-subjectivity cannot be achieved by outsiders. Thus they maintain that a man can never understand a woman's point of view, a White cannot understand what it means to be Black, an atheist cannot realize what it means to have faith in a god. These denials of the possibility of empathy and inter-subjectivity have been made for many years but it is only recently that many citizens and scientists have taken to saying that because an outsider cannot comprehend completely what it is like to be an insider, his partial understanding is worthless and even dangerous. If so, the citizen is quite right to protect his interests and to refuse to cooperate with scientists. Malinowski's (1938:99) rhetorical question, 'is it necessary in order to understand your best friend to have made love to his wife?', has been forgotten.

With the questioning of positivism has come the partial abandonment of the natural science paradigm. We are not here concerned with the complex debate which has had the effect, at least for the time being, of dividing the social sciences, and sociology in particular, into a variety of partially competing schools of structuralism, functionalism, critical sociology, hermeneutics and so on. For the style of inquiry of social science has not been greatly altered by these debates, though the interpretation of data is of course significantly dependent on the epistemological and methodological framework in which the interpretation takes place. But quite independently of this philosophical upheaval, which has effected even a social science as close to the natural sciences as psychology, the natural science paradigm would have had to be modified if it was to be retained for use in social science. For the social world is reactive and it reacts to, among other things, the activities of social scientists. As Goldstein and others (1966:38–9) put it, 'Social and behavioral scientists are particularly vulnerable to the possibility that the very performance (and publication) of an experiment may change things in such a way that the same results would no longer be obtained.' In short, once we realize how things are, we like to alter them; if we have discovered how social institutions work, we think we also know how to make them work differently. The more social science becomes a part of social life, the less its mode of inquiry conforms to the natural science paradigm. Whether this complication can be resolved by working with a dialectical or feedback model, or whether, as some pessimists maintain, it merely makes manifest the fundamental impossibility of ever achieving a satisfactory science of society, need not concern us here. Despite the problematic status of the philosophical foundations of social science, social inquiry continues, and for the most part makes use of a battered natural science paradigm, modified to take account of the facts that scientists, like citizens, are mere mortals, and that citizens, and even scientists, are continually learning from their participation in a society of which social science has become an inescapable part.

The retreat from positivism has been accompanied by a re-characterization of knowledge. As mentioned earlier, during the nineteenth century the knowledge gained by social inquiry was typically perceived as a source of enlightenment. During the twentieth century there has been a shift; this knowledge has often been seen as a source of power to be used by those who control it for their own advantage, rather than for the enlightenment and benefit of all mankind. But now a third perception has also emerged: increasingly some social groups and agencies are coming to view the findings of social inquiry as a form of property. The notion of knowledge as property has appeared in two contexts, in the Third World and with minority groups in industrialized societies. Power, of course, may be thought of as a kind of property, and a government department may well regard the findings of a social survey that it has sponsored as both a source of power, the blueprint for an exercise in social engineering, and as a form of property that it must not give away to a rival department or to the general public. But power is an active form of property, and the notion of property that has newly developed around social inquiry is essentially passive. Knowledge in the form of social data has come to be regarded as a kind of private property, an asset possessed by an individual or a group which may be treasured but is not intended for use and which is available for sale or gift only under restrictive conditions, if at all. We may regret the prevalence of this view, particularly when it leads to export taxes on knowledge which may well fail to make any significant impact on intellectual colonialism. But we cannot dismiss. this attitude, whether found in the West or in the Third World, as merely an irrational and short-sighted response either to the failure of social science to offer much enlightenment or power, or to the fear that any enlightenment or power would accrue only to scientists and sponsors to the detriment of the interests of citizens and their governments. On the contrary, the notion that some kinds of knowledge are secret, and not to be broadcast for all to hear, has a long history in Western civilization and the other great traditions, from the Garden of Eden onwards. Indeed, Young (1975:55–6) describes how one of the grounds for resentment by some citizens in Papua against his work among them as an anthropologist was his apparent misuse of sacred and ritual knowledge, which should be treasured and exchanged, as if it were empirical and technical and therefore usable without restriction.

This attitude towards information about social life is paralleled in the attitude now adopted towards the material manifestations of social life and culture. In the West we have tended to justify the presence in our museums of cultural trophies – loot – from all over the world by reference to the universal values of science. The argument is, or was, that we are not impoverishing the Lapps, or the Bushmen, by displaying their artefacts in our museums. Instead we are doing all mankind a service by rescuing them from destruction. The Elgin marbles are on display in the British Museum where, it is said, they can be seen by many more people than would have been possible had they remained on top of the Acropolis, waiting to be ground down to powder by Turkish soldiers. This argument is clearly based on the premiss that works of art and representative material objects, like knowledge itself, are sources of enlightenment. But now there are demands for the return to their original habitat not only of the glories of the Parthenon but also the bronzes of Benin, painted masks from the Sepik, bark paintings from Arnhem Land and so on round the world (cf. Robinson, A. 1976; Phillips 1976). Some museums are beginning to recognize that the objects they display continue to serve other functions. For example, certain masks held in the Museum of Man in Ottawa are visited every year by Iroquois priests who feed them. Other objects in Canadian museums may be borrowed by Indians for ceremonial use (Nooter 1975:161).

Social scientists have responded to these shifts in the distribution of power and in the perception of knowledge in a variety of

65

ways. In later chapters we shall discuss the effect these changes have had on how data are collected and how the findings of research are disseminated. The same changes have repercussions on how scientists see the relation between their scientific work and their citizenship, their membership of the wider society. For if knowledge is power, it will be used and if it is property it must be protected. The scientist has to decide whether to leave these tasks to others or to become involved in them himself.

The common thrust of these attacks on positivism and the natural science paradigm has been to induce social scientists, in their collective capacity, to become more involved politically. The value-free and politically neutral stance has been attacked as being political by default, and as providing covert or implicit support for the existing order. Scientists have been called upon to make the political implications of their professional activities explicit, and to realize that their true interests as scientists lie in trying to change the present order of things. Attempts have been made to commit professional associations, set up originally to include all members of a profession in a country, to a specified partisan political stance, while in other cases members with similar political views have formed their own caucus within their association (cf. Barnes 1969). Efforts of this kind were made particularly vigorously in the United States during the Vietnam war, a war which not only divided opinions sharply among the general public but in which social scientists were engaged in their professional capacities by the military on an unprecedented scale (Klare 1972:88–116; Deitchman 1976:18–35, 56–76). Charges of unethical conduct were made by scientists against colleagues from whom they saw themselves divided politically, though the facts were often vehemently disputed (cf. American Anthropological Association 1976a; Geddes 1975:352 fn.). But the pressures to politicize social science have by no means been confined to the United States and certainly preceded the American involvement in Indochina. For example, Nadel (1953:13) tells how, after carrying out fieldwork as an anthropologist in Nigeria, he returned in 1935 to London and gave a talk to an academic audience on the ideals of Indirect Rule, to which he regarded his own inquiries as a contribution. To his surprise, he was attacked by West African students attending the meeting for lending his support to a policy intended to repress Africans (Foster 1969:177).

Most of the efforts to get professional associations of social scientists to take a political stand on such matters as opposition to imperialism, racialism and sexual discrimination have been premissed on the view that knowledge is power, and that social scientists have a particular responsibility to see that the knowledge they themselves contribute from their research is used for good and not for evil. The idea of knowledge as property has however been present in some debates. For example in north America in 1969 the African Studies Association experienced an attempt to convert it from a scholarly, ostensibly non-political, body to one which actively supported struggles by Black people throughout the world (Challenor 1973). What is interesting about this incident is that, according to a critic, its outcome was to convert the Association into a Black American racialist body rather than to Africanize it (Van den Berghe 1973). If what this critic says is true, this is a good example of the process whereby a body of social scientists, committing itself to furthering some goal whereby a section of the population will benefit, adopts the view that membership of the body must be confined to those in that section, whether this be Blacks, or women, or Indians or whatever. Some movements stop at this degree of exclusiveness, but there is always pressure to go on and make the language of discourse, the concepts and methods of analysis, similarly exclusive to the group.

Social science developed in the West, and has been exported to the rest of the world. Intellectuals in countries wishing to free themselves from Western dominance may therefore decide to reject it as a foreign importation. Alternatively they may put social science on the same footing as natural science or military hardware and try to ensure that it is applied in their own interests and not those of the West. A third course is to argue that social science is not a Western innovation but only a belated Western discovery of traditional indigenous wisdom. Thus Saksena

(1967) claims that the analytic categories of structural functionalism, as developed by the American sociologist Talcott Parsons, are all to be found in ancient Hindu texts. Other Indian intellectuals reject the idea that social science has any validity in India. A third, and the largest, Indian group works within the broad theoretical framework of Western social science, some members applying Western concepts and techniques unchanged and others adapting them to local cultural and social conditions (Saran 1958). The same diversity of responses appears with other social groups who opppose themselves to the dominant tradition in Western social science, and to the interpretation of themselves that it offers. Thus Deloria (1969:86) protests that by analysing the condition of modern North American Indians in terms of universalistic categories like marginality, as being 'between two worlds', White anthropologists have stifled the creation of modern tribalism. Mafeje (1971:261) takes the opposite line, and protests against the use of the concepts of 'tribalism' and 'feudalism' to describe conditions in the Third World; class formation and regional particularism are more appropriate analytical concepts. 'To be able to contribute to that kind of universalism, as social scientists, we need generalizable concepts with high explanatory power – and "tribalism" is not one of them.' Likewise 'matrifocal family', a term coined in a technical context, has acquired a derogatory connotation (Blauner and Wellman 1973: 322). Objections by members of less powerful groups against the ways in which scientists of dominant groups analyse their social life are matched by criticisms raised against these scientists' assumption that their analytic categories have universal applicability and validity. Indeed, many of the generalizations announced by social scientists as being eternally and ubiquitously true turn out, on closer inspection, to apply only to White north Americans or to first-year psychology students (cf. Clinard 1966).

Black sociology is claimed by some of its practitioners to be a social science concerned with the social life of Blacks that can be comprehended only by Blacks. Forsythe (1973:225–6) maintains that Dilthey, Weber, Peter Winch and the symbolic interactionists hold that culture can be learnt about only by immersion in the social context. 'White radical sociologists cannot get this type of information, either because they do not know the "language" of Blacks or because Blacks allow Whites to see only what they want them to see.' It might seem to follow that Whites must study Whites, and Blacks study Blacks, and never the twain shall meet. But on the other hand, if the task of Black sociology is to include, as Staples (1973:168) advocates, explaining that, though Black is beautiful, White is not necessarily ugly, we have again a social science that is universalistic in its domain of explanation, if not in its practitioners.

Thus analytic categories are seen not as value-free tools developed for universal use but rather as tied to a particular intellectual stance, a particular political position or a user belonging to a specified delimited social group. If one group uses an analytic scheme as part of the means whereby it rationalizes and justifies its exploitation of another group, then the oppressed group must develop its own analytic scheme as part of its attempt to understand its exploitation and to liberate itself. When these propositions are held widely, the notion of a universalistic social science disappears. In the enthusiasm of nation-building or group liberation, some intellectuals may wish to demonstrate their independence conceptually as well as politically and economically. The advice given by Uberoi to his fellow Indian social scientists, to distinguish between cultural uniqueness and political independence and 'to define our relevant problems and pursue their solutions, not worrying about the sources of ideas' (Abbi and Saberwal 1969:192), then becomes a plea for moderation.

Opposition to the idea that social science is a source of universal enlightenment, and that therefore the more social inquiry the better, has taken many forms. Changes in the balance of power between scientists and others, and changes in the perception of knowledge, help to explain why, since 1945, opposition has taken the forms it has (cf. Shils 1967). But some of the instances of opposition can be explained much more simply. People dislike hearing the things scientists find out. So they stop them inquiring, or stop them from publishing their findings. For in relation to the public at large the social scientist stands in a different position from his colleague in natural science. Several writers on the epistemological foundations of social science have stressed that one of its distinguishing features is that the scientist does not have any privileged access to his data. He is a citizen like those he studies, and in interpreting their actions he can use only the same kinds of knowledge and experience as they themselves use. But while a large body of meta-sociological writing is concerned with the implications of this fact less attention has been given to its converse, that, at least to some extent, the citizen is also a scientist (Giddens 1976:153). He too can reason scientifically and, even without any scientific training, he can easily learn and make habitual use of the findings of inquiries in social science if he comes to hear about them and they are relevant to his activities. Thus while the natural scientist may sometimes safely disregard his lay critics, the social scientist has to pay heed to them, for they too have experience of social life and have learned to operate successfully in a social environment. This inescapability of lay criticism becomes greater as social science becomes more a normal part of secondary education. But even where this has not yet occurred, there will always be some citizens who are better acquainted at first hand with the social scene from which the scientist has drawn his data and who will not be inhibited from criticizing him by their unfamiliarity with his framework of scientific analysis. On the contrary, citizens with local knowledge who are unfamiliar with social science are much more likely to reject technical terms as preposterous nonsense, though they usually accept as authoritative the equally unfamiliar and incomprehensible jargon of natural science. In my view, this annoying characteristic is an inherent feature of social science and not merely, as some have supposed, an index of its methodological immaturity.

This feature has become important not only in industrialized countries subjected to a relatively high amount of investigation from sociologists and psychologists but also in Third World countries where empirical inquiry in social science has mainly been carried on by anthropologists working in rural areas. University students are quick to claim greater knowledge of their own

70

recently non-literate communities than that possessed by an expatriate anthropologist who may have stayed only a year or two and who may have worked through an interpreter. Students who are sympathetic to social science in general may yet be critical of the way it has been applied to their own communities, and are supported by other members who are not students (Strathern 1974). Thus for example a writer describing himself as 'a true blooded black Papua New Guinean' complains about the impression of his country given by the writings of Margaret Mead. He writes 'I guess it would be just the same as what my people would think if I visited America and came back to tell them that Americans ran nakedly in public, not knowing that only a handful of streakers do it' (Nokenkam Moa, in Weeks 1975:34). Just as in industrial countries health administrators may object to scientists who publish findings showing that their hospital, or their country, compares poorly with others, so in the Third World may local intellectuals object to reports claiming that the traditional institutions of their countries were less developed, or less sophisticated, than those of their neighbours (Hau'ofa 1975). This criticism may be just as vociferous when the anthropologist concerned is not an expatriate but a member of a local community, as evidence from New Zealand and Fiji shows (Crocombe 1976). New nations, and ethnic groups newly conscious of their corporate identity, tend to be intolerant of criticism and in some cases have imposed a blanket prohibition on all further inquiries. The widespread outcry in Mexico that followed the publication of a Spanish translation of Oscar Lewis' book *The children of Sánchez* in 1965 (Beals 1969:11–15) shows that objections to the publication of unwelcome facts and critical comment are not confined to new nations or ethnic groups struggling for recognition. The 'Springdale' affair, in which members of a small town in New York State objected strongly to the publication of a disguised account of their political and social life, shows that even in the homelands of empirical social research the same social processes are at work (Vidich and Bensman 1968:315–475; Barnes 1967:209–10).

If social science were a luxury that we could do without,

these restrictions on its pursuit might still be regretted but would not be crippling. If, on the other hand, we believe that, in a world characterized by rapidity of change, lack of consensus, imbalance of power, and massive powers of destruction, social science is a necessary tool for survival, then we must try to conduct our inquiries in such a way that, as far as possible, these resistances are not engendered.

Even so, the scientist cannot hope to succeed every time. The pursuit of knowledge may be his highest goal, but other people have other priorities. Thus for example Weaver (1971) describes how she took care to send drafts of her report to her informants for checking, to work with a local assistant, and to provide her gatekeepers with a copy of her academic proposal for further research, together with an interpretation of this in lay language. Nevertheless her gatekeepers were reluctant to allow her to proceed with further research, being concerned to discover whether she would make money out of her inquiries and whether her assistant would be given a degree. We have only her side of the story, but even so it seems that the gatekeepers, the council controlling a North American Indian reserve, were understandably more interested in not being exploited financially, as they saw it, and in securing advancement for one of the citizens, than in contributing to the pursuit of knowledge, as defined by this scientist. This trend will certainly continue. As we shall see in Chapter 8, citizens as well as scientists have begun to organize in order to exercise control over the inquiries made about themselves.

At the present time a great deal of routine social science is conducted within the spirit, if not fully within the letter, of the natural science paradigm. Increasingly, however, the social scientist, whether he likes it or not, is obliged to take account of the power to prevent, modify or hinder his inquiries exercised by other parties in the process. He has also to allow for the ways in which they perceive his inquiry conceptually, and what they hope or fear about its likely outcome. They too have interests in the inquiry. These we examine in the next chapter.

5 A diversity of interests

Social science, as we have seen, constitutes an extension of some of the basic aims of the natural sciences to the study of the social world. Given his commitment to the pursuit of knowledge, is the whole of social life a legitimate hunting ground for the omnivorously curious social scientist, or ought he to confine himself to certain areas only? In particular, are there areas which, however intellectually intriguing they may appear, cannot be investigated without such major intrusions on the rights and interests of citizens, in particular their right to privacy, that the scientist must forgo them? Privacy has been described as 'a two-way street consisting not only of what we need to exclude from or admit into our own thoughts or behavior, but also of what we need to communicate to, or keep from, others' (Ruebhausen and Brim 1965:1189). If we accept this view the citizen has a need to conceal as well as to reveal, to know as well as to be left in ignorance. Likewise a collectivity, or mankind in general, has a need to know some things about individual citizens and no need to know other things. Mankind has a need to know general propositions about social life established by scientific inquiry, though whether it has any need to be kept in ignorance about discoveries in social science, actual or potential, is a matter for debate.

When we query whether, at the level of generalizations about social life, knowledge is always better than ignorance, we usually have in mind the efforts of military sponsors to promote inquiries into destructive or harmful topics. We tend to ask about the desirability of limits on the freedom to inquire into everything when it seems that the scientist himself, rather than his sponsor, is becoming a threat to the powerless citizen. These questions arose, for instance, in connexion with a covert inquiry made in the middle sixties in the United States into homosexual fellatio in public lavatories. Some of the scientist's colleagues suggested that he should avoid this research topic, and argued that in an area of such sensitivity it would be best to 'let sleeping dogs lie' (cf. Katz, J. 1972: 326–9). The scientist argued against them that there are probably no 'sleeping dogs' in the realm of social interaction and certainly none so dormant as to merit avoidance by those whose commitment should be to the enhancement of man's self-knowledge. So far as his own study is concerned, Humphreys points out that the phenomenon he was studying was in fact the object of attention of the police, the press, and other agencies of social control, and that their acts are very much more harmful to the citizens involved than was anything done by the covert observing scientist. Nevertheless Humphreys was well aware of the potential danger to the citizens he described and took great care to conceal their identity. On one occasion he went to gaol rather than alert the police to the existence of the inquiry he was making. He argues that the publication of his study is unlikely to increase or decrease the amount of homoerotic activity that takes place in public lavatories, but that it may help to correct the superstition and cruelty that have characterized the reaction of society to this activity in the past (Humphreys 1975:168).

In general the debate has been about the extent to which the requirements of the quest for knowledge through scientific inquiry should be allowed to override the interests of those citizens on whom the inquiry is to be made. Some scientists have argued that citizens may legitimately be made to suffer so that mankind may benefit, whereas others maintain that the citizen has every right to refuse if he wants to. It would be as unreasonable for social scientists to treat citizens as freely exploitable for scientific ends as it would be, according to one commentator, for a surgeon to accost a healthy man with the request, 'Pardon me, sir, may I rip open your abdomen in the interests of science?' (Wilson, in Newcomb 1953:4). A third view is that, unlike surgeons, social scientists do not seriously interfere with the well being of citizens, so that a conflict of interests does not actually arise.

74

This debate concerns all branches of experimental and observational social science, but anthropologists have also to deal with another possible conflict of interest. As traditionally practised, anthropological inquiry is the study of disappearing social conditions. Although for most of the time that man has existed on earth he has lived by hunting and collecting, it is only in the last couple of hundred years or so, just as this form of subsistence is about to disappear, that it has been studied effectively. Subsistence agriculture and animal husbandry has been practised for a very much shorter time, and has been studied for significantly longer, but even so intensive studies of pre-literate societies of all types have begun to be numerous only just as these societies are being transformed into industrial societies or, more often, into communities that are dependent on industrial societies for most of their tools and their markets. Lévi-Strauss (1966:126–7) has described this never-to-be-repeated overlap of the old and the new, mediated by anthropology, daughter to the era of imperialist violence, and bounded in time.

Some anthropologists have therefore an interest in studying disappearing societies, and hence, we may argue, in preventing or delaying their disappearance. Not all anthropologists would support a policy of non-interference, and even Verrier Elwin, mentioned in Chapter 3, advocated only that tribal land rights should be respected, and that tribal people themselves should be trained to do the work of administration and development. Yet the process of acquiring the intellectual and material resources needed to protect themselves from more powerful neighbours may entail so radical a change in style of life that it can scarcely be defended as a way of preserving a traditional non-literate culture. Some anthropologists perceive an ethical problem in deciding whether to give priority to studying communities who have only recently been brought into the administrative ambit of a wider society or to providing them with the least problematic of the benefits of industrial technology, medical aid (Grayson 1969). Others claim that the two objectives do not interfere with one another, and that preserving the right of these communities to exploit their natural environment is equally important.

Some social scientists are so confident in their methods of analysis and techniques of investigation, or are so blinkered by them, that they are ready to specify in advance precisely what they need to know, and will shut their eyes to avoid being surprised by unexpected discoveries. But many more are uncertain at the beginning of an inquiry about what topics they can safely ignore, and prefer to take full advantage of any new facts they may happen to stumble on as the inquiry proceeds. Yet to gain support from others, scientists usually have to declare what they want to find out. Even if the initiative for an inquiry comes from citizens or sponsors, there still has to be some kind of statement of what the inquiry is aimed at. Successive discussions with sponsors, gatekeepers and the citizens themselves serve to delimit the inquiry, and the classes of data to be collected may be carefully listed in an attempt to identify an area of consensus to which all the parties can subscribe. A good deal of effort may be directed at steering the inquiry away from controversial aims, as well as from kinds of data that are expensive or tedious to collect. On grounds of time and money, and to gain the approval of the other parties, a scientist may have to forgo inquiries into many topics that he would like to learn about. In these circumstances a scientist may develop alternative strategies to gain the knowledge he seeks but which others had hoped to hide from him. Thus for example, in a study of a factory the scientist in charge wanted to ask citizens about their preferences among the four unions operating there. The management of the factory insisted that questions on this topic should not be included on the questionnaire administered to the citizens, and eventually the scientist agreed to the deletion. Subsequently he found out about the views of citizens on this topic by a different method (Form 1973:95–103). In discussion at a conference, the scientist was criticized by a colleague for violating his agreement with the factory management by behaving in this way. While defending his action, the scientist concerned seems to have recognized the force of this criticism, for he replied: 'Would I again be the bastard that I was? Probably so . . .' (Form 1973:116). I think he was being too apologetic. It seems to me that scientists should endeavour to convey to the public at large that they are insatiably curious, and that they cannot define in advance which areas of knowledge will be irrelevant to their particular inquiry. In practice, many social scientists are, of course, myopic, blinkered, easily satisfied; many sound research designs call for only a very restricted input of data; many examiners and editors are old-fashioned, conventional, resistant to new classes of data and new forms of analysis; allowing a research report to become a complete history of the inquiry is disastrous. Yet in principle social scientists ought to be omnivorous, and potentially interested in everything, so that the constraints which the scientist accepts on modes of inquiry and forms of publication can be seen for what they are, and not as constraints on his scientific interests. We credit physicians with omnivorous curiosity about health, so that if we take a sick child to the doctor we are flattered rather than offended if he inquires spontaneously about our own state of health. But we can be confident that he will not gossip with other patients about our aches and pains. When talking to a novelist we accept that some transformation of ourselves may appear in next year's novel; interviewed by a journalist, we realize that some mutilated but identifiable version of what we do and say may be printed in tomorrow's newspaper. Social scientists should aim at securing public recognition for combining the journalist's sceptical curiosity and the novelist's empathic perspicacity with the physician's professional reticence and fidelity to the data.

The interests of the scientist impinge on citizens to varying extents, depending on the aims of the inquiry and the mode of data collection that is adopted. The formal interview and the encounter with the research assistant administering a questionnaire, as well as the questionnaire sent for completion by the citizen in his own time, have become recognized features of social life in most industrial societies. Members of the public know how they are expected to respond. There has been less public recognition of the role of participant observer, though an increasing amount of data is being collected by scientists adopting this mode of inquiry. There are many fewer participant observers than there are interviewers, but the diversity of contexts in which they carry out their inquiries is much greater. The role has become socially recognized in some tribal communities exposed to saturated study for many years and maybe in some kibbutzim, communes and other special institutions easily accessible to social scientists. As the role gradually becomes part of the general consciousness, the insatiable curiosity of the social scientist should be emphasized as one of its essential attributes. The term 'participant observer' is usually applied to a social scientist who participates in the activities of some community or social unit, usually filling an existing social role modified to allow for his transient status. He observes and records what he sees and hears, usually quite openly (*pace* Janes 1961:446–7). Though he may conduct formal interviews and administer questionnaires, much of his information comes from the ordinary activities of the community which, in general, would have gone on in much the same way had he not been present. Some writers have said that it is unethical for an observing scientist to utilize, for example, data gathered at social parties for scientific purposes; it is, they argue, a betrayal of friendship. I agree with Riesman and Watson (1964:267) that 'It is exploitation if the guise of friendship is assumed for an unfriendly purpose, but if the friendly interaction is entered into in good faith, with other objectives being *in addition to* and not *instead of*, we see no serious violation of ethical standards' (their emphasis). But 'good faith' surely involves the scientist in drawing attention to his professional insatiable curiosity.

Scientists share a common commitment to the pursuit of knowledge but sponsors have in common with one another nothing more than the possession of resources and an interest in using them to promote social research. There is little that can be said about ethical dilemmas that can apply equally to a government department, a charitable foundation and a commercial enterprise. Nevertheless it is important to remember that sponsors, like citizens, have interests and enter into negotiations with the scientist usually from a position of strength. The foundation is in some sense in a more vulnerable position than the government agency or the commercial enterprise, since although it may be more open-handed with its funds, it is more dependent on public legitimation of its activities. Portes makes the point that 'the task of dispensing funds for socially legitimate causes is almost as difficult as that of earning them'. Sponsors who claim to be interested only in some aspect of the general good have continually to seek moral legitimation for their activities, and hence depend on maintaining a favourable reputation among those social scientists who are their potential beneficiaries. Therefore a private sponsor, or even a publicly-endowed body, is likely to seek to differentiate itself to a visible extent from the short term policies and interests of government. By providing evidence of social pluralism, it enhances its own crediblity. Most of the short-term policy objectives of the US Government in Latin America are aimed at supporting the status quo in Latin America and are seen, in academic and other circles, as reactionary. By contrast, some of the research projects in Latin America supported by private US sponsors, the foundations, have been aimed at facilitating social change and have been welcomed by local scholars. This wish to differentiate themselves from official government policy leads to 'the paradox that foundations have shown greater receptivity to collaborative projects with the socialist Cuban government than with "friendly" regimes in Paraguay or Nicaragua' (Portes 1974:20).

Klaw (1970) calls the relation between natural scientists and their governmental sponsors a Faustian bargain, and his label may be applied also to the social sciences. Yet the moral hazards of accepting financial support vary widely from one occasion to another. A private or corporate sponsor may be more demanding than a governmental agency, and a sponsor that seeks a full pound of flesh from one scientist may give another a completely free hand. The government may, for administrative convenience, provide separate channels of support for 'pure' and 'applied' research, and attempt to control the latter closely while deliberately holding back from interference with the former. The greater the part played by government in public life, the greater the dependence of scientists on the government, rather than other sources, for support; but also the greater the diversity of governmental interests, so that it may be easier to find some agency interested in supporting any given research project. But the names of governmental agencies are poor guides to their range of interests, though any agency with a sufficiently cryptic name is usually safely assumed to be disguised. Agencies differ too in the specificity of their interests and in their freedom to support research that is peripheral to their publicly-stated interests. Thus the various inquiries by the Rothschild committee and similar bodies have been concerned to establish rules defining the circumstances in which UK branches of government may support so-called pure and applied research. The existence of bodies like the Research Councils, with an explicit interest inter alia in promoting pure research, makes it feasible to argue that they should have sole responsibility for research of this kind, and that other governmental agencies must spend their money only on research topics that fall firmly within their own bailiwicks. A striking example of how the interests of governmental sponsors cannot be deduced from their ostensible area of responsibility is provided by the US military. Following the end of the Second World War, when there was a large increase in the amount of social inquiry carried out but before arrangements for providing federal financial support for that research had been separately institutionalized, the various military branches of government supported many research projects, which, at least so far as the social sciences were concerned, had little or nothing specifically to do with warfare (Kelman 1968:97). Thus for example the experiments conducted by Asch on pressures to conformity, described in Chapter 6, were financed by the US Department of the Navy. During the McCarthy era in the United States, research on sensitive topics like Soviet and Chinese culture was less liable to political censure if carried out under military aegis than under civilian sponsorship, and Mead (1972:127–30) defends her participation in such research while also arguing that, in post-Camelot conditions, all research of this kind should be removed from military sponsorship. Civilian federal funds for social research did become available during the sixties and it then became reasonable for the US Department of Defense to claim that, at least in its research

80

in foreign areas, it was 'interested only in those so-called cultural and social factors that have a clear relationship to defense activities' (Berreman 1969; cf. Deitchman 1976). Yet despite this clear division of function, an increasing number of social scientists, so Berreman claims, sought research funds from the Department of Defense as the only place where funds could readily be found, or found at all.

If there are many possible sponsors, with a diversity of interests, then a scientist may be fortunate enough to find one or more from whom he can accept support with a clear conscience. Likewise if there are social scientists of many different ethical and political persuasions, a sponsor may be able to find one of them willing to inquire into some topic in which he is interested. In these circumstances, it should be relatively easy to follow the advice given by Orlans (1967:5) to social scientists who object to a possible sponsor's objectives: 'don't decry the morality of its staff, but try to change their objectives and, in the interim, don't take their money' (cf. Likert and Lippitt 1953:603). But this kind of free market with an adequate plurality of buyers and sellers of the skills of social science is unlikely to prevail for long, and the market model does not take account of the differences in power between sponsors and scientists. There is therefore always the temptation to emulate Mrs Baines in *Major Barbara*, and to argue that money may be redeemed by being diverted from an evil source to good ends.

Independent foundations provided significant support for social research in Britain in the immediate post-war years, though the Colonial Social Science Research Council began its operations while the Second World War was still in progress. In the seventies in Britain and in several other Western countries, most support for social research comes from the government, though from its civilian rather than its military branches. Most large government agencies have routinized their use of, and support for, social research, so that the social scientist entrepreneur finds himself negotiating with other social scientists who are employees of his would-be sponsor. Scientifically qualified civil servants can challenge him on his own ground, and thus can exercise more effective control not only over the topic of his inquiry but also over the way in which he conducts his inquiries. For example, Rein (1976: 89–90) describes how even so apparently technical a matter as the choice of standardized educational test to be used in a field experiment can generate an ethical dilemma, if a sponsor insists, for broadly political reasons, on the use of tests that scientists consider invalid. Similarly, the evaluation of research findings, which at first glance might seem to be a purely technical procedure, is in fact greatly influenced by the political context in which the research has been carried out, a context mainly defined by the sponsor, as well as by the values held by the scientist as citizen (cf. Sjoberg 1975: 37–45). Even with the most innocuous inquiries a sponsor may be more likely to perceive the ensuing knowledge as a source of power rather than of enlightenment. Political pressure on government agencies, even those charged with responsibilities for supporting pure research, encourages them to use the tax-payer's money for research proposals that are purported to be useful. Social scientists may exploit this fact when seeking financial support by describing over-optimistically the likely practical significance of their proposed research, and some forms of application for research funds pose this temptation explicitly. It is a brave social scientist who will be prepared to say firmly, as Rutherford did of his research on atomic fission, that his proposed inquiries have no practical application at all. It is a brave bureaucrat who will provide funds for such 'useless' topics, particularly if they can easily be identified from their titles by hostile politicians. 'Lesbianism in Lesotho' is said to be a recent example. Federally funded research projects in the United States have also become vulnerable to the predatory scrutiny of hostile politicians (Starr 1977). In these circumstances social scientists are tempted to pay lip-service to the notion of knowledge as power, and to tailor their scientific curiosity to match the interests of their sponsors, however sceptical they may be at heart.

Although most of the financial support for pure research in social science, i.e. research not directly linked to a proposal for social action, has come from government and private philanthropic foundations, support for applied research and requests for professional advice have come from private and nationalized commercial enterprises as well as from government. Psychologists in particular have carried out consultancy work of many kinds for various industries (Baritz 1960). Most of this work has been conducted within the natural science paradigm. The workforce or the potential customers or some other aggregate has been the object of study, and the aims of the inquiry have been set by the sponsor, who claimed ownership of the knowledge obtained from the inquiry. Negotiation has been between scientist and sponsor, or scientist and gatekeeper, rather than with citizens, and ethical issues have rarely been raised. Some research organizations have endeavoured to ensure that the pursuit of knowledge as enlightenment has gone hand in hand with the achievement of knowledge as power, or, to shift this aim slightly into the clinical language of the Tavistock Institute, to maintain the doctrine of 'No research without therapy, no therapy without research'.

Some social scientists seek to avoid completely the Faustian bargain. Evans-Pritchard, for many years a government anthropologist, spoke from experience when he said 'He who sups with the administration needs a long spoon' (Barnes 1977:53), and some social scientists would appear to reject all direct government support. For instance, Hiatt (1969), with the war in Indochina in mind, argued that a social scientist must be committed to the concept of a university as a place where no subject of investigation is held to be sacrosanct and that acceptance of government contracts is incompatible with this commitment. But the government is a many-headed Hydra, and some heads are more benign than others (cf. Glick 1970; Hiatt 1970); likewise some contracts are more restrictive than others. Beals (1969:2) puts the position plainly:

... the scientist of any persuasion rarely has all the freedom he desires and often must compromise his honesty. A major reason for this is that, with few exceptions, he must be employed if he is to eat and study or use the methods and findings of his discipline.

Shallice (1972) makes the important observation that although a sponsor, by offering support for research into a specified topic, may secure information that would not otherwise come to light, the new line of inquiry may then acquire a momentum of its own. Scientists become intellectually interested in the new field for its own sake, a new sub-specialism develops, and soon the initiative for suggesting new topics for inquiry lies with the scientists rather than with the initial sponsor. He suggests that this process has occurred with research into sensory deprivation. The initial impetus to conduct research in this field may well have come from the military, with its professional interest in interrogation techniques, but continuing research activity has been sustained by the intellectual interest of scientists who have become adepts in this area. Shallice argues that the use of sophisticated methods of interrogation by the British Army in Ulster from 1971 demonstrates that military operations were being approached from a scientific perspective, and that the soldiers concerned utilized their knowledge of the professional psychological literature on sensory deprivation; psychologists must take responsibility for this. He would like the editors of scientific journals to take more account of the likely practical applications of research findings, particularly when the research has been sponsored by military agencies, and, where the applications are likely to be socially damaging, to refuse publication. Thus this is a plea not that scientists should refrain from inquiries that may lead to knowledge that may be used for evil, but that editors should use their influence to turn the attention of their scientific colleagues towards inquiries more likely to lead to socially helpful applications. The number of scientists is limited, yet the number of topics into which they might inquire is virtually unlimited; editors should discourage choices that are socially damaging and not select for publication on the basis of technical competence alone. In other words, if military and similar sponsors want research done on topics likely to lead to potentially destructive results, they should not be given gratuitous help by unthinking scientists. This is a plea for mobilizing editorial power, such as it is, to counteract the power of sponsors in controlling the choice of research topics. Editorial power, as Reynolds (1972:713) points

A diversity of interests

out, is comparatively weak and, in any case, we have to remember that research on noxious topics has often proved to have some beneficial outcomes; potential good and potential evil have to be compared without full knowledge of either.

Sometimes intellectual curiosity as a scientist merges into political interests as a citizen. In much of the controversy about behavioural genetics, including the effect on intelligence of genetic differences, some scientists have called in the name of greater scientific understanding for more research, while those opposing them have argued that research in this area will yield, at least at the present time, little enlightenment and will lead only to greater racial and ethnic discrimination (cf. Walsh 1971). Thus two prominent geneticists argued in 1971 that in the 'racial climate' of the United States at that time, research on racial differences in intelligence, however well intentioned, could easily lead to unnecessary accentuation of racial differences and therefore should not be encouraged. Five years later, while continuing to assert that research on this topic has neither theoretical nor practical applications, they conceded that the topic has aroused a good deal of understandable passion and that without research unwise actions might flow from erroneous views about these differences (Cavalli-Sforza and Bodmer 1971:801–2; Bodmer and Cavalli-Sforza 1976:679–80).

Gatekeepers and citizens may have attitudes about the acceptability of sponsors that are just as relevant to the process of inquiry of those held by the scientists. Thus for example the Himalayan border countries project of the University of California was initially financed from private American sources. In 1968 a member of the Indian parliament disclosed that the project was now to be partially financed by the United States Department of Defense for a period of three years. The project at once came to grief because of Indian opposition (Berreman 1969). Glazer (1972:134–9) records his embarrassment when, after he had assured the Chileans whom he studied and with whom he collaborated that he was not sponsored by any United States government agency, he discovered that he had unknowingly accepted support from SORO, the Army agency responsible,

85

inter alia, for Project Camelot. Several years after the event he declared himself to be 'still haunted' by the fact that several copies of his doctoral dissertation were sent to SORO.

During the Vietnam war, much of the controversy about social research turned on the sponsorship of inquiries by the CIA, even though the main sponsor seems in fact to have been the Department of Defense. The CIA is manifestly and appropriately a covert organization, and it is reasonable to assume that it is never telling the whole truth. It is therefore peculiarly unfitted to act as a sponsor of research activities in which the suspicions of gate-keepers and citizens have to be taken into account. If the real objectives of a research project are benign, why cannot they be stated openly, by a sponsor whose word will be believed? Why would the CIA be involved unless there was something to hide? But before we begin to congratulate ourselves that nothing so sinister could happen here, or could happen again in the United States, we should remember that in Britain, as in most Western countries, the sources of a sponsor's wealth are often obscure, and that there is in principle no reason why the most benignly named institution should not be a front for some organization even more sinister than the CIA. The major private sponsors have taken a good deal of trouble to declare the sources of their funds; for the most part they are the profits of private industry. By taking money from such sponsors scientists may feel that they are en-dorsing, or tolerating, the system that produces these profits, or alternatively that they are diverting a small portion of ill-gotten wealth to good ends, depending on how they variously view the matter. The open identity of the sponsor, and in most cases the evidence of the sponsor's source of wealth, enables the citizen as well as the scientist to decide whether or not, or how far, he is willing to become involved in the process of inquiry. If the identity of the sponsor is secret, he is being asked to buy a pig in a poke.

When a citizen's right to privacy is recognized, either by custom or in law, a gatekeeper may consider that he has a duty placed on him to protect the citzens from unwarranted invasions of their privacy which they are not powerful enough to resist on their own and which the scientist wishes to make in the name of science. In some cases the gatekeeper may mainly be protecting his own interest, under the guise of protecting the privacy of the citizens, but in others this may not be so. Thus, for example, the function of the Bureau of Research in the United States Office of Education, in vetting questions to be included in questionnaires for use in education research, has been defined as serving 'as an honest broker between the scientist who presses for scientific freedom, and the public which, generally speaking, places considerably greater emphasis on the value of personal privacy' (Conrad 1967:359). Much the same sentiments are often expressed by gatekeepers even when there is no right to privacy embodied in the law and when the gatekeepers' own interests are not threatened by the inquiries proposed. A gatekeeper may wish to protect children or employees from being asked questions by the scientist which, in the institutional context of a school or factory, they may not feel powerful enough to refuse to answer. The gatekeeper is in effect seeking to redress the imbalance of power between scientist and citizens by intervening on their behalf. But in practice it is often difficult to differentiate between the gatekeeper's own interests and his interpretation of the true but unexpressed interests of the citizens he controls. On the other hand there is no guarantee that the scientist is any better qualified to speak for the interests of mute citizens than is their gatekeeper, and the scientist's interests are quite likely to conflict with theirs. Universities whose members carry out research may consider that they should protect the interests of the community on which they depend for financial and moral support, and may therefore impose constraints on the kind of research that their members carry out under the academic banner. In some American universities all proposals for research involving citizens must be vetted, usually by an academic committee, to ensure that the rights of the citizens are adequately respected, as judged by the university (e.g. Vargus 1971:246).

The research process is thus one in which several different parties are involved whose interests and obligations are partly parallel and partly divergent. In general it is the scientist who is the entrepreneur who takes the initiative in trying to get the parties to cooperate and who has to negotiate with them so that they can cooperate fruitfully, so that new value, in the form of knowledge or action, emerges from the joint endeavour. It is against this picture of a diversity of interests, and of a variety of views about how the process of inquiry should proceed and how its outcome should be perceived, that we can now turn to consider in greater detail the two main phases of the process, the collection of data and the communication of results.

6 Collecting data

Social inquiries take many forms and the ethical issues they raise vary accordingly. At one extreme is the national census, typically occurring only once every ten years, when citizens are required by law to answer a limited number of questions about themselves and about members of their households. The aggregated anonymous results of censuses are published fairly quickly but the individual schedules remain, in most cases, inaccessible to the public, and to social scientists, until long after the individuals concerned are dead. Interaction between scientist and citizen is minimal. At the other extreme is the collaborative investigation of some social institution, extending over several years, with sustained contact in a variety of contexts between the scientists and the citizens, resulting eventually in some publication in whose preparation both groups have been involved. The Glacier project, carried out by the Tavistock Institute of Social Relations during the forties, fifties and sixties in a factory in north-west London, is an example of a lengthy inquiry, though the contexts of interaction between scientists and citizens were in this instance fairly narrowly defined (Jaques 1951:11–16; Barnes 1977:26–9). Most inquiries fall between these two extremes. The importance of paying attention to the rights of the citizens, and of the other parties to the inquiry, in a lengthy collaborative inquiry is easy to see. But even with national censuses, the rights of the citizens to privacy and secrecy have often been vigorously asserted. A significant number of citizens objected on principle to providing the information required from them in the last United Kingdom census in 1971, and some were fined for breaking the law. People objected particularly to stating their country of origin, parent's country of origin, ownership of car, educational qualifications

89

Who should know what?

and employer's address. Some people objected simply to providing the information, while others feared that, despite the stiff guarantees protecting the confidentiality of census returns, the information on their schedules would be misused. The guarantees protect the citizen's privacy but social scientists often chafe at the restrictions placed on access to detailed census information. The extent of the guarantees is not always stated unequivocally, or is misunderstood, as was shown by an incident in 1971. The Social Survey division of the Office of Population Censuses and Surveys sampled one in every 150 of those women who, in the recent census, had declared themselves to be former nurses, so as to provide information for a committee investigating the state of nursing in the National Health Service. Whether this follow-up survey infringed the guarantees given at the time of the census was debated publicly (*Nursing times* 1971; Hewitt 1977:12). The Registrar General himself is reported to have said that the census was a 'monstrous invasion of privacy', though Madgwick and Smythe (1974:87–97), in their critical account of the erosion of privacy, admit that, despite its serious shortcomings, the census was very far from being the worst example.

Objections of this kind go back a long way. Even in the eighteenth century, when a proposal for a British census was first discussed in 1753, one member of Parliament objected that it would be to 'treat us like oxen and sheep . . . As for myself, I hold this project to be totally subversive of the last remains of English liberty . . . ' (*Hansard* 1813:1320; Glass 1973:17–20). In defending the indirect procedure he had used in the British census of 1851 for assessing the strength of support for the various religious bodies, Horace Mann (1855:142) argued that to ask every person in the country to state his religious belief would be 'far too inquisitorial to be ever adopted in England', though presumably he was well aware that precisely that question had been asked in the Irish census of 1834 (cf. Pickering 1967:382; Thomson, D. M. 1967 & 1972:121). The inquisitorial aspect of the census attracted the opposition of the Women's Freedom League in 1911, who chalked 'No Vote No Census' on the walls

90

Collecting data

of the houses where they spent the night of the census (Fulford 1957:240). Yet the information required of the citizen in a national census, because it has to be collected from everyone, is invariably much less 'inquisitorial' than that called for by the government in innumerable other contexts affecting only specified categories of the population. The information called for by social scientists is often much more comprehensive, constitutes a much greater invasion of privacy, and is sought for from only some members of the community and not from others. When censuses are opposed, it is not surprising that social scientists cannot get the information they seek simply on demand.

In talking about empirical inquiries made by social scientists it is convenient to make an initial distinction between the laboratory and the real world. Any laboratory is, of course, part of the real world in that it exists in time and space and not merely in the imagination, and also in the sense that, so we assume, people's behaviour in the laboratory is sufficiently closely related to the way in which they behave in the world outside the laboratory for us to be able to infer from one environment to the other. The laboratory is a specialized and delimited environment, where conditions can be kept constant or varied at will, observations and recordings can be made intensively, and where it is considered legitimate to ask people to do things they would not normally do outside. Nevertheless the citizens who enter the laboratory remain citizens, just as the scientists are also citizens, and even though they may have agreed to forgo some of their rights as citizens for the duration of the experiment, there are limits to which the scientist can accept this abdication or can subject them to harm. For example, it is generally believed that the solidarity of a closed group may be enhanced by making initiation into membership an ordeal. An ordeal experienced by initiates in many parts of the world was circumcision (cf. Allen 1967). Two psychologists in the United States, studying the effect of the severity of initiation on liking for the group, required the citizens they studied in a laboratory to read out a list of obscene words (Aronson and Mills 1959). This ordeal was, as Aronson and Carlsmith (1968:11) comment, 'rather pallid' in comparison

91

with what happens in the real world, but ethical considerations prevented them from using any stronger substitute stimulus. In the dramatic Stanford prison experiment discussed later in this chapter, in which volunteer students were subjected to physical pain, psychological humiliation, anxiety and extremely unpleasant memories (Zimbardo 1973:249), the scientists nevertheless ruled out, for ethical, moral and pragmatic reasons, the use of threats or promises of severe physical punishment and did not allow homosexual or racist practices to flourish, though these are features of the real prisons they were trying to simulate (Haney et al. 1973:72). Yet though the laboratory may not be exempt from all moral constraints, it remains an environment in which citizens can be put to considerable distress, and induced to display cowardice, fear, anger, conformity or other characteristics they would rather not have exhibited (Schultz 1969:223).

In this sense the laboratory is a privileged moral environment, where to some extent the rights and duties of citizens can be set aside temporarily. What is problematic is the extent to which this should happen, the kinds of considerations that might justify a greater or lesser departure from the ethical bonds of ordinary life, and what procedures should be adopted to recompense for the damage that may be done by this departure. Outside the laboratory, a scientist may be able so to arrange things that certain citizens are willing to behave as if they were in a laboratory, and, for example, accept invasions of their privacy that they would not normally tolerate. But these citizens, and the scientist himself, are likely to be surrounded by other citizens who are not parties to the bargain, and hence the extent to which events in the field, in the real world outside the laboratory, can be coaxed into scientifically desired forms by a relaxation of moral constraints is likely to be small. Nevertheless ethical issues arise in field as well as laboratory experiments, and in the field are not confined to experimentally manipulated situations.

In some kinds of social inquiry lying is an integral part of the research design. Scientists tell lies to citizens and observe what the citizens do and say. Premeditated lying is characteristic of the inquiries carried out by psychologists rather than by sociologists

92

and anthropologists, and within psychology it is a feature of experimental work in the social psychology laboratory rather than in the field, i.e. in the real world. In the couple of decades after the end of the First World War, there was a rise in the incidence of deception in social psychological and personality research, as reported in American journals (Menges 1973:1030). Lying is an explicit form of deception, and has been discussed most extensively by experimental social psychologists, some of whom have argued that deception is both undesirable and unnecessary in psychological inquiry (Vinacke 1954; Kelman 1972: 997). As used by psychologists, deception occurs when the scientist, acting openly in that role, tells lies to citizens expecting that they will believe him to be speaking the truth. Deception is certainly practised also by sociologists and social anthropologists, but usually in some other form; it may be seen by them either as a regrettable necessity before mutual confidence between scientist and citizen can be established, or as a continuing necessity when the scientist pretends not to be a scientist at all. The same mode of deception as in psychological experiments is however found in many clinical trials of new medicines when a control group is used. A doctor gives patients placebos which he hopes they will think are effective medicines when in fact they are not.

I think that few people would argue that the use of deception in clinical trials is wrong, particularly if a double-blind test design, in which neither doctors nor patients know who are receiving placebos, provides the best check on the value of the new medicine; the misfortune of the patients who receive only placebos is matched by the risk run by those who are given the real medicine. But in psychological experiments usually all, rather than only some, of the citizens are deceived, and some psychologists argue that other types of experimental design exist which are as effective as those that entail deception. Others, with that wish to reduce as far as possible by empirical inquiry the residual area left to moral judgement which seems to characterize the psychological profession, have tried to investigate how much difference deception makes to the outcome of experiments, and to discover in what conditions citizens do not mind being deceived (Berscheid et al. 1973; Shulman and Berman 1974). Against them, it is argued that the violation of the personal rights of citizens is always wrong, whether or not it has any effect on experimental results (Waterman 1974).

Those who object to the use of deception tend to argue against it in principle, but widespread discussion of deception has been triggered off by particular experiments in which deception has led to distress, or where the results obtained by the experiment have been disturbing. One experiment that has become a classic in social psychology involved deception, but little or no distress. In the 1950s Asch carried out experiments designed to discover to what extent individuals would resist pressures to conformity. In the laboratory, seemingly honest student volunteers were asked to state publicly which of three lines on various cards matched in length a standard line on another card. Only one of the students had not been briefed beforehand on what he should say; he was the only 'naïve subject', as such persons are usually described. The six or eight others were all 'stooges' or 'confederates' and had been told by the experimenter what to say. The object of the experiment was to discover to what extent the naïve subject continued to believe the evidence of his own eyes in the face of false testimony proclaimed by the stooges (Asch 1956).

Asch attached great importance to revealing the deception to his naïve subjects at the end of the experiments, and thus perpetuating the perception of a laboratory as a specially privileged environment in which normal rules of conduct and mutual trust could be temporarily suspended in safety, for everything would come right in the end. Even so, the necessity for deception created various practical difficulties. Both the stooges and the naïve or 'critical' subjects, as Asch calls them, were asked to keep the details of the experiment confidential, so that the experiments could proceed within the same institution using the same design. Asch did not reveal in his published report the names of the three institutions of higher learning where he did the experiments, saying that 'It seems proper not to identify them by name.'

Presumably Asch thought that the demonstrated propensity of most of the naïve subjects to conform to the majority consensus of opinion might reflect poorly on their moral qualities. But now that the results of the experiments have become part of received psychological wisdom, their inbuilt deception causes further trouble. Students of psychology who are required to replicate the experiments as part of their professional training have to carry them out very early in their course, while they may reasonably be expected to be still naïve, before they learn from their textbooks what is supposed to happen. The same hazard affects all replications of well-known experiments that involve deception, and leads experimenters to devise more and more elaborate ways of eliciting spontaneous responses from increasingly un-naïve student-citizens. Deception escalates, so that, for example, the debriefing phase in the experiment, when the scientist abandons his role of manipulator and speaks frankly to the citizens as fellow human beings, becomes in more sophisticated experiments a second sham; the citizens are merely being led up a new and even more devious experimental garden path (e.g. Festinger and Carlsmith 1959; cf. Kelman 1967:2–3; Rochford 1974). Once a citizen has experienced this kind of two- or three-stage deception, there is no reason why he should have any further trust in what the scientist tells him. Particularly if he has done his homework he may well anticipate, accurately or inaccurately and cooperatively or antagonistically, what he thinks the experimenter wants him to do. The 'screw you' phenomenon appears and the experiment loses its validity (Bickman and Henchy 1972:2–3; Schultz 1969:222).

Other psychologists defend the practice of deception in experiments. Much of the controversy about the Milgram experiments on obedience, in which citizens were tricked into thinking that they were administering electric shocks (Miller, A. G. 1972b:75–224; Milgram 1974), turned on the fact that the work was done under the auspices of a university, Yale, in the department of psychology. Some of the defenders of the experiments argued that any man who volunteered to take part in the experiments would know (a) that he might well be misled deliberately, as happens in many such experiments, and (b) that he would know that the university authorities would never allow him to be really harmed. Milgram admits that more of the citizens than he expected chose to administer, so they thought, strong shocks to the victim and that some of them experienced stress while so doing. But he argues that at no point did they run the risk of injurious effects resulting from their participation, and points to the evidence of a questionnaire adminstered to the participants some time after the experiments had been carried out. 84 per cent of them stated that they were glad to have been in the experiment, and only 1·3 per cent indicated negative feelings. These favourable responses must surely be due mainly to the careful debriefing that took place immediately after the experiment had been completed.

A careful postexperimental treatment was administered to all subjects. The exact content of the dehoax varied from condition to condition and with increasing experience on our part. At the very least, all subjects were told that the victim had not received dangerous electric shocks. Each subject had a friendly reconciliation with the unharmed victim, and an extended discussion with the experimenter. The experiment was explained to the defiant subjects [those who refused to give shocks] in a way that supported their decision to disobey the experimenter. Obedient subjects were assured of the fact that their behavior was entirely normal and that their feelings of conflict or tension were shared by other participants. Subjects were told that they could receive a comprehensive report at the conclusion of the experimental series. (Milgram 1974:194)

Milgram further defends his work with evidence to show that at least some of the citizens reported that they had learned a good deal about themselves and about human beings in general from their association with the experiments. This benefit, which it must be if we accept the premiss that knowledge is better than ignorance, can be achieved only if citizens are dehoaxed and if the rationale of the experiment is explained to them.

Some commentators defend deception, at least in some instances, on the grounds that the amount of distress engendered in psychological experiments is often only slight, and that there is evidence to show that debriefing can be effective in alleviating tension that may have been produced. It is only through debriefing soon after the experiment finishes, rather than months or years later when they may happen to read about the experiment and recognize that they took part in it, that the citizens directly involved can hope to learn much from their participation. A good deal of attention has been given by psychologists to the process of debriefing and to the hazards likely to be encountered as citizens begin to realize how they have been duped (Festinger 1953:170; Aronson and Carlsmith 1968:32–6, 70–73).

Some psychologists maintain that debriefing is sometimes unnecessary and even undesirable. For example, certain psychological tests, like the Roschach and other projective tests, depend for their validity on the naïvety of the citizens to whom they are administered. If a citizen knows what criteria the tester will apply and how his responses will be marked, he can try to modify his spontaneous replies in the hope of producing a result more to his liking (Krout 1954). It then becomes a battle of wits between citizen and tester in which the latter, by complicating the test, hopes to be able to infer what the citizen's spontaneous replies would have been had he known nothing in advance about the test. Debriefing a citizen after he has taken a projective test makes him less naïve the next time he is tested, so that continued use of the test undermines its validity. This phenomenon is found to some extent with all psychological tests that become part of the ambient culture, and is seen notably in the growth of coaching specifically aimed at securing high performance in intelligence tests. Projective tests seem to be particularly sensitive to the naïvety of the citizen, and hence he is unlikely to receive anything like a full explanation of how they are constructed. At the same time they are designed to uncover aspects of his personality that he may not be aware of, and have therefore been singled out as being morally questionable (Shils 1959:129).

But some psychologists have gone a step further and argue that debriefing, or more accurately dehoaxing, is not always necessary, even when naïvety is not in question, particularly in covert field experiments, where citizens in the real world may not realize that they have been under the scientist's scrutiny in some social setting that, unknown to them, he has arranged to suit his own ends. Citizens may not wish to gain that insight into themselves that they might get from an explanation of the experiment, particularly if they had behaved in some reprehensible way. In a covert field experiment, it is argued, the amount of manipulation that a scientist can achieve is small, and the citizens face only the kind of life situation they might normally encounter and which they can easily deal with whatever happens. They should therefore not suffer any loss of self-esteem.

I think this line of argument has some force, but it is open to objections. Absence of debriefing entails the loss of the opportunity to learn. The citizen cannot, for example, learn that he is slower than average in going to help a (staged) victim of an accident unless he is dehoaxed afterwards; without dehoaxing, he loses the stimulus, which might be quite powerful, to modify his behaviour. It is true that if the scientist is relatively powerless, his manipulation of the real world may be harmless; it is merely 'a simple acceleration of natural events' (Bickman and Henchy 1972:4). For example, in an experiment designed to discover how much racial discrimination there was in the allocation of municipal housing, students, men and women and Black and White, posed as married couples in various combinations and made inquiries about flats that had been advertised as vacant. The officials responsible for their allocation were tricked into dealing with inquiries which were in fact bogus; they were not dehoaxed, and their decisions provided evidence for illegal discrimination which they might well have wished not to be published. Yet few people would regard the actions of the students as unethical or unjustifiably harmful to the officials, whose identity was disguised in the report (McGrew 1967). More people would welcome the publication of evidence that the law was 'typically' being broken.

Yet even if a scientist does not have so free a hand to manipulate events in the real world as he has in the laboratory, a scientist in a position of power might easily cause more distress in covert field experiments than Milgram ever did in the laboratory. At present, the laboratory is institutionalized as the legitimate stalking ground of the psychologist and, to a much lesser extent, his colleagues in other social science disciplines. The citizen who enters this danger area may submit himself voluntarily to unspecified physical and psychical hazards but he believes that when he returns to the real world he will be safe again. If psychological, or even socio-logical, experimentation in the real world becomes commonplace, it too will become institutionalized and part of the public consciousness. Psychologists have begun to conduct experiments in the real world rather than the laboratory because the main aim of their discipline is to understand how people behave in the real world; the laboratory, and its rats, are only surrogates. But whereas citizens volunteer, albeit not always freely, to enter the laboratory, citizens become involved in field psychological experiments unknowingly. In some experiments they are put to only minor inconvenience, while in others they are presented with staged situations they may choose to ignore but which may still generate distress. Even in ignoring a staged situation they may be providing data for the watching covert psychologist, as in a Good Samaritan experiment (Piliavin et al. 1969). Debriefing sometimes follows, as in the Paddington station experiment (Sissons 1971), in which travellers were asked the way to Hyde Park as a ruse for observing some aspects of non-verbal communication, but most field experiments leave the citizens unaware that they have been participants. Absence of debriefing prevents citizens from learning directly from their participation, but their reliance on the authenticity of what they see going on around them is not undermined.

But if field experimentation becomes institutionalized, the 'pollution' of the research environment, as Kelman (1972:999) puts it, will spread from the laboratory to the real world. Like frequent mock air raids and practice fire drills, covert field experiments may lead the citizen to mistake the genuine event for a staged one; he may, for example, leave the real accident victim to die because he is tired of rushing to aid psychology students masquerading as accident victims. This saturation is unlikely to occur widely but may well be encountered in those

99

localities where scientists and students constitute a significant fraction of the population, as in some small university towns. Already in some of these, where large classes of social science students regularly carry out their practical training in social inquiry locally, the citizens show the effects of saturation and are reluctant to answer the same questions yet again. The students are fresh each year while the citizens remain the same. Likewise, in some repeatedly studied rural communities, resistance has developed. Portes (1973:155) reports that in one Chilean rural district, farmers refused to complete questionnaires, arguing that three years of supplying information to visiting Chilean and United States economists, water law experts, engineers and sociologists had brought them no benefit at all. The saturation level for obtrusive inquiries of this interrogatory kind is probably easier to reach than for staged events, but the danger of saturation cannot be disregarded.

To overcome the ethical objections to deception, and the methodological complications that follow from the institutionalization of deception, Mixon (1974) and others have advocated experiments in which the scientist speaks honestly to the citizens and asks them to act out the roles he indicates to them. The technique of role-playing or 'reality practice' is used in the socio-dramas and psycho-dramas of Moreno (1953) and others and must be distinguished from the concealed role-playing in the field that occurs in most covert research. The citizens are asked to behave as if they really were the characters whose roles they have been assigned. Role-playing, it is claimed, is a better way of investigating in the laboratory how citizens behave in specified conditions that are difficult to observe and study in the real world. The play-acting must be done realistically; merely asking people to imagine how they would behave is likely to yield invalid results. This discrepancy between imagined and actual behaviour is well demonstrated in a field experiment in which nurses were tempted to break hospital regulations by giving an excessive dose of an unauthorized medicine to a patient in response to a telephoned instruction from an unknown 'doctor'. Ten out of twelve graduate nurses, and all twenty-one student nurses, on being asked to

100

imagine themselves 'as vividly as possible' in this situation, said they would refuse to give the medicine; in a real test, twenty-one out of twenty-two qualified nurses were on their way to the patient's bedside to give the medicine before being intercepted by a waiting scientist (Hofling et al. 1966).

Unfortunately Hofling and his colleagues did not repeat their inquiry, with role-playing nurses actually receiving telephone calls known to be bogus, rather than sitting in a classroom at a desk; the results might have been closer to those obtained in the real test. Mixon reports that getting citizens to act out the Milgram obedience experiments enabled him, and them, to understand why Milgram's deceived citizens acted as they did, though his conclusions have been challenged (Tajfel 1977). Though role-playing provides a useful technique for making inquiries and coming to important discoveries by effectively harnessing the full ability of the citizens to make their contribution, it certainly does not enable the scientist to escape from consideration of ethics. The ethical issues in role-playing are well brought out in the Stanford prison experiment, discussed in a later section. Nor does it meet fully the requirements necessary for satisfactory experimental designs from which valid conclusions can be drawn, though it may have more value as a way of exploring or generating new ideas (Cooper 1976). After reviewing the literature extensively, A. G. Miller (1972a:634) concludes that 'the prospects for role playing as an alternative to deception are very poor'.

Whereas deception has been a lively issue among psychologists, their colleagues in sociology have been more concerned with confidentiality and the achievement of trust between citizens and scientists. One reason for this difference is that almost all of the knowledge gained by psychologists is expressed in nomothetic terms, whereas sociology, in its empirical and applied aspects, often organizes its findings ideographically. Some sociologists may still see as their ultimate goal that set of determinate equations sketched tantaltzingly by Homans (1949:330) which would reveal that 'There would be neither "exceptional" groups nor "random" variations in group characteristics but only different solutions of the system of equations.' Many natural scientists who

Who should know what?

write impatiently about slow progress in social engineering see social science in these terms. But even Homans suggests that this goal may be unobtainable, and the present practice of empirical inquiry in sociology is better characterized by Gouldner (1965b:7) when he notes that the applied sociologist 'makes use of the *concepts* rather than the generalized propositions of pure social science'.

The contrast between psychology and sociology in this respect can be seen in the way in which use is made of information on individuals. At the end of the nineteenth century, at an early stage in the development of psychological experimentation, the people on whom experiments were performed were highly trained professionals, or 'reagents' as they were sometimes known (Schultz 1969:215). Twentieth-century psychology has however been essentially the study of naïve amateurs. Indeed, since the most readily available supply of people willing to be experimented upon has been from students studying psychology, the problem facing the experimenter has been, as mentioned earlier, to utilize students as soon as they become willing and/or compliant but before they cease to be naïve. In these circumstances the personal identity of the individuals who participate in psychological experiments is usually quite irrelevant. Furthermore virtually all results in experimental psychology are published only in aggregated or impersonal form. The individuals become entities with specified qualities: age, sex, race, x years of schooling, y pounds annual income, voted for Z in the last election, and so on. The correlations found to exist between the citizen's responses and his attributes are seen as at least a first approximation towards some relation which will be eternally and ubiquitously true. On the other hand, most sociological inquiries are much more deeply embedded in the historical and spatial context in which they are made, and the loss of information that is inevitable when disguises are used is likely to be significant, because of its effect on both the validity of the results and their general interest. Kruglanski (1975:105) distinguishes theoretical or universalistic research and what he calls context-concerned or particularistic research in psychology, but it is the former that accounts for the greater part of psychological inquiry, while the latter is characteristic of sociology and even more so of anthropology. In general, therefore, sociologists do not want to use disguises except where they must, whereas psychologists lose nothing of value by making their subjects anonymous. The units discussed by political scientists are often so large and select that they cannot be effectively disguised, whatever the scientist may wish. Sociologists and anthropologists typically report events from the real world, where citizens are responsible for their actions, and where attribution in print may therefore have serious consequences, whereas the citizen usually does not have to answer to his fellows or to society for how he behaves inside the psychological laboratory.

These differences between the disciplines may explain why the topic of deception, which has attracted so much attention from psychologists concerned with ethical issues, is not mentioned in the code of the British Sociological Association (cf. Riesman and Watson 1964:261). For there is no analogue in sociological inquiry, for example, to Milgram's experiments. Yet a more serious charge has been made that some industrial sociologists have advocated the use of deception, not as a necessary though regrettable feature of research, but as an acceptable characteristic of ongoing social organization. March and Simon (1958:54) discuss 'felt participation in decisions'. They say that 'most students of the subject argue that (provided the deception is successful) the perception of individual participation in goal-setting is equivalent in many respects to actual participation. Thus, actual influence over the specific decision being made is of less importance to the individual than acknowledgement of his influential decision.' They make no suggestions for eliminating deception, nor do they discuss what happens when it ceases to be successful. Yet the alleged generation of a false consciousness of participation via the ballot-box in liberal democracies forms the basis of much radical criticism.

The one kind of deception that does concern sociologists is concealment. The sociologist either entirely conceals the fact that he is acting as a scientist and an observer, and pretends that

103

he is simply a citizen of some other sort; or else he admits to being a scientist engaged in some kind of empirical inquiry but partially conceals what he is trying to find out. The full concealment of covert research is possible only under a limited set of conditions, but partial concealment is a pervasive concomitant of field research (cf. Junker 1960:35). For whether or not the fairly straightforward kinds of experimental deception practised by some psychologists in the laboratory can be abandoned, it is difficult even to imagine a real world in which deception does not occur continually. In the circumscribed context of a laboratory experiment, or an encounter in the real world between an interviewer and a citizen who is asked to complete a questionnaire, where the range of interests involved may not be very great, then maybe citizens and scientists can be entirely honest with one another. But other forms of inquiry, notably the technique of participant observation that is typical of most research in social anthropology and of a substantial amount of sociological research, entail sustained interaction between scientists and citizen over months and years, far too long for either side to remain permanently on its best behaviour (cf. Colson 1976:265). Yet inquiries of this kind clearly depend to a much greater extent than do laboratory experiments and questionnaire completion on the development of mutual trust between those who have to exchange information and services in a wide range of contexts. How can the inevitability of deception be reconciled with the necessity of trust?

This question can be posed with reference to any enduring social relation, and is not specific to the relation between scientist and citizen. Most of us manage to remain on terms of trust with many other people without having to adopt a policy of absolute honesty. But whereas our relations with friends, relatives and workmates are for the most part based on a similarity of temperament or a complementarity of interests, there is likely to be divergence of interest and often of temperament as well between scientist and citizen. Whatever other aims he may have, the scientist has a commitment to the pursuit of knowledge, a commitment that citizens do not necessarily share. Indeed, they

104

may see it as incomprehensible, frivolous, dangerous or wrong (cf. Portes 1973:153). Furthermore, the process of social inquiry, even when data collection extends over a couple of years or so, is quite brief compared with the time taken by most citizens to absorb a thorough understanding of their social environment. The scientist cannot spend 'Twenty years agrowing' to gather his data. Hence there is great pressure on him to adopt a policy towards the citizens that will facilitate the formation of significant positive relations with them with minimum delay. The citizens may have firmly held views about the qualities of the scientist which, initially, may be quite false; for example, they may think that he is much more powerful, and therefore potentially much more useful to them, than he actually is. The scientist may be tempted to exploit this false assessment of his abilities to gain information, but he is then skating on thin ice, and the longer he skates the thinner the ice becomes.

The British Sociological Association (1973:3) recommends that in this type of situation the sociologist should subscribe to the doctrine of 'informed consent' on the part of subjects and accordingly take pains to explain fully the objects and implications of his research to individual subjects (cf. Katz, J. 1972:521–724). But in fact it may often be as difficult, or as self-defeating, for the sociologist to explain in advance to the individual citizen exactly what the objects of his inquiry are as it is for his psychologist colleague conducting experiments in the morally privileged environment of the laboratory. To state in advance what hypotheses the scientist hopes to falsify or confirm is to invite citizens to testify not according to their own lights but according to what they think he wants, or alternatively does not want, to hear. This for example, Blau (1964:28) argues that bureaucratic situations are so likely to engender feelings of insecurity in the scientist who studies them that on pragmatic grounds, quite apart from ethical considerations, he should not resort to concealment and deception. But Blau then goes on to say, as if in an afterthought, that 'Refraining from deception does not imply, of course, revealing one's hypotheses to respondents, since proper research procedure may require these to remain concealed.'

Unfortunately not all citizens recognize 'proper research procedure' when they see it.

The best discussion of this topic is by Berreman, in his essay 'Behind many masks', where he argues that deception is an integral part of all social relations, and that the relation between scientist and citizen cannot be an exception to this rule. Given this view, he states his doctrine that the scientist does not need to be more open and honest with the citizens than they are to one another and to him. His argument in support of this precept is based on the distinction made by Goffman (1969:92–122) between back and front regions of social space. Any individual, whether citizen or scientist, prepares himself in secret in the back region for the social roles he enacts in public in the front region. The scientist seeks to understand the public performance by peeping behind the mask, by seeing into the back region to learn what is really going on behind the scenes. The citizens, at least initially, are anxious that the scientist should see them only on their best behaviour in the front region. The scientist behaves in the same way. Berreman says 'the ethnographer will be presenting himself in certain ways to his informants during the research and concealing other aspects of himself from them. They will be doing the same. This is inherent in all social interaction.' He then goes on to claim that it is 'ethically unnecessary and methodologically unsound to make known his specific hypotheses and in many cases his area of interest. To take his informants into his confidence regarding these may well preclude the possibility of acquiring much information essential to the main goal of understanding their way of life' (Berreman 1972:xxiv).

I think that Berreman has identified the dilemma more clearly than other commentators, but I can give only qualified support to his proposed solution. Nor indeed is his solution always possible. We can contrast Berreman's comments, made primarily with reference to his own research in the Himalayan foothills, among a largely illiterate peasant community, with the experience of Form (1973:93), who carried out the inquiry into industrial relations in a Fiat factory in Italy mentioned in Chapter 5. He wished to interview workers in the factory, but the management of the company proved to be a suspicious gatekeeper. The managers wanted to know what the inquiry was aimed at discovering, and Form provided them with copies of the research proposals that had been submitted to the sponsors of the project, the National Science Foundation and the (United States) Social Science Research Council. The contrast is striking. Any gate-keeper or citizen, with an appreciation of how social inquiries are financed, knows that sponsors habitually require a full state-ment of the scientific and practical aims of any proposed in-quiry they are asked to support. In this context scientists tend to be over-ambitious rather than vaguely reticent in describing what they want to discover. Is then the scientist to refuse the citizen who wishes to see the research proposal, on the ground that if he does so, he will modify his behaviour or his responses to ques-tions because he now knows what the scientist is trying to find out? Or is it only the powerful gatekeepers, the management and the union officials in Form's case, who are to be let into the secret, while the workers remain 'naïve' subjects?

These questions are made harder to resolve when, as often happens, the scientists and the citizens do not come into direct contact at all. In the Fiat example, the workers were to be inter-viewed by a locally recruited team and indeed Form had to negotiate with the management about how this team should be recruited. One of the obvious ways of minimizing the risk that the information collected by interviewers is not systematically biased is to conceal from them just exactly why the information is needed. If they know precisely what the scientist hopes to discover they may cheat or unconsciously bias their observations. The same consideration applies when the scientist relies for part of his data on observations made by citizens and reported to him orally or in writing. Thus, for example, in his study of Corner-ville, Whyte made use of observations of interaction in a gang made by one of its members (Whyte 1941:662). How much the scientist takes interviewers and citizens into his confidence under these conditions must depend in part on how well-formed are the hypotheses he is trying to test and how sensitive to prior knowledge the process of data collection is. Yet even if we accept some hierarchical structure of awareness and ignorance that reflects the differentiation of power and responsibility within the research team, a situation in which a partially naïve interviewer collects information from a citizen who is much better informed is unlikely to yield reliable results.

The dilemma then is to reconcile the power of sponsors, gatekeepers and, certainly sometimes, citizens to demand to know all there is to know about a project and the necessity, in order to obtain valid data, of concealing a good deal about the project from citizens, and maybe from gatekeepers as well. There seems to be no easy way out, and if the scientist wishes to treat the citizens on a basis of equality irrespective of whether they have the power to insist on this, his freedom of manoeuvre is further restricted. If the citizens are themselves powerful, it will be the scientist who strives to achieve equality with them rather than the other way round. Berreman's statement that for the scientist to take such citizens in his confidence is 'ethically unnecessary' no longer applies.

One way out of the dilemma might seem to be the presentation of a variety of different statements, for different audiences, of what the project aims at. One version of this tactic was, in fact, practised by Berreman. The aims of his study, carried out in 1957–8, were to provide an ethnographic description of an area little known to the outside world, to analyse kin, caste and community ties, and to study the effects of recent governmental reform programmes; presumably these are the aims he reported to his sponsors, various governmental and academic agencies in the United States (Berreman 1972: ix, 2). Four months after arriving in the selected community, on the first occasion suitable for making a public statement, Berreman told his new neighbours that following India's achievement of independence it had become necessary for Americans and Indians to know one another, particularly the relatively unknown Indians of the Himalayan foothills who would play an increasing role in the development of India (Berreman 1972: xxiv–xxv). This explanation for his presence among them worked satisfactorily, in that he was never challenged by members of the community, nor it seems by anyone

108

else in India, for concealing his real aims. Had he declared to his neighbours the aims set out in his book, they might well have been even more suspicious and uncooperative than they were. Eventually he gained more of their confidence, and after returning to the United States published a full and sympathetic account of their social life. In his book he describes how Brahmins and Rajputs, despite their high caste status, sacrifice animals, eat meat, drink alcohol, ignore the great Hindu gods, marry widows, marry across caste boundaries, share wives and have more than one wife, and sell women to men from the plains (Berreman 1972: xxxviii–xxxix). Yet on his return to the village after an absence of ten years, he was welcomed back as an old friend. No one's interests seems to have been harmed.

Yet although Berreman's mode of inquiry is not close to the natural science paradigm, the cultural gap and the barriers to communication between him and the citizens he studied allowed him to operate as if he was an observer from another planet. The citizens had no comprehension of what an anthropologist aimed to do, and none of them was able to read his book about them. More importantly, at least in the ten years that elapsed between Berreman's visits, no one in India who might have intervened in the affairs of the village – officials, missionaries, traders – acted on the basis of the information contained in the book. Under these circumstances, Berreman, if he was to carry out the study, may well have had no option to being vague and misleading about his objectives, and he harmed no one by acting in this way.

Where citizens already hold well-formed perceptions of social inquiry, a scientist who wishes to innovate may adopt a more traditional topic for investigation as a cover for his real interest. Thus Clegg (1975: viii, 81) aimed to make a critique of conventional ways of conceptualizing power but concealed this aim from the citizens, employees on a building site. He told them he was trying to compare management practice with the norms set out in books on management. They applauded his common sense, but we do not know what they thought of his book when it appeared later.

Another technique, recommended by D. Katz (1953: 88), is

explicitly to reveal to the citizens some of the subsidiary and inessential aims and findings of the inquiry, while remaining silent on crucial issues. This may perhaps have sufficed with community studies in the fifties, when Katz was writing, but neither his recipe, nor Berreman's mixture of vagueness and flattery, would have satisfied, for example, the Fiat management, or any other gatekeeper or group of citizens familiar with present-day social science and who will be able to read whatever is published. Yet Berreman's analysis of front and back regions still holds. The scientist's task is to find a way of gaining the confidence of people with whom he cannot be entirely honest, who have considerable power to obstruct and prevent his inquiry, and who are quite unlikely to be entirely honest with him. In general, the more the scientist is able to take the citizens into his confidence the sooner he is likely to be taken into their confidence, which is what he wants. But if his data are to be valid, to some extent he must continue to conceal from them what he is trying to find out. His only route out of this dilemma, so it seems to me, is to aim at gaining the confidence of the citizens *as a scientist*, as someone whose special craft requires him to be chary of disclosing all his aims and interests, at least initially. This attribute complements the omnivorous curiosity which, I have argued in Chapter 5, ought to characterize the social scientist. The position of the social scientist is in this respect somewhat similar to that of the doctor examining a patient. Patients accept that if a doctor were to begin his examination by telling the patient of all the signs and symptoms he is interested in, and the reasons why each of them may have diagnostic value, the patient, with or without the best will in the world, is likely to cheat. Yet the reticence of the doctor does not undermine the patient's confidence in him, at least not if it is limited to the context of the examination. An inquiry by a psychologist into, for example, symptoms taken to be indicative of mental illness would be likely to be vitiated in the same way as the doctor's if the objectives of the inquiry, and the diagnostic symptoms, were fully explained to the citizen before the inquiry began (Cannell and Kahn 1968:580). The citizen may be tempted to give himself the benefit of the doubt even in reporting such comparatively 'hard' attributes as age and address if he knows why information on these topics is being sought. On the other hand, a citizen who is given no indication of the purpose of an inquiry, when faced with an ambiguous question (as so many items on questionnaires are), has to guess in the dark what the scientist really meant to ask about; uninformed citizens are not necessarily more reliable sources of information about themselves than those who have been fully briefed. In general, the scientist's task would be facilitated if members of the public were to accept that he is constrained by the requirements of his techniques of inquiry, in much the same way as is a physician, in the explanations he can give for his questions. Without this acceptance in the ambient culture, the scientist has to try to establish it afresh with each new encounter with citizens and gatekeepers and even with sponsors as well. Even when this initial constraint on the role of scientist is accepted, social scientists must expect a lack of consensus, as with doctors, about when, if ever, they should tell all.

This seems a better and safer tactic than providing a different story for each different audience. A vague statement that the scientist is 'studying the community' or, as in Lynd's study of Middletown, studying 'the growth of the city' (Lynd and Lynd 1929:505) may perhaps have been adequate in those contexts where social inquiry had not become a recognized recurrent activity. Nowadays more and more people realize that such broad descriptions must be a cover for something more specific and, particularly if it is hidden, more threatening. If citizens and others realize that there is a hierarchy of definitions of the inquiry, ranging from the bland publicity handout to the detailed scientific specification, and if they believe that access to these definitions is restricted by power considerations alone, they are likely to distrust the scientist, and rightly so. By demonstrating that as far as possible anyone interested can find out as much as he likes about the inquiry, its aims and methods, and that the only restrictions are those entailed by the process of data collection itself, the scientist may hope to gain the confidence of the people he works with.

Who should know what?

When a scientist is working openly, and has gained the trust of the citizens, they may still be cautious in what they say to him, just as they are cautious in talking to one another. A scientist who demonstrates that he can keep a secret may eventually be told more than would a fellow citizen, because the scientist is perceived as being different, as marginal to the community, and as someone whose metier it is to be a repository of secret information. The more the scientist establishes himself in the role of confidant, the greater the responsibility he incurs for ensuring that the secrets entrusted in him do not leak back into general circulation. What constitutes a secret, and from whom it must be concealed, is of course something that cannot be determined in advance. Communities differ very widely in how they evaluate information as public or private (Junker 1960:34; Simmel 1968; Spiro 1971; Barnes 1977:35–36), and in the extent to which notions of privacy are given legal force (International Commission of Jurists 1972). Even within a culture, a piece of information that is private in one context may become public in another (Warner and Stone 1970:123–43; Barnes 1967:208–9), and what is treated as private in one generation may become public in the next. So diverse are cultural evaluations of privacy that privacy can be used as a variable in cross-cultural analysis (Roberts and Gregor 1971).

The scientist's responsibility to respect the confidentiality of his data is particularly great when citizens are engaged in illegal activities and need to conceal their actions from the police and similar agencies. In making inquiries of this kind the scientist has to decide to what extent he is willing to connive in, or participate in, or perhaps even encourage, illegal acts. The liability of the citizen to take active steps to prevent or report acts of wrongdoing he may know about varies widely from one jurisdiction to another, as does the extent to which he is under an obligation to cooperate with the police if asked to do so (cf. Broeder 1960). But though the risk that the scientist, as a citizen, will be judicially punished because of his association with criminally-acting citizens may vary, his moral responsibility to them always remains. Polsky (1971:141) asks what is the scien-

tist's duty as a citizen and comments that '. . . our very understanding of "citizenship" itself is considerably furthered in
the long run if one type of citizen, the criminologist, conceives
his primary duty to be the advancement of scientific knowledge
about crime even when such advancement can be made only by
"obstructing justice" with respect to particular criminals in the
short run'. Yet he goes on to emphasize that the scientist must be
prepared to face the legal penalties which he risks in this mode
of inquiry. Polsky also stresses the importance of the scientist
being clear in his own mind and to the citizens he studies about
the extent to which he is not prepared to break the law in the
pursuit of scientific understanding (cf. Humphreys 1975:228–31).
Porter (1977) makes the same point when he says that, for him,
'murder is going too far'. As Whyte (1955:317) puts it, '. . . the
fieldworker cannot afford to think only of learning to live with
others in the field. He has to continue living with himself' (cf.
Barnes 1977:31–2).

Even in the most law-abiding community, citizens may wish to
draw a distinction between what they say to the scientist for the
record, and what they tell him for his own enlightenment, off the
record. Some citizens seem to be very hesitant to speak for the
record if asked to do so in advance, but once having spoken
may be readier to let the scientist make use of their testimony.
Communities vary widely in their attitude to open note-taking
when citizens speak to a scientist. In many instances a scientist
has reported that he could not use a notebook openly when
presumably the citizens must have known that he would later
write down all he could remember of what he had heard and seen.
Others have tolerated notebooks but objected to tape recorders,
while in my own experience a citizen once complained that I was
not writing down what he said; did I think him a fool whose words
were not worth recording? A covert inquirer who secretly tapes
the conversations of his companions runs the risk of being un-
masked if his recorder is discovered. But is it right for a scientist
working openly to tape citizens without their knowledge? One
answer to this question was found by Chambliss (1975:38), when
engaged on a long-term study of criminals. He wanted to make

sure that his record of conversations was accurate, but found that a formal request to be allowed to use a tape recorder inhibited citizens from talking freely. He therefore decided to tape them without their knowledge. At the end of every interview he told the person what he had done, removed the tape from the recorder and handed it over. He explained that he wished to use the tape only for scientific purposes. Only in one instance, when a man described a murder he had committed, did the citizen not hand the tape back to him.

Under colonial conditions, the authority of the anthropologist as apparently a member of the expatriate elite may often have been sufficient to ensure that citizens endeavoured to give the impression of cooperating with his inquiry by answering his questions, even if the answers they gave were in fact misleading or insincere. This kind of relationship is not confined to the colonial world. Some writers have referred to a 'culture of repression', a state of mind in which subordinate groups become accustomed to submit passively to all intrusions that come from above or from outside, and hence will supply scientists with information about their beliefs and activities that they would deny to a neighbour. They may of course falsify their information, or try to say what they think the scientists want to hear, but will endeavour to give the impression of cooperating willingly (Huizer 1975:67). Information collected in this context is likely to be unreliable or misleading, though it may give an impression of completeness when entered on a questionnaire form. The field scientist who relies on being identified with a superordinate group may seem to gather his information more quickly, though there are ethical hazards in appearing to support a group merely as a trick to obtain information (Kelman 1972:998). His colleague who seeks to identify himself more closely with a subordinate group and to gain the confidence of its members may have to proceed more slowly but may arrive eventually at a fuller understanding of what is going on.

At least, it would be comforting if this was always the case. If the citizens, though repressed, are all stout egalitarian democrats at heart, then maybe the egalitarian scientist eventually gets closer to the truth than his quicker authoritarian colleague. The evidence available from many monographs on poor and powerless categories of people bears this out. But what happens when the citizens themselves are basically hierarchical and authoritarian in their way of life, as for example in many communities in India and Polynesia, as well as, nearer home, military communities, hospitals and so on? In these contexts the scientist may well have to adopt a similar stance if he is to gain the attention of the citizens. He may still have to negotiate his supply of information, but he is likely to have to deal separately with each stratum in the community. Likewise in a society polarized into rival factions, it may be suicidal for a scientist to adopt a policy of being ready to be friends with anybody. He may try to divide his time between one faction and another, but this is always hazardous, physically if not morally (cf. Roy 1965:269). Even if the scientist wishes to remain neutral and above the battle, the citizens may refuse to recognize this as a possible stance. Thus Brunt (1974:312) describes how, at the beginning of a study of a divided community, he explained his intentions to the municipal council. '... I tried to stress the "objective" and "neutral" nature of my work. This produced hilarity among the council members, who pointed out to me that "neutrality" does not exist.'

Some degree of association and identification with the values and customs of the community, or some segment of it, is necessary if the citizens are to tolerate the presence of the scientist in their community. For this a price has to be paid, and the greater the disparity between the scientist's own preferences and those of the community, the heavier he will perceive this price to be. The price may not necessarily have ethical implications; a scientist who gives up smoking in deference to the views of the citizens (e.g. Béteille 1975:107) may be making a difficult gesture but no moral issues are insolved. But the same anthropologist also considered that he could not violate the sentiments of his Brahman hosts, and stopped inviting Untouchables to visit him at his house, thus giving support to a system of discrimination to which, as a citizen, he was opposed. In an industrial context, 'co-option' into friend-

115

ship, as S. M. Miller (1952:98) describes the process, may inhibit the scientist from questioning the basic values of his friends-for-the-time-being, however deeply he may be opposed to them. Indeed there must be some amount of compatability between the values of the scientist and those of the citizens he studies. Without this, he cannot expect to gain much insight into the reasons why they act in one way rather than another, for no scientist is simply an infinitely adaptable collector of data, a man without qualities (cf. Barnes 1977:32–3). He always remains to some extent a citizen, with his own moral code. If he cannot achieve sympathetic understanding with them, he should switch to some other topic of inquiry. As Douglas (1976:99) says bluntly, 'One should have feelings, but not passionate and well entrenched commitments. It's one thing for a noncustomer to study massage parlors. It's another for a nun to study them, or a politically ambitious city attorney.'

Any scientist working in the field may expect to establish some personal relations of friendship with certain citizens, as well as collaborating professionally with others. Some scientists have no difficulty in distinguishing between personal and professional relations, at least in principle, though the distinction may be difficult to apply in practice. But sometimes the culture of the citizens may not recognize this distinction even in principle. They may well place a higher value on even new-found friendship than does the scientist, and demand a higher price than he is willing to pay. This is hazardous, particularly if he regards friendship in the field as merely a tool of research, as some do. Thus Varma (1967:539) recommends as a rule of thumb for the field investigator that 'no more commitment should be made to subjects of study, one's research staff, or colleagues than one can honestly keep'. He advocates a means-end connexion between personal friendship and obtaining data, and allows for the development of friendship (presumably he means genuine personal friendship) only providing that 'it does not make for undue stress on the researcher's time, energy and resources'. Many social scientists would reject this instrumental view of friendship, particularly when, as with Varma, the scientist is studying citizens with whom he has long-standing associations. In our terms, this view is an attempt to accommodate participant observation within the natural science paradigm. Varma is certainly right to caution his colleagues against raising the expectations of citizens unduly. But while many citizens find the notion of separating personal from professional commitments even in theory to be bizarre, many scientists find this separation difficult and disasteful to make in practice.

For these reasons the scientist should in general seek to establish and maintain an anomalous status for himself, and should avoid identifying himself completely with the community he studies, or with any segment of it, even though he may participate energetically in social action that arises from his research. Complete identification is indeed often impossible, for the citizens may have no wish to acknowledge their identity with him. But even where it is a possibility, it should be avoided, for it is incompatible with the autonomy of the scientist. This is a restriction inherent in his role that most citizens, and some scientists, find hard to accept. In this sense, the scientist is always a disappointment to the citizens. He remains, as Hughes (1956:86) puts it, a marginal man, keeping 'the delicate balance between loyalty to those who have admitted him to the role of confidant and to his colleagues who expect him to contribute freely to the accumulating knowledge about human society and methods of studying it'.

This necessary balance is however not simply between the interests of citizens and professional colleagues. In every community there is some diversity of points of view. The scientist has to balance the advantages of being associated with one viewpoint, and thus of gaining a fuller understanding of the aims and relations of its supporters, against the necessity of learning about their opponents as well if he is to understand the struggle between them adequately. If he has to collect all his data by himself, he cannot avoid being a somewhat luke-warm supporter of any side, wherever his own sympathies may happen to lie. Sometimes the local social scene may be so sharply polarized that he cannot straddle the local cleavages without being seen as a traitor by both sides. For this reason, in a study of a small American city by a team of two Black and two White anthropologists, published as *Deep South*, each couple kept to its appropriate side of the colour line. Members of the team could meet only surreptitiously to compare notes (Warner and Davis 1939:234). The members were certainly deceiving the community in what they were really doing, at a time when the racial divide was clear-cut. The community seems never to have been dehoaxed, though its identity is no longer so well hidden (Davis et al. 1965:viii). In polarized situations the scientist's task is made easier if citizens are prepared to accept that, though the iniquities of their opponents are blatant, the ignorant scientist must be given the opportunity to discover them for himself.

Polarized or dichotomized local social contexts are found not only in ethnically divided communities but occur ubiquitously within every complex society. In industrial situations the social scientist may have great difficulty in not being identified with management by the workers, and maybe vice versa as well. If a social scientist inquires into the working of welfare agencies, there is a strong tendency for him to become identified with the professionals rather than with their clients, even though he may regard the latter as the focus of his interest. If he seeks to involve clients actively in the research process, they may object to conniving at what they perceive as 'police spying'. Thus Davies and Kelly (1976:223) report that in a study of an agency intended to help unemployed young people in Manchester, where in the eyes of the clients the field investigator had become identified with the professionals, they 'had to agree that, in the circumstances, our participant observer techniques had been even more subversive of the defences of these young people than the records kept by the various State agencies with whom they had been dealing'.

Whether or not there are major divergences of interest among the citizens, the scientist, if he is to pursue his inquiry at all effectively, is often forced to deceive them, by commission and omission, about his true intentions and opinions. My thesis is that this deception is inevitable, and that scientists should try to foster a public image of themselves as persons who must neces-

118

sarily act in this way in their professional activities. In claiming the privilege of acting in a way for which the layman would be censured, the scientist incurs a responsibility to protect the interests of citizens, particularly when they are not powerful enough to protect themselves.

It is not only the scientist who practises deception and concealment. Sponsors are not always honest with citizens. For example, in the 1960s the CIA provided funds for the support of a wide variety of organizations, including some engaged in social science research, whose activities were thought to further the political goals of the CIA. As a condition for its support, the CIA tended to impose a ban on the publication of the fact that it was supplying the money, presumably in the belief that it would be counter-productive to reveal the identity of the sponsor. But the ban itself sometimes impeded the research. Thus in 1966 the Center for International Studies at the Massachusetts Institute of Technology decided 'regretfully' not to take any more contracts from the CIA for the simple reason that although the results of the research were published openly, the ban on mentioning the existence of the contracts prevented disclosure of the sponsor for whom the work was being done (Pool 1967: 271). In the following year a committee chaired by the Secretary of State declared that covert support to institutions of higher learning was contrary to United States national policy and was to cease.

Secret sponsorship affects not only a naturally secretive body like the CIA. An opinion poll conducted by an agency such as the Gallup organization, known to be interested in the distribution of opinion in the country rather than in promoting any particular opinion, may well be conducted quite openly, without any attempt to conceal the identity of the agency. But a similar poll, conducted by the research branch of a political party, or by foreign scientists, might well yield distorted results if the identity of the sponsors became known. At least, this is the assumption that led to a remarkable guideline issued in 1967 by a group of United States federal agencies supporting research in foreign countries. Following the cancellation of Project Camelot, the federal government was anxious that research projects carried out in foreign countries with support from US government funds should be seen to be entirely above board; there was to be no pretext for thinking that such research was really disguised espionage. Hence 'the fact of government research support should always be acknowledged by sponsor, university and researcher', and 'when a project involves research abroad it is particularly important that both the supporting agency and the researcher openly acknowledge the auspices and financing of research projects'. But what about opinion polls? The statement of policy continues: 'If the research is of such a character, as in opinion sampling, that the objectivity of its research techniques is substantially destroyed when respondents know of the project's auspices, then it is doubly important that either the host government or collaborating local researchers, or both, be fully informed about the nature of the project' (American Anthropological Association 1968). In other words, everyone must know except the citizens themselves! The assumption seems to be that, in this context, an opinion poll, like some of the procedures in experimental social psychology we have discussed, is a technique in which deception is an integral, and not accidental, part of the research design. Fortunately, valid opinion polls can usually be conducted without deception of this kind. It may well be that more often it is the general public that is deceived, when believing that there is such a thing as a 'public opinion' on every conceivable issue (Marsh 1978).

I do not know of any analogous discussion in Britain about concealing the source of financial support for research projects. In this country sponsors are more likely to complain that scientists are remiss in forgetting to publicize the support they have enjoyed from their sponsors. Nevertheless the issues raised in the American discussions about covert sponsorship have a bearing on research wherever it is carried out. The Faustian element is present in every relation between scientist and sponsor and not merely when the sponsor is a branch of government. Although, as discussed in the previous chapter, the scientist may be satisfied that he has adequately protected his soul, the citizens may need to be convinced of this before they are prepared to trust him.

If he is not willing to discuss where the money comes from, the citizens have every ground for being suspicious.

Deception and concealment of objectives occur when citizens know that the scientist is a scientist. In covert research a scientist seeks to conceal from the citizens that he is a scientist. Covert research takes many forms, from hiding under beds to posing as a convert to a religious sect, and the attitudes of social scientists towards research of this kind vary from unqualified disapproval to easy or enthusiastic acceptance (Weick 1968:373–4). Some covert research is scarcely to be distinguished from the use of unobtrusive measures of social behaviour. Use of these is usually commended as creating no artificial disturbance to the social phenomena being studied (Webb et al. 1966). Thus for example an early inquiry into national differences was carried out by eavesdropping in public places (Landis 1927), yet this relatively innocuous investigation attracted the editorial comment that the right of citizens to have private discussions in public places had been violated. Later, some more debatable kinds of academic covert research became quite common. For example, during the fifties, several studies of occupational groups were carried out by doctoral students at the University of Chicago who 'worked at the job they studied without revealing their professional interest to their fellow workers' (Roth 1959). In this context there may perhaps have been no reason in principle why the research should have been carried out covertly; the student-scientists could presumably have told their fellows on the shop floor what they were trying to do without greatly altering the design of their inquiries. In some cases they worked in industry primarily to support themselves financially as students. Yet even when the job comes first and the research second, the scientist who works openly is likely to have to redefine his relation with his fellow workers. As Junker (1960:36) says, 'If he escapes the problems of a spy, he takes on those of a traitor.'

In other instances of covert research in industrial settings, covertness seems to have been an integral part of the plan of inquiry. For example, in the studies of 'gold bricking' and re-striction of output carried out by Roy (1952, 1953, 1954), he presented himself to his fellow workers on the shop floor as a worker like themselves. Had he presented himself as a researcher, both management and unions would certainly have wanted to influence the kind of observations he made, and the workers might well have behaved differently. This kind of deception is often defended as being the only way in which a scientist can gain information which, so he believes, citizens will be willing to impart to a newcomer who identifies himself with them but which they wish to hide from outsiders. But this defence is at best incomplete, judged in moral rather than technical terms. Even if we accept the view that scientists should be free to seek the truth wherever it may be found, a scientist who has collected information in this way has to face alone, without the benefit of consultation with the citizens concerned, the consequences of revealing, in one form or other, the information they wish to conceal.

Douglas, a sociologist well known for his studies on deviance and suicide, defends vigorously his use of an impressive battery of techniques to secure information about citizens, without alerting them to the fact that they are being investigated, when they are unwilling to let the truth be known. He defends this mode of investigative field research on the grounds that all the citizens concerned are carefully protected by the cloak of anonymity, and that compared with the activities of other investigators in America, for example the massive news agencies 'which every day purposefully set out to expose and destroy the projects and careers of thousands of individuals and groups', the methods used by social scientists are genteel and harmless (Douglas 1976: xiv; cf. Reynolds 1972:695). Maybe his comparison is sound, at least for the United States and for those aspects of social life in which he is interested. But the cloak of anonymity is probably a more effective form of covering on the nude beaches of California than in many other social settings. In any case, social scientists should be cautious about relying on the transgressions of others to justify their own shortcomings.

Some commentators maintain that all covert research is ethically wrong and that if information cannot be acquired by scientists operating openly, it should not be sought at all. Warwick (1975:212) says uncompromisingly, with Humphreys' covert study of fellatio in mind, 'Social research involving deception and manipulation ultimately helps produce a society of cynics, liars and manipulators, and undermines the trust which is essential to a just social order.' Covert research by impersonation, Erikson (1967:371) claims, is attempted only by scientists looking down the social ladder rather than up. Scientists masquerade as workers but not as managers, as privates rather than generals. Covert research thus conforms to the nineteenth-century model, with the elite scientist gathering data in the slums, rather than on a model based on negotiation with citizens. Other commentators point out that although a scientist who carries out his inquiries unbeknown to management and workers alike does not, on the shop floor, intervene one way or the other to alter the relation between the two sides of industry, nevertheless one side may be able later to make much more effective use of his findings. A scientist who studies a workforce covertly but with the knowledge and connivance of management is much more open to criticism on ethical grounds, particularly if the management, as sponsor, can influence how the inquiry is conducted and what, if anything, is published (cf. Barnes 1977:12). Under these conditions the scientist comes close to accepting knowledge simply as a source of power.

Masquerading is not confined to covert research. To facilitate his inquiries a scientist working openly may claim personal attributes he does not have. These masquerades usually do not artificially lower the status of the scientist, as they do sometimes in covert research. On the contrary, the false claim is made to bring the scientist into a social vantage point from which he can make his inquiries more effectively. Unmarried women carrying out field inquiries in traditional communities may claim to be married, or even widowed, so as to avoid the social constraints imposed on the unmarried. Atheists and agnostics may attempt to give an appearance of religious conformity, or at least of a desire to become religious, in order to be accepted into the society they are studying. In one instance an Indian social scientist working openly in an area where he was a stranger pretended that he belonged to a caste higher than his own, and thus gained access to religious ceremonies. A pretence of this kind, if undetected, may well yield more data for the scientist, but also is hazardous, for if the deceit is discovered by the citizens they may reject him completely. Yet where the cultural attributes of the scientist are not readily translatable into the culture of the citizens, some distortion in their perception of him as a person is probably inevitable, however honestly he describes himself. For example, when I began making inquiries in western Norway, I reported honestly to members of the family with whom I lived that I had a wife and children in England. Because, unlike most Norwegian married men, I did not wear a wedding ring they inferred that, although I was being honest with them, I intended to present myself to others in the community as unmarried, and therefore legitimately occupied in talking to unmarried women. But whether this sort of masquerading is really intended or inadvertently implied, and whether unmarried scientists pose as married or married scientists pretend to be unmarried, no harm is necessarily done to the interests of citizens. Only the conscience of the scientist suffers, when he has to continue to deceive those who begin to take him into their confidence about their own affairs.

Another line of argument is that, unlike some procedures in psychological research, deception and concealment are not inherent in the design of research into spontaneous activities in the real world; patient negotiation will eventually enable a sympathetic and resourceful scientist to gain the agreement of all concerned to the collection of information on all aspects of social life. If this is so, we merely have to balance our wish to be honest against the urgency of our need to find out. This argument may be sound, when, as in our example of managers and workers, the scientist is studying responsible and informed citizens, with whom negotiation is possible in principle however hard it may be in practice. Suppose instead that the inquiry takes place not in a factory or chain store but in a mental hospital. Rosenhan (1973) describes an experiment in which, with the connivance of the administrator of a hospital and its chief psychologist, he was admitted as a patient, was diagnosed as schizophrenic, and then proceeded to make observations on how doctors and nurses behaved in relation to patients. The object of his inquiry was to investigate whether psychiatric diagnoses are constructions in the minds of the observers (doctors, nurses and the like), or whether they are valid summaries of characteristics displayed by the observed (patients). If the inquiry had consisted in Rosenhan spying on the staff and reporting back to the administrator, the similarity with a management-sponsored covert inquiry in industry would have been close. Fortunately, Rosenhan's research design was quite different. The other seven scientists in the inquiry gained admission to mental hospitals without anyone at all in them knowing that they were pseudopatients, and their bogus status was never detected by the hospital staffs, even though over a quarter of the authentic patients voiced their suspicions of these cuckoos in their nest. The data collected by the scientists might perhaps have been constructed from interviews with doctors, nurses and patients, but even if that were done the testimony of patients would, from the definition of their status as mentally ill, be liable to be discounted by those who disliked it. Had the inquiry been made openly, the presence of acknowledged scientists on the ward making observations would in all probability have altered the behaviour of doctors and nurses, at least initially, though a somewhat similar inquiry had been made earlier in which the scientist found open observation an advantage (Caudill 1958:xv; Barnes 1977:11–12). The disguised report of the inquiry criticizes the conduct of mental hospitals in America in general terms and makes yet another challenge to the validity of the concept of schizophrenia, but it is not directed against the staff of any identifiable hospital. The inquiry constitutes a striking example of how knowledge as enlightenment may be obtained by the benign use of deception and where the use of deception in obtaining the information increases rather than decreases its credibility. Yet there is a price to be paid, in the pollution of the research environment, if ill citizens receive poorer care because they are thought wrongly to be healthy scientists operating covertly (cf. *Lancet* 1977). The scientist, too, pays a price, for he has to act deceitfully towards citizens he may admire and respect. Indeed, two anthropologists who deceived patients, their relatives and staff in a palliative care unit for the dying maintain that the moral cost is so high that covert role-playing in the field should be employed in social inquiry only when no alternative method of gathering information is available (Murray and Buckingham 1976:1190).

Some inquiries are carried out more covertly than others. Margaret Mead describes how, at an early stage in her career as an anthropologist, she carried out research semi-covertly, presenting herself as a 'helpful wife' of her husband, who was studying tribal myths and folktales. At the time, she defended the fact that she did not take notes as informants spoke to her by claiming that 'Such unawareness was essential to the successful prosecution of a study involving intimate details of contemporary life.' Many years later, in the revised edition of her book, she writes 'I am still uncertain as to whether the sacrifice of genuine authenticity that one must make whenever the fieldworker's actual role is altered by disguise is not the more important issue' (Mead 1966:xxi–xxii).

It is certainly true that the scope of open inquiry can be extended significantly by negotiation. For example, industrial pilfering might seem at first glance to be a topic of legitimate interest that the social scientist can hope to study at first hand only covertly; indeed, attempts to study this topic openly have been successfully obstructed by interested gatekeepers. Yet approval for open inquiry into behaviour as morally problematic as this has on occasion been gained by patient negotiation. Even so, there seems to me no reason for assuming that in the end, patience always wins, and that every possible form of actual behaviour can be studied openly; not does the progress of social science depend on all conceivable forms of inquiry becoming possible. As I see it, there will always remain many areas of social life that would be interesting to investigate but which are inaccessible to open inquiry. The moral problem of whether or not these should be tackled by covert inquiry will still be with us.

Most discussions about covert research relate to situations

in which the citizens could, if they so wished, take the scientist fully into their confidence and tell him everything he wants to know. But in some situations citizens are not free to open their hearts to even the most persuasive and trustworthy scientist. Yet these same situations may be of particular theoretical interest and of major practical importance, so that a better understanding of how they operate may be sought by scientist and citizen alike. Meetings of the British cabinet fall into this category, and the battery of objections that would be raised against allowing a covert social scientist merely to listen quietly to them, let alone to try his hand at mediating between ministers, makes the suggestion ludicrous. The deliberations of juries also belong to the same category, for their secrecy is embodied in the legal process and does not stem merely from the idiosyncratic coyness of jurors. Though they reach their decisions in secret, jurors are responsible to society for the decisions they take. Any move to improve the jury system must be based on some working hypothesis about the way in which juries gradually achieve a consensus, and the best way to check this hypothesis is to match it against the way juries behave in practice. But how can this be done if secrecy is an essential feature of a jury's deliberations? Mock trials may provide a partial answer, but can scarcely be equated with authentic events. Tape recordings made covertly might seem to supply the data required; jury trials are numerous, and there is greater chance that a disguise would be successful than with a unique organization like, say, the British cabinet.

A much discussed attempt in America to study jury deliberations in this way shows well the hazards of this variety of covert inquiry. A presiding judge and counsel agreed to recordings being made in six civil cases in 1954. The tapes were edited to remove names and places that might enable the cases to be identified, but were then played to a judicial conference that was not as closed to the press as was supposed. Covert taping thus became public knowledge and as a consequence legislation was passed to prohibit any recording of jury deliberations (Amrine and Sanford 1956; Broeder 1959; Burchard 1958; Ruebhausen and Brim 1965:1193; Vaughan 1967; Katz, J. 1972:67–109; Barnes 1977:

22–6). It is worth noting that, in the extensive discussions of the ethical issues involved in this affair, little attention seems to have been paid to the interests of jurors, whose secretly expressed opinions might be exposed to publicity; commentators have been more concerned with the effect that taping might have on the course of justice and the integrity of the courts. Would the same balance of emphasis be found today?

Some social scientists have condemned covert research without qualification, declaring that it is spying and therefore wrong. Many other people think the same. For example, W. H. Auden wrote of Mass-Observation 'Still worse is the person who sits in the corner, saying nothing, and then goes home and writes it all up in a little black diary. He is a spy, and should be treated as such' (Madge and Harrisson 1938:62–3). But suppose the quiet person in the corner had gone home to write a poem based on what he had seen and heard; would Auden then have objected so strongly? The ethics of spying are perhaps even more difficult to unravel than the ethics of social research, yet most commentators who have charged their fellow social scientists with spying have used the term merely pejoratively, without specifying when, if at all, they think that spying may be justified. Boas (1919) was one of the first to protest against American anthropologists acting as spies and clearly held that it was wrong for a true scientist, openly professing himself to be acting in that role, to act as a spy for his government; but he did not imply that spying is wrong in itself (cf. Stocking 1968:273). Since the ethical issues raised by espionage are complex and eminently debatable, spying is quite useless as a yardstick for determining whether any specified mode of social inquiry is ethically good or bad (cf. Kelman 1968:77). We have to deal with the ethical problems of social research on their own terms, and cannot merely argue by analogy with spying. To give an extreme example, we can scarcely argue that Bettleheim (1943) behaved unethically because he did not reveal to his SS gaolers in a concentration camp that he was trying to preserve his own integrity, and his life, by studying them.

Can we avoid the difficult ethical problems raised by research that entails deception and concealment by switching to a more open and honest mode of inquiry? As mentioned earlier, several psychologists have advocated role-playing as a means whereby citizens can participate in the process of inquiry as moral and intellectual equals. But role-playing does not automatically provide an ethically impeccable road to scientific knowledge. Indeed, the generation of anguish and loss of self-esteem, which in psychological experiments is regretted even more than the necessity of deception, can occur in role-playing even when little or no deception takes place. The Stanford prison experiment (Haney et al. 1973; Zimbardo et al. 1973) has been linked in controversy with Milgram's experiments on obedience but the objections to the role-playing at Stanford have been focused on the physical pain, psychological humiliation and anxiety experienced by the participants, features which were lacking in Milgram's work, as much as on the anguish and loss of self-esteem. In the Stanford experiment, volunteers from various colleges in the United States and Canada who had agreed to participate in a study of prison life, and who were paid fifteen dollars a day for doing so, were incarcerated in a mock-up prison built on the campus of Stanford University. The volunteers were assigned at random to the roles of guard and prisoner. The only element of deception seems to have been in the arrest of the prisoners by members of the Palo Alto police force; the volunteers were not told that this was a fake, and that the experiment had already begun. Zimbardo (1973: 254) admits that this was a breach, by omission, of the ethics of the 'informed consent' contract between him and the volunteers. The experiment was intended to run for a fortnight but after only four days Zimbardo intervened to release four of the prisoners because of 'extreme depression, disorganized thinking, uncontrollable crying and fits of rage' (Zimbardo et al. 1973: 48).

Zimbardo argues that although the responses of the volunteers were much stronger than he expected, the experiment was justified in that new knowledge was gained and that the cost, mainly borne by the volunteers who were prisoners, was offset by what they learnt about themselves. He says that in restrospect they looked upon the experiment as a 'valuable didactic experience . The sponsor, the (United States) Office of Naval Research, gained from the experiment, he says, by being seen to have supported basic research that gained much publicity and which yielded new information. The sponsor was stimulated to support research into problems of racism in the military corrective system (Zimbardo 1973:248–9). But Zimbardo did not convince all his critics; an attempt to follow up the inquiry with further research on prisoner–guard relations ran into difficulties.

In this case the volunteers had agreed in advance to participate in an experiment in which, they were told, there would be an invasion of privacy, loss of some civil rights and harassment. The prisoners may not have expected such rough treatment as they got, but we cannot argue that they were taken unawares. Nor would many people wish to argue that individuals should not be free to volunteer to suffer in a good cause. The intervention of the scientist to terminate the experiment when, unexpectedly, individuals began to suffer considerable anguish, was a responsible act, though we might query whether the intervention was made later than it should have been. How much was learnt from the experiment is also open to debate but most people would share with the experimenters their surprise at discovering the brutality of the gaolers towards the prisoners, and the extent to which prisoners and scientists were captured by the roles they had been assigned.

Some of the criticism directed at the experiment is based on the argument that it was undertaken not in order to discover facts that could be brought to light only in this way but simply in order to generate popular support for prison reform (Savin 1973 a and b). This is a modification of the much more common criticism, that politicians and others attempt to increase support for policies by claiming unjustifiably that their efficacy has been tested scientifically. In this case, the objection is that politicians and others used the *process* of scientific testing, rather than its outcome, as a means of increasing support for their policies by giving the experiment publicity and thus stimulating public interest. In other words, the process of inquiry was being subverted from its proper function; while purporting to be a technique for discovery, it was in fact a stunt. Clearly there is some danger of this happening, whether or not citizens happen to be maltreated as part of the inquiry. But whose interests are threatened by this? This abuse, or new use, of experimentation does not make any additional demands on the interests of the citizens directly involved, though maybe the sponsor is being misled. The chief threat, as I see it, is to the integrity of the scientist. The search for knowledge is difficult enough as it is, without introducing into the search additional criteria aimed at achieving maximum political effectiveness for the process itself. Publicity may well be an integral part of an ongoing programme of action research in the field, but in the Stanford example it seems as if the publicity and political commitment were unintegrated and uncontrolled adjuncts to a realistic experiment in the fairyland of the laboratory. If pseudo-experiments in the laboratory have publicity value, it may be appropriate to make use of them for political ends; but it is dangerous to confuse these stunts with honest experiments.

One of the most interesting features of the experiment is the effect that role-playing had on the participants. Indeed, it was the unexpectedly intense reactions that were generated which led Zimbardo to terminate the experiment prematurely. Role-playing may be a way of avoiding deception, as Mixon urges. But the Stanford experiment shows that role-playing can become a collective *folie* in which people behave towards one another in ways that, under normal conditions, they would regard as reprehensible. Since the role-playing is actually carried out, even if in a fantastically constructed microcosm, the participants cannot excuse their conduct, as they may have been able to do in Milgram's obedience experiment, by saying that they were sure that, despite appearances, no harm was being done. In the Stanford experiment, people were 'carried away' by the roles assigned to them. Zimbardo and his associates tell how one of the citizens, 'Prisoner 819', who was about to be released prematurely from the prison following an uncontrollable crying fit, still wanted to be able to prove to his fellows that he was not the 'bad prisoner' they said he was. 'He had to be persuaded that he was not a prisoner at all, that the others were also just students, that this was just an experiment and not a prison and the prison staff were only research psychologists.' The scientists were carried away just as strongly as were the volunteer student citizens. One of the scientists, the 'warden' of the prison, writes: 'I am startled by the ease with which I could turn off my sensitivity and concern for others for "a good cause".' Likewise, on hearing a rumour that a mass escape plot was being planned, the whole team of scientists, without thinking, responded as custodians; 'Instead of collecting data on the pattern of rumour transmission, we made plans to maintain the security of our institution.' Role-playing, then, may seem to be a technique of inquiry in which scientists and citizens can cooperate as equals in arriving at the truth; no one is being deceived, or tricked into doing things he would not really do if he knew all the facts. But if the roles are unequal, and the actors whole-heartedly enter into their parts, they may still behave in ways they may not want to follow even at the time, though they are fully aware of what they are doing. For example, Guard A in the Stanford experiment described himself before the experiment began as a pacifist and non-aggressive individual; by the fifth day, on his own initiative, he attempted to force-feed a prisoner, and reported: 'I hated myself for making him eat but I hated him more for not eating.'

The guards and prisoners in the Stanford experiment were volunteers, and had agreed beforehand to a temporary deprivation of their civil rights. Their participation in the experiment, Zimbardo claims, had no long-term deleterious effects, and most of them have become advocates for penal reform (Zimbardo 1973:249). But it would, I think, be rash to argue from this evidence that role-playing experiments of this kind are always justified. The fact that the responses of the participants were unexpectedly intense suggests that the technique may be hazardous, even if in this instance its effects were, in the long run, beneficial to the participants as well as to the wider society. At the very least, some circulation of roles between scientists and citizens would seem to be called for, so that scientists do not become habituated in suppressing their sensitivity and concern for others for the 'good cause' of scientific inquiry.

Our discussion of role-playing shows that even when scientists use a technique of inquiry that they are invited to prefer on ethical rather than technical grounds, they still have to face serious ethical issues. These issues take various forms depending on whether the inquiry is made in the real world or in the laboratory, whether the scientist comes into contact with the citizen only in a narrowly delimited context or over a wide range of activities, whether the contact is fleeting or sustained for months and years, and so on. Nevertheless these issues are always there, and if in the past scientists have not recognized their existence because they operated within a natural science paradigm, conformity to that paradigm is now more widely recognized as itself being a decision with ethical and political implications. Nor can the embattled scientist escape from ethics by retreating, once his data have all been collected, to the academic ivory tower to transform them into a scientific report in peace. For the dissemination of the results of his inquiry is a process with just as formidable ethical hazards, as we shall see in the next chapter.

7 Communicating results

Most successful empirical inquiries in social science lead to the preparation of a report, which may or may not be published. All the parties in the process of inquiry are likely to have an interest in what is written in the report, but their interests are different. The scientists have an interest in the pursuit of knowledge and its dissemination, and this can most readily be achieved by publication. Most scientists are also interested in furthering their own careers, and this aim too is facilitated by publication, provided that what is published stands up to the critical scrutiny of their peers. The sponsor may have merely a general interest in promoting the pursuit of knowledge, as with some foundations and those governmental agencies that are specifically concerned with the advancement of knowledge. But other government agencies and most commercial sponsors have a more instrumental attitude to research. They look for guidance in executing specific tasks in policy or in relation to their competitors. Particularly in those cases where competitive interests are involved, whether these are commercial or factional or military, the sponsor may wish for a full report of the inquiry for its own use but may be opposed to publication of the report. The citizens may be interested in seeing what is said about themselves, whether in a private report or in public print, both because their own personalities are involved and because of the possible use that may be made of the report to alter their own conditions of life, for better or worse. Gatekeepers are usually not directly concerned with publication but in so far as they consider themselves responsible for the protection of the citizens, they too may be concerned with the consequences of their decision to allow access to them. Gatekeepers who control access to documents

134

rather than people are much more likely to be concerned with questions of publication.

In general, then, scientists like to see as much published as possible, whereas the interests of the other three parties may be adversely affected by unrestricted publication. Yet we may argue that a plural democratic society depends for its survival on the maintenance of a free flow of ideas, critical as well as constructive; if so, the short-term interests of sponsors and gatekeepers, and of the citizens directly affected by the inquiry, have to be matched against the longer-term interest which they all have in the maintenance of informed criticism and comment. If, for instance, an inquiry into arrangements provided for the rehabilitation of ex-prisoners shows that these arrangements are ineffective, a report stating this fact may be perceived by those responsible for operating them as criticism of their work, even if they are not personally identified in the report. But a democratic society depends for its existence on the possibility of informed criticism of the working of all its social institutions, even if the criticism is disliked by those concerned.

There are several ways of trying to reconcile this diversity of interests: the report may be disguised; its contents may be vetted by sponsors, gatekeepers or citizens or all three, or its wording may be negotiated with them; a plurality of reports may be prepared, each intended for a different audience; and so on. Sponsors and gatekeepers are usually more articulate than citizens and exercise more power over the scientists, so that their interests in controlling publication are comparatively well defined. Yet citizens as a collectivity, and even as individuals, may endeavour to exercise some control over what is included in a published report. Often the only scarce asset held by the citizen, of relevance to the scientist, is information, whether about his opinions or about events he has seen or participated in. If he wishes to influence what the scientist says, he can be selective in what he tells, or can profess to opinions he would like to see attributed to himself even if he does not actually hold them, and so on. Alternatively he can play safe and refuse to provide any information at all. Very frequently, scientists try to get sincere, even true, responses by promising that the citizen shall remain anonymous. The assumption is that a man will be more likely to report honestly that, for instance, he conceals the amount in his wage packet from his wife, or that he voted Liberal in the last election, if these facts about himself are not published for all his neighbours to read but are drowned in some summary statement about percentages of men in some unspecified locality doing this or that.

When citizens can recognize themselves in print, and do not like what they read, they may act to protect their interests, usually by attacking the scientists. Thus in the 'Springdale affair', the citizens whose actions had been described, albeit pseudonymously, in a book publicly lampooned the research team in a Fourth of July parade (Vidich and Bensman 1968:315–475). A more common reaction is to threaten a libel action, on the grounds that the reputation of an individual or corporate body has been compromised. The commonest active response of all is to refuse any further cooperation with the scientists concerned, or with any social scientists whatsoever, as seems to have happened at 'Springdale'.

The use of pseudonyms to protect the identity of citizens was one of the first indications of the inapplicability of the natural science paradigm to social inquiry. There is a long history of pseudonyms in literature and political pamphleteering but they seem to have been little used in the early professional publications of social science. Anthropologists wrote openly of the tribes they studied and sociologists described communities under their real names. But in 1929 the Lynds' study of Muncie was published under the disguise of *Middletown* and in 1932 Margaret Mead published *The changing culture of an Indian tribe* without revealing the real name of the group she was talking about. There seems to be no analogue in natural science to this use of pseudonyms, for the objects of study are not moral agents with rights and duties and interests that must be respected. In medical science, of course, pseudonyms have been used for many decades to protect the identity of patients whose conditions were described. Likewise faces in medical photographs have been blanked off to

136

hinder recognition, though these disguises have sometimes been omitted from photographs of 'natives' (Western 1975:5). In both medical and social science, one set of persons studies a wider set. The relation between doctor and patient is one of structured inequality, unlike that nowadays between scientist and citizen. Perhaps therefore it is not surprising that medical science, apart from some heterodox areas of psychiatry, although disguising its patients, has not made any of the further shifts away from the natural science paradigm that are beginning to be made in social science.

In justifying their use of a pseudonym for the city they studied, the Lynds appealed simply to the notion of privacy.

A community as small as thirty-odd thousand affords at best about as much privacy as Irvin Cobb's celebrated goldfish enjoyed and it has not seemed desirable to increase this high visibility in the discussion of local conditions by singling out the city by its actual name. (1929:7)

They further protected the identity of the city by rounding various statistics which might otherwise have given clues.

In social science a pseudonym is usually only a partial disguise. Most individuals are able to recognize themselves, as in 'Springdale', even if others cannot. The identity of a city or province is hard to conceal, and many colleagues come to share the secret where scientists work, particularly when they make inquiries over many years. Yet even if a disguise is transparent it may still serve a useful purpose. Thus Mead did not attempt to conceal that her disguised Indian tribe was located in the United States, and she admits that anthropologists and members of the tribe itself will know which group she is describing. Nevertheless, she says, 'where pride in group identity enters into a picture which also includes disintegration, demoralization and despair, the group as well as the individual must be shielded from casual reproach' (Mead 1966:xx). Likewise Berreman (1972:lviii) explains his use of a pseudonym for the village he studied in northern India by saying 'The employment of pseudonyms is done for the protection of privacy rather than for concealment. Anyone who set about it could easily locate "Sirkanda".'

137

The same might be said about many of the disguises used by sociologists and anthropologists. If these disguises are transparent, or penetrable, why are they thought to be useful and necessary? I think the answer lies in the uncertainty and ambiguity that is an essential feature of social life. An analysis of a community sets out, in unambiguous and unchanging print, the facts of the case or some gloss or perception of the facts; it reveals wrongs and imperfections, and also good deeds that have been done unobtrusively. As a citizen of 'Plainville' remarked, while admitting the honesty of what had been written about his inadequately disguised town, 'it still hurts to see things carefully laid out' (Gallaher 1964:303). In Goffman's terms, it shows what goes on behind the scenes as well as up front. Hence, so it seems to me, the citizens are less likely to become offended if they are not confronted inescapably with what the scientist regards as the truth about themselves, even if they agree with his verdict. It is easier for the citizens to avoid facing up to the picture of themselves if their real name is not on it. Furthermore the disguise may give them some useful protection if a powerful outsider tries to use it as evidence against them. If he uses real names the scientist may be seen as challenging the citizens to deny the truth of what he says, a confrontation he and they may both wish to avoid.

In most instances where pseudonyms are used, the disguised citizens should have no difficulty in recognizing themselves as they appear in print. But sometimes the disguises consist of more than merely changes of name. Other details may be altered, as for example the rounding of statistics practised in *Middletown*. Imprecision and the use of multiple pseudonyms may add to the uncertainty and confusion. These may be seen as ways in which the scientist attempts to protect himself against the possible hostility of citizens whose imperfections he has illuminated, just as much as devices whereby the scientist protects the citizens against punitive action from outsiders. If, for example, he describes citizens carrying out illegal or reprehensible activities he may wish to protect himself from charges of libel; but he may also feel obliged to protect them from prosecution on the basis of the evidence he supplies, and to protect himself from the charge of being an accessory.

When he participates in illegal activities the social scientist may put others at risk as well as himself; when he publishes an account of these activities he certainly increases the risk of legal sanctions being taken against the citizens, however well he disguises their identity. One of the stronger criticisms made against Humphreys has been that by going to their homes to interview, under a false pretext, some of the men he had observed earlier committing fellatio in public lavatories he put them at risk of being revealed to their families and the police as deviants, as well as being confronted with the knowledge that Humphreys knew them to be deviants. When his book was first published he defended his action, but a few years later he changed his opinion and said that he would not do the same again. At the time of the study, despite great moral anguish, he was confident that whatever pressures were put on him he would not reveal the identity of the men he studied. Now he writes, 'Since those days of uncertainty, however, I have spent three months of a Federal sentence in a county jail and am no longer so certain that I could have withstood the pressures of the criminal justice system' (Humphreys 1975: 230).

Simple pseudonyms, provided they are not mistaken for real names, merely diminish rather than distort the data. But when quantities are rounded, and details of time and place altered in such a way that the reader cannot tell how much is genuine and how much is disguise, the scientist is presenting his data in distorted form. His obligation as a scientist is to make sure that the distortions are insignificant, while his duty to the citizens is to ensure that the distortions constitute an adequate disguise. The usual rule of thumb for disguises is that the data should be presented in such a form that an outsider cannot identify any citizen while any citizen can recognize himself through the disguise (Humphreys 1975: 172). If citizens are to be involved in the preparation of a report on an inquiry, their contribution to the process can be substantial only if they can recognize themselves or their community through the disguises introduced to protect their

139

interests. There is of course no reason a priori why the limits to the penetrating power of the citizen's perspicacity should ensure that the distortions introduced as disguise are scientifically insignificant; furthermore the definition of an 'outsider' is clearly problematic. Nevertheless the rule provides a useful check on unnecessarily elaborate disguises. In some books and articles disguises seem to have been used merely because it has become customary to do so, without there being any apparent need for them. Indeed, Gibbons (1975) argues that when the citizens have given their 'informed consent' to being studied, disguises are unnecessary. Yet sometimes they give their informed consent only on condition that disguises are used.

Occasionally a scientist may consider it necessary to thicken his disguises, so as to ensure that the citizens he describes cannot even recognize themselves. This may be done even when there are none of the hazards associated with publishing details of illegal or reprehensible acts. For example, in a recently published book, the author reports that

All names have been changed, and sometimes sexes; institutions, affiliations and research topics have been changed or described in general terms . . . If the same name happens to appear in more than one place, it does not refer to the same individual. (Platt 1976 : 7)

With such circumspection, we might well think we were about to hear something really iniquitous; alas, all that is offered is an account of the *Realities of social research*. This unusually opaque disguise is necessary, the author argues, because 'my respondents are members of the group most likely to read this book. This makes it harder to preserve their anonymity, where this is necessary, than in most research reports.' Luckily, citizens in general are not so sensitive as Platt thinks her colleagues to be; or, more probably, they are more sceptical of the truth contained in the reports of social scientists. I am reminded of the adage that academic politics are comparatively bitter just because the spoils are comparatively meagre.

Occasionally an author attempts to protect the identity of the community he has studied by adopting a pseudonym himself.

140

The anthropologist who studied the small town coded as 'Plain-ville' presented himself to the citizens as a scientist who was studying the community and, despite initial suspicions, he was accepted in this role. But 'every serious informant requested, and was promised, the protection of complete anonymity, and it was for this reason, rather than because of any desire on his part for secrecy, that all place names and personal names, including his own, were withheld or altered' (West 1945:xv). In a recent account of a gang in Glasgow the author delayed publication for several years and then published under a pseudonym, in order to protect himself as well as members of the gang (Patrick 1973:9).

This device of pseudonymous authorship has not been widely used in social science and is unlikely to achieve any substantial increase in protection. An anonymous author cannot easily defend what he has written against his professional peers without revealing his identity. If he wishs to be given professional credit for what he has written he must reveal who he is, as the author of *Plainville* did eventually. The pseudonyms of authors attract the probing curiosity of professional librarians, who tend not to bother about deciphering code names for communities and citizens.

When a scientist uses pseudonyms and blurs the data in his report, he usually makes his own decision about how much disguise is necessary to protect the privacy of the citizens. When the book or article appears in print, the citizens, if they notice the event, are presented with a *fait accompli*; the damage, if there is any, has already been done. One way of ensuring that statements objectionable to citizens do not appear in print is to involve them in the process of writing up. For example, Bott and her colleagues, after collecting most of their data, prepared draft detailed accounts of the social relations of two married couples, using fictitious names and disguising their identities. These drafts were then discussed with the couples concerned. The four citizens eventually agreed to the publication of these accounts of their private lives, though they did not necessarily accept the truth of what was said about themselves. The process of 'working-

141

through' the material with the citizens helped the scientists to revise their analysis at several points, and was productive in that much confidential material could be published without breaking faith with the citizens who supplied it. Bott says that 'all four individuals seem to have come through the experience without harm' (Bott 1971: 47). This process of 'working-through' took the equivalent of one person's working time for more than a year, and Bott notes that it would be impracticable to go through this lengthy procedure for all the material a scientist hopes to publish. Nevertheless, in the Glacier Project, Jaques and his colleagues circulated drafts of each section of their book to each of the groups in the factory who were concerned, and discussed it in detail with them. The revised and agreed drafts, which gave the true name of the factory but no names of individual employees, were then all reported to the Works Council of the factory, and were checked and revised by that body before being reported to the factory generally and finally published to the world at large (Jaques 1951: 17).

Few scientists follow such an elaborate procedure as this, but many refer their first drafts to the citizens in order to gain a check on the accuracy of their observations and conclusions, without necessarily envisaging the possibility of irreducible disagreement between scientist and citizens. Thus for example, Bell (1959: 49) says

After writing the first draft of the Haskell County Kansas Study I took the manuscript to the community and went over it with my major informants. In many ways this was the most productive part of the fieldwork. It enabled the informants for the first time to understand what I was attempting to accomplish.

This must have been the experience of many scientists. But the dividing line between fact and interpretation is usually problematic, and citizens may be just as keen to point out errors of interpretation, as they see it, as errors of fact. It is hard to draw a clear line between a proper respect for a citizen's right to privacy and excessive respect for the accuracy of his interpretation of events. Jaques adopts the extreme view that no interpretation of

142

events should be published until the participants and the scientists have reached agreement on what it is; until then, the topic is 'not ready to be written up' (Jaques 1951:16). This policy may perhaps have been appropriate in the particular circumstances of the Glacier Project, but clearly cannot apply to the description and analysis of events where citizens are in conflict with one another. In a sharply divided community, approval of what the scientist has written by one faction may well entail automatic rejection by its rivals. It seems to me that a scientist should grant a veto on publication neither to the citizens nor to his sponsor. Nevertheless, the process of working-through, wherever it can be carried out, does give the scientist a much better understanding of how he can honour his obligations to the citizens and to his sponsor, as well as providing him with additional information about how they interpret the data he has analysed. Indeed, these interpretations are essential data, and have to be taken into account in any well-grounded analysis The scientist who cannot involve the citizens in the writing-up stage of his inquiries is at a great disadvantage cognitively, and also runs a greater risk of harming the citizens inadvertently. The citizens may not agree with everything that the scientist proposes to say about them, and his stay among them is, in general, unlikely to have led them to settle all their differences with one another. Involvement in writing-up gives them an opportunity to repudiate interpretations they cannot accept at a stage when the scientist can still make constructive use of their disagreement with him.

Wallis (1977) has given an excellent description of this process of negotiated publication, carried out in a context where, if he had followed Jaques' advice, he would have been unable to publish anything at all. Leaders of the group of citizens he studied, the Church of Scientology, objected vigorously to what he proposed to write about them. After negotiation Wallis agreed to make some of the alterations they sought but refused to make others. His book (1976) appeared with an appendix written by a member of the Church, rebutting Wallis' thesis. His account of the circumstances in which he carried out his study, and of the negotiations about what he should say in his book, also has an appendix by a

143

Church member warning readers against being misled by Wallis' work. Whether or not Wallis misrepresents Scientology may be debated; publishing dissenting appendices is a tactic with hazards as well as advantages. Nevertheless Wallis has, in my view, provided us with an admirably clear and frank discussion of the process of negotiation whereby a social scientist collects data and presents his analysis of the collective life of a group of citizens more powerful than himself and differing radically from him in the interpretation of events.

So far we have discussed the communication of the results of social inquiry only by the written word. Pseudonyms may give limited but adequate protection when the results of an inquiry appear in print, but the dangers to the privacy of citizens posed by some other media of communication are harder to avoid. Photographs of citizens used as book illustrations may nullify the protection given by pseudonyms, yet anthropologists, if not other social scientists as well, sometimes include photographs in their publications without consulting the citizens depicted in them (Hicks 1977:216–17).

A medium used increasingly by social anthropologists, and to a lesser extent by sociologists, is film. An ethnographic film constitutes an effective record of social behaviour which complements and substantially amplifies, though it does not replace, the written word and which has great value for teaching. As with the written report, the personal identity of the citizens who appear in the film is usually not of interest to the scientists, students and members of the general public who see the film. Yet the candid camera makes a much greater intrusion into the privacy of the individual than does an ethnographic notebook, an intrusion which usually cannot be repaired by some device such as blanking off faces, as in medical photographs, or photographing citizens only with their backs to the camera. Exactly where and when the film was shot is often indicated only vaguely, with some loss of scientific value. The citizens concerned are able to recognize themselves, and their neighbours, more readily on film than in a book. If only public and approved behaviour is shown, maybe no one will feel offended, but many ethnographic films seek to

144

show much more than this. Allowing a film to be screened everywhere except near where it was shot might be a way of avoiding embarrassment but to follow this policy is to revert to the natural science paradigm, with the insulation of citizens from the results of the research carried out upon them; few citizens would agree to shut their eyes to local secrets which are to be revealed to every stranger. Many groups of people who have been filmed for scholarly purposes have welcomed the creation of a permanent visual record of their lives, particularly for the interest they hope it will have for their children and grandchildren. Nevertheless there seem to me to be serious obstacles in creating a visual archive which would adequately mirror the pattern of social life without giving unwarranted offence to those citizens who are shown undisguisedly to be corrupt, venial, lazy, mean or whatever the local version of evil happens to be. Filming activities which the citizens perceive as innocuous, or about which there is consensus, presents fewer ethical problems, however esoteric or bizarre or morally charged these activities may appear to distant viewers. There are of course political issues which are raised by the process whereby ethnographic films which have been made initially for purposes of research become transformed into items of mass entertainment, and fuel for cultural prostitution, the conversion of an authentic way of life into a fragmented series of tourist attractions. The sponsorship of social research by mass media may be as beset with ethical and political hazards as is sponsorship by the military. Yet within a relatively homogeneous society, where questions of cultural imperialism do not arise, the impossibility of providing effective disguises for those who appear in scientific films is even clearer. Citizens should be fully aware of how they are to appear on the screen, and be willing to be filmed, if the inquiry is not to end with a shout of 'Never again!'

Disguises of various kinds may be effective in protecting the interests of citizens when a report is published, but confidentiality is at risk from the very moment when the scientist is told or allowed to see something that would normally be hidden. There are many ways in which scientists can attempt to ensure that

145

their field notes remain in safe custody, and that particular care is taken of any documents that link disguises to real names. In recent years a new hazard has arisen from the legislation which has been enacted in several countries allowing citizens to have access to any official or unofficial dossiers that may have been compiled on them, and from the power of the courts, in some cases, to subpoena field reports written by social scientists as part of their data collection. A scientist's field notes are seldom written in such a form that information on any given citizen can be isolated from data about many other members of the community, so that to acknowledge one citizen's right to know what a scientist has written about him may endanger the confidentiality of information received from or about others. In relation to the courts, social scientists may be regarded either as analogous to priests and doctors, whose confidential sources of information may be respected, or to journalists, who from time to time have been sent to prison for refusing to reveal their sources. Both kinds of hazard have arisen recently, and scientists need to be more careful than many have been in the past in how they protect their field data (King and Spector 1963:205). The problems that arise from legislation on these matters are discussed in Chapter 9.

Although in recent years scientists have become more concerned with protecting the identity of the citizens they study or from whom they receive information, we should remember that sometimes citizens prefer to appear in print under their real names. Confidence in oneself, and pride in one's own culture, may lead one to seek publicity rather than shun it. A community whose members feel that they have nothing to hide may interpret the use of a pseudonym as evidence that the scientist wishes to publish lies. James West's use of a pseudonym for 'Plainville' was regarded by some of his citizen-critics as proof that he had double-crossed them and written an untruthful book to make money for himself; why else, they asked, would he use a pseudonym? (Gallaher 1964:292).

A good example of a group insisting on the use of real names is provided in Madan's (1965) study of a rural group of Kashmiri Brahmins. It was the citizens, rather than the scientist, who insisted that the identity of their village should not be disguised. This insistence was, of course, a compliment paid to the scientist as well as an expression of the citizens' confidence in the admirable qualities of their own distinctive way of life. Yet their action might also be seen as a way of exercising some control over what he said about them, for he too is a Kashmiri Brahmin whom the citizens endeavoured to recruit to their village and whom they certainly wished to make answerable for anything he said about them. Some of the information he gained was, he thought, given to him as a potential fellow villager rather than as an anthropologist. He says, 'This raised for me the ethical problem of what I had come to know. It was obvious that at least some households had taken me into the domain of their privacy, and thus bound me to secrecy' (Madan 1975:151). The absence of pseudonyms must certainly have served to strengthen this constraint.

Whether or not they appear in print under disguises, citizens are unlikely to welcome every statement made about them, even where no breach of privacy or of confidentiality has occurred. The scientist may consider that he will be completely hamstrung if he cannot say that the citizens are less than perfect, but the citizens may be annoyed that their imperfections have been drawn to their own attention even in disguised form. Fair comment may be the lifeblood of democratic society, but why pick on us to comment on? This sort of consideration applies to the public image of social inquiry in general, but is particularly acute where scientists expect to be in continuing contact with a community over a period of several years, during which various publications about the community will appear. The scientists then have an interest in building up good relations with the community so that the inquiry can get started, and in maintaining the fund of goodwill through the years despite the appearance of publications that depict the community with all its imperfections. Thus for instance, in the code of professional conduct drawn up for the Cornell Program in Social Psychiatry (1959–60:148), reference is made to the importance of protecting the goodwill that a project may have obtained in a given research site. 'Proposed publications which are deemed to be very likely to impair seriously the relationship of the program to the research site through the disclosure of confidences, facts or critical evaluations (explicit or implicit) of local persons, groups, and practices will not be approved for publication.' Maybe the insertion of the strongly qualifying phrase 'very likely to impair seriously' was intended to preserve the possibility of making some criticisms of the citizens. Nevertheless it is clear that quite apart from any considerations of privacy and anonymity scientists have to decide where their publications should lie between the two extremes of innocuous platitudes that are scientifically worthless and scientific discoveries that may be derogatory to some of the citizens who supplied the evidence.

Much the same considerations apply when it is likely that the social and political status of the citizens, and their views about right and wrong behaviour, will change while the present generation is still alive. Values that are held firmly at the time of the inquiry may, a decade or two later, be firmly repudiated, and conduct that at the time was admirable may later become a moral and political liability. Yet while the scientist may be able to anticipate in a few contexts, as for example with cannibalism, that a customary and well-accepted practice is likely to be repudiated by the citizens he studies within a few years, and that therefore he must be particularly careful in the way in which he publishes his data, in general he cannot possibly predict what embarrassment, moral offence or political danger may be engendered later by the publication of a report which, at the time, all concerned may endorse and welcome. Mead (1966:xxii), writing with reference to data collected 'without an open declaration of purpose', e.g. covertly, draws attention to the need to protect the anonymity of citizens for many years, when conditions may change. She notes, for instance, that the label 'animist', which citizens may accept willingly at one stage of political and cultural development, is now bitterly resented when it is applied to the members of a proud nation-state. In general terms this is good advice, though I recall meeting certain members of a proud nation-state who were proud to be recognized as animists, as having successfully resisted the blandishments of Christianity and Islam. Yet if the scientist cannot predict how the ideas of citizens and the political orientation of the regime will change, he can at least be sure that change of some kind is likely, and should try to be particularly careful in reporting aspects of social life where change is most likely (cf. Mead 1969; Colson et al. 1976:495).

Paying proper regard to the interests of citizens whose circumstances may change in the future may however merge into accepting censorship from other groups who wish these changes to take place. For example, in the 1930s an Indian sociologist carried out an inquiry into the social life of a mountain community of his own state. He described in his doctoral dissertation the system of polyandry that operated in the community. When a book, based in part on the dissertation, was published in 1975, women politicians protested that the author, who had become Chief Minister of the state, had portrayed the women of the community in a vulgar and distorted fashion. They demanded that the book, which contains a foreword by Indira Gandhi, should be banned. The author defended himself by claiming that, in some copies of the book, certain pages, where he stated that the custom was no longer practised, had been omitted. What seems to have happened is that a form of marriage, which is the norm in several Himalayan societies, has become offensive not to the members of these societies but to the inhabitants of the plains who, in the context of a desire for modernization and for an increased tourist trade, wish to deny that their state still contains communities with a style of life different from their own. The scientist-politician concerned gave way under pressure from his opponents, not from the people whose lives he described. Thus we have what Berreman (1976) describes as 'an example of perverse political pressure on scholarship'.

While pressure from the citizens who are described in the report, or from sections of the public, may influence its form and contents, more direct pressure is often imposed on the scientist by gatekeepers and sponsors. In most national archives there is a clear division between open and restricted material. It often happens that a research worker gains permission to see documents that bear on his topic of inquiry but which have not yet passed into the public domain or which may never do so. In this situation, the government department concerned acts as a gatekeeper controlling access not to the citizens but to documents related to them. Similar conditions prevail when a social scientist is granted access to documents and records kept by a firm, to correspondence and unpublished documents in private hands, to confidential academic records and the like. In all these cases, the cloak of secrecy is temporarily and partially withdrawn in the interests of greater understanding. Often, the gatekeeper imposes some condition on the scientist in return for granting access. He may be required to submit for approval by the gatekeeper any passage destined for publication in which he quotes from a confidential document. Sometimes the gatekeeper may insist that nothing shall be published about the inquiry without his approval, irrespective of any direct use that may be made of citations from confidential documents. Or the gatekeeper may take some intermediate position, allowing, for instance, free use of citations in an unpublished doctoral dissertation but prohibiting confidential citations in openly published work.

Recent controversies about the Wilson memoirs, the Crossman diaries and the Pentagon papers have brought this aspect of gatekeeping to public notice. But attempts to control publication are not confined to gatekeepers. Some sponsors may endeavour to insist that, as a condition for receiving financial support, the scientist will undertake not to publish anything that has not first been vetted by the sponsor. Others merely require that their sponsorship shall be mentioned in any publication arising out of the inquiry so that their altruistic support for scientific research shall be properly rewarded. Where a sponsor not only offers financial support but also controls facilities for publication, it may claim the right of first refusal to publish. Thus for instance, one Australian sponsor imposes, as a condition for providing financial support, the requirement that nothing at all arising from a research project shall be published without its permission, but then goes on to note that this permission shall not be withheld unless it proposes itself to arrange for publication.

150

In practice, it is more often pressure applied by a sponsor or gatekeeper, rather than the scientist's sensitivity to the risk of offending the citizens, that produces innocuous platitudes or which results in no publication at all. Political regimes that lack open debate and argument tend to have ruling elites that are intolerant of criticism, and which will not attach their imprimatur to statements that reflect adversely on their activities. Sponsors likewise may feel that their largesse should protect them from criticism, and a scientist may be reluctant to offend the patron on whom he depends for financial support.

It is therefore advantageous if the rights of the scientist to publish, and the rights of the gatekeepers and sponsors to control what he says, are brought up for discussion as early as possible, before too great an investment of time and effort is made in an inquiry that will lead nowhere. Even when the rights of scientists and sponsors are defined clearly in advance there may still be vigorous discussion before an agreed report can appear. For example, Whyte (1959:95–102) describes vividly his difficulty in getting his sponsor, the National Restaurant Association, to approve publication of a book on the industry which included an account of how its workers were disenchanted with their jobs. After much negotiation, Whyte agreed to publish his discussion of attitudes to jobs in an appendix. But on an earlier occasion, his gatekeeper successfully exercised its right to prevent publication.

Prior discussion with gatekeepers is appropriate when the scientist is trying to negotiate access to whatever it is that they guard; but in some contexts scientists have sought to get past gatekeepers without being noticed. For instance, one sociologist reports that, while carrying out a community study, he decided that he would have no scruples in deceiving his main gatekeeper. He gave the gatekeeper a false account of his objectives, and tried to avoid being noticed while making his inquiries (Van den Berghe 1967:185). In this instance, the gatekeeper was the South African government, the scientist's real objective was to study race relations, and he justifies his actions by categorizing the regime as a racial tyranny. His inquiries were in no way facilitated by the government, and his report is a condemnation of the social system that the government upholds (Van den Berghe 1964:259). His actions have not been censured by his professional colleagues, and indeed they merely demonstrate, in the clearest possible form, how ethical considerations cannot be divorced from considerations of politics and power. The South African regime will not be transformed merely because a social scientist has criticized it. There have been serious constraints on empirical social inquiry in South Africa for forty years or more, so that he cannot be accused of spoiling a previously good research site for his colleagues. But the world is full of tyrannies, large and small, and many are not as well publicised as is South Africa. If research, whether covert or not, is concealed from an administrative gatekeeper and is eventually brought to light, the disclosure may lead to the imposition of further constraints on social scientists. But in these circumstances we might argue that the exposure of injustice justifies the deterioration in the conditions for empirical research, and that a regime that cannot tolerate criticism will move towards greater repression irrespective of the feeble goads administered by annoyed social scientists. Each context and each inquiry has to be looked at on its merits, but the difficulties of deciding on the right course of action when carrying out social research under tyrannical regimes serve to emphasize the premiss of an open pluralist society on which the possibility of sustained empirical social inquiry is based.

Pseudonyms and other disguises are means whereby the citizen's right to privacy is protected; other people are hindered from discovering facts about him that he does not wish them to know. But does the citizen have a right to be protected from finding out about himself? Most people, in general, would answer no; the increased self-awareness and understanding that come from social inquiry are usually cited as two of its greatest potential benefits. But while this may apply in general, there may be particular kinds of information where the answer is not clear-cut. The situation is analogous to cèrtain kinds of medical information. If a patient knows that his physical condition is such that he is likely to die, then, so it is argued, he is likely to struggle to remain alive with less determination; the prophecy will be self-fulfilling. Also he may be made unhappy, whereas in ignorance he might have remained cheerful. In the social field, tests that predict undesirable outcomes are liable to become self-fulfilling, and some scientists have therefore argued that an individual should not be told how he has performed on them. For example, some have urged that the results of tests that are held to indicate a propensity for juvenile delinquency should not be passed on to the children who take the tests. Knowledge that one's performance on such a test shows that there is very little likelihood of one becoming delinquent might also be a self-fulfilling prophecy, and might in any case be a welcome reassurance. But in the context in which these sorts of tests are administered to a group of children, it would be futile to reveal the results only to those who had done well and to conceal them from the rest; hence nobody can be told (cf. Kelman 1968:37–8).

The same argument is sometimes used with reference to less normatively charged kinds of information, and where the likelihood of prophecies becoming self-fulfilling is less. For example, knowledge that one's IQ is below normal (as half the population's must be, by definition) may be depressing and lead to an unwarranted lowering of ambition. But to be told that one's IQ is above normal may lead to an equally unwarranted lowering of effort, with results that are just as damaging. In the case of IQs, which have been the subject of continual controversy (Brim 1965), the citizen is to some extent shielded by the cautious attitude of some psychologists towards raw scores. McGuire (1972:79), for instance, states that a score should not be given 'even to anyone entitled to have it without the statement by the psychologist as to how far it is likely to be a fair estimate of the subject's true level of intelligence'. What is interesting is that although McGuire shows a good deal of sensitivity in discussing exactly who should be told what about the citizen – psychologists, psychiatrists, social workers, general practitioners, etc. – he does not even mention the rights of the citizen to know about himself.

Yet empirical research shows that prophecies of this kind may be self-fulfilling even if the citizen himself is not told about his performance. In 1964 Rosenthal and Jacobson (1968), employing

153

a typical deception technique, told some school teachers that certain of their pupils had been identified by means of a new test to be academic 'spurters'. The teachers were cautioned not to discuss the test results with either the pupils or the children's parents. At the end of the year the pupils were tested again. The scientists found that those children designated as 'spurters' had in fact done better than the rest, and were liked more by their teachers. In fact, the prophecy of success was a pure artefact; the 'spurters' had been selected at random. Supplementary data suggested that the spurters' success was mainly due to the expectation their teachers had that they would do well (cf. Zanna et al. 1975).

As with medical information, it is not always clear when the receipt of social information about himself will be to the citizen's benefit or not. It is easy for the social scientist to adopt the paternalistic stance of the typical doctor, and to be chary or reticent in passing information to the citizen, particularly when the citizen is a child. Nevertheless, if our fine phrases about enhanced self-knowledge from participation in research are to have substance, the citizen has surely a right to know unless there is a very clear indication that the knowledge would be harmful to him. This must be particularly the case when the citizen is an adult and when he takes the initiative in deciding that he wants to know about himself.

When a book or article is published, it becomes public; anyone who wishes can read it. There is even a convention in the world of science that anything published becomes thereby automatically and universally known. In practice there are many impediments to the flow of knowledge: censorship, high prices, limited editions, language barriers, information overload and the like. But these impediments, luckily, work imperfectly. Hence when a social scientist publishes the results of his research, he should assume that anyone whatever may read what he has to say. The citizens he describes may study his report, and so may their friends and enemies. We have discussed how the scientist can negotiate with citizens, gatekeepers and sponsors so that the interests of all parties in the process of inquiry are adequately

154

allowed for in the outcome of the research. But what responsibility does a scientist have to citizens who cannot or do not articulate their interests, or whose interests change with the passage of time? These questions were raised in yet another incident in the war in Vietnam. In 1957 Georges Condominas published in French an anthropological account of Sar Luk, a Montagnard village in South Vietnam. No disguises were used and individuals were mentioned by name. In 1962 the US Department of Commerce published, for the official use of the US government, an English translation of this work, which was then distributed to the Green Berets for use in the war. The translation was made without the permission of the author or his publisher, and he learnt of its existence only years later (Condominas 1973:4). The author protested strongly: 'How can one accept, without trembling with rage, that this work, in which I wanted to describe in their human plenitude these men who have so much to teach us about life, should be offered to the technicians of death – of *their* death!'

Pirating is a breach of national or international law on copyright, and on this score the Department of Commerce acted wrongly; but that is a minor matter, since there might well have been an English version of Condominas's book had publishers been quicker to recognize its merits. The important issue is the use to which the pirated book was put, and it is about this that Condominas protests. But though I sympathize with his feelings, and hope that, similarly placed, I would have reacted as he did, we must also look at the obligations that he had towards the people he studied. Because of what he published about them, American aggression could be directed against them in a more sophisticated and perhaps more effective form. Had he disguised their identity, maybe they would have suffered during the war no more than other groups did. Had he known how much use was to be made of ethnographic intelligence by the United States forces, he might have taken the precaution of using disguises, or have refrained from publication entirely. These are all imponderables that, helped by hindsight, we can suggest that a percipient anthropologist might try to take into account, but it would be quite

155

unreasonable to expect that these are considerations which the Montagnards should have tried to weigh when negotiating with him about what he should be allowed to say about them. The principles of professional responsibility adopted by the American Anthropological Association include an obligation on the anthropologist to 'reflect on the foreseeable repercussions of research and publication on the general population being studied' (American Anthropological Association 1970). I think it is not unacceptably paternalistic for an anthropologist to foresee repercussions that the citizens cannot envisage. Yet how foreseeable, at the time when Condominas wrote his book in French, was the harnessing of ethnographic information in the conduct of a terrible war? And would the plight of the Montagnards during the war have been alleviated if nothing had been published about their way of life? The brutal destruction of Sar Luk in a counter-offensive by South Vietnamese troops during Diem's regime seems to have been unconnected with the existence of the book (Condominas 1977:xiv). To my mind this incident shows that while social scientists have an obligation to attempt to foresee the likely consequences of publication, particularly when the citizens concerned are poorly placed to do so themselves, and to modify the form of their publications accordingly, this exercise of caution cannot be relied upon to eliminate all cases of injustice and exploitation facilitated by ethnographic information. The recipe for eliminating injustice and exploitation, if one exists, must be sought elsewhere. The goal will not be brought nearer by refusing to publish anything at all.

Despite the ostensibly universal availability of publications, some social scientists have tried to segregate their audiences, and to modify their publications to take account of the interests of different sets of readers. Some make use of language barriers, omitting in the version intended for local readers material which might be disliked and which they make available only in the version of the report intended to circulate elsewhere (Street 1969: 97). In Australia, Aboriginal men are sometimes very concerned that photographs of sacred paintings or cult objects should not be seen by Aboriginal women, but may not necessarily object to them being seen by men anywhere, or by women outside Australia. Hence in a recent case it was proposed that a book with photographs should be published outside Australia, while the Australian edition should have no illustrations (cf. Hamilton 1971). A policy of this kind already operates in museums, in that Aboriginal sacred objects displayed openly in museums overseas are in Australia removed from public view. In another country, an anthropologist who published an undisguised account of various secret initiation rites performed by a community all of whose members were, at the time, illiterate has asked any of his readers who may visit the area not to reveal to the citizens the knowledge they have gained from reading his book.

All expedients of this kind are unstable, for illiterate tribesmen and tribeswomen learn to read and begin to study anthropology; a compromise that is satisfactory to one group of Aboriginals may offend the religious susceptibilities, or the political ambitions, of another group; as Condominas's case shows, books are bought and translated by enemies as well as friends. Thus while negotiation about what may be published and where, and a pessimistic attitude about possible repercussions, are necessary elements in the process of social research, they are certainly not sufficient to ensure a utopian outcome.

Disseminating the results of social inquiry is indeed just as difficult and hazardous a matter as collecting the data on which they are based. There is no easy way to communicate knowledge if adequate attention is to be paid to the interests of the parties involved. In communicating results the intertwining of political considerations with ethical questions is closer than in collecting data. For the finished product of the inquiry, the report describing the correlation between variables or the state of affairs round the village pump, is the knowledge towards which all the earlier stages of the process of inquiry are only preliminaries. Knowledge is a public commodity which can be used for good or ill, and what is problematic is the extent to which a scientist continues to have responsibilities for the entity he has created. This is one of the main questions discussed in the next two chapters.

8 The professionalization of social science

In the last two chapters we have discussed in detail the ethical hazards encountered in social inquiry. In the light of this discussion let us now look again at the historical development of empirical social science research in the twentieth century. Striving for professional status and recognition, and conforming to well-established schools of thought in the philosophy of science, social scientists stressed that their inquiries were 'value-free'. By this they meant that sociology and psychology, just like physics, chemistry and engineering, were sciences that, actually or potentially, embodied eternal truths independent of time and space. Though sociologists and psychologists, like chemists and engineers, might well be concerned with political and social questions in their off-duty capacity as citizens, they were not, or should not be, influenced in their work by the political views that they might hold. Those few individuals who confounded their roles as scientists and citizens were shunned by their fellows who were primarily concerned with preserving the purity of the professional ivory tower.

But whereas it may not be too difficult to sustain the belief that a natural scientist can keep separate, say, his inquiries into the bending of girders and his opinions about nationalizing the banks, it is much harder to keep apart a social scientist's inquiry into, say, the causes of strikes and his opinions about an incomes policy. Because they study political and social phenomena, social scientists are more likely to have articulate political opinions than are their colleagues in the natural sciences. Hence it is not surprising that some social scientists should react against the effort to gain intellectual respectability by isolating social inquiry from political commitment and instead seek to establish an explicit connexion between research and social action. One of the first attempts came in 1935, with the foundation in the United States of the Society for the Psychological Study of Social Issues. The Society for Applied Anthropology was formed in 1941, and the Society for the Study of Social Problems was started by American sociologists ten years later. All three bodies are based on the premiss that the knowledge gained by social inquiry can be utilized for the amelioration of real social conditions, and that citizens who are also trained in the social sciences are particularly well qualified to advise on, or to initiate, ameliorative social action. From this stance it is an easy step to become concerned with the ethics of both social inquiry and the application of the expertise of social science to current social problems.

This concern can stem either from a commitment to social action, whereby the social scientist becomes directly aware of the interests and powers of fellow non-scientist citizens, or from the opposite, a wish to remain secure within the academic ivory tower despite the onslaughts or temptations of the wider world. It may perhaps also spring from a formal and routine commitment to lofty ethical principles, embodied in a professional code. Codes of professional practice, of which the Hippocratic oath of the medical profession is the most venerable example, have long been a symbolic attribute of professional status, and the process of professionalization may include the adoption of an appropriate ethical code (Hobbs 1948). Indeed, in the early 1920s, this aspect of professionalization was itself institutionalized, in a 'Campaign of the International Association of Rotary Clubs for the writing of codes of standards of practice for each business and profession'. Each Rotary Club received the outline of a theoretical model code (Gundaker 1922:230). These codes, in many cases, probably have little effect on the conduct of members of professional associations (Baumhart 1961; Hobbs 1968:165), and serve as a basis for the regulation of disputes within the profession rather than as a means for protecting the public interest (Gotlieb and Borodin 1973:237–8). Nevertheless social scientists, either in seeking to achieve professional status or because of a heightened awareness of the impact of their activities on others,

159

have put a good deal of effort into constructing codes or, contrariwise, in explaining why they are unnecessary (cf. Orlans 1973:51–80).

Ethical issues are more likely to arise, or at least are more likely to be recognized as such, when the findings of a scientific inquiry are put to practical use rather than merely published in the world of scholarship (cf. Harris 1952; Foster 1969:174). Hence it is not surprising that the Society for Applied Anthropology should claim to be the first behavioural organization to concern itself with a formal code of professional ethics (Chapple 1951), though the American Psychological Association had established a special committee on scientific and professional ethics as early as 1938 (American Psychological Association 1952:426). The same Association later drew up a formal code of ethics, based on an analysis of what had happened in over a thousand actual incidents (Hobbs 1968:165; cf. Evan 1960–61; Golann 1970:206). Codes were drawn up specifically for two large investigations based on Cornell University during the 1950s (Bronfenbrenner 1952; Cornell Program in Social Psychiatry 1959–60). The Nuremberg trials stimulated discussion about the ethical obligations of doctors and the adequacy of their enunciation in the Hippocratic oath, so that the medical profession came to be a model to which social scientists who were aware of their ethical responsibilities could appeal (Berg 1954:108; Williams and Ouren 1976). Applied anthropologists, though generally suspicious of the unmodified natural science paradigm, also thought of themselves as analogous in some respects to engineers and sought to proclaim their comparable ethical responsibilities (Chapple 1952). Yet it was not until after the cancellation of Project Camelot in 1965 that the main professional bodies of American sociologists and anthropologists, divided among themselves by the Vietnam war, began to argue in earnest about professional ethical codes. The old paradigm has been tarnished and, as mentioned in Chapter 1, ethics has become fashionable with social scientists, notably with anthropologists (e.g. Berreman et al. 1968; Jorgenson et al. 1971; Chilungu 1976). In 1976, for example, elections to the committee on ethics of the American Anthropological Association were contested, and statements by rival candidates stating the policies on ethics that they favoured, appeared together with their photographs, in the house journal of the Association (American Anthropological Association 1976b). The same journal runs a regular feature, 'Ethics and the anthropologist', and a collection of articles on this topic has appeared as a book (Rynkiewich and Spradley 1976; cf. Appell 1971).

In Britain there has been no catalytic event analogous to the cancellation of Project Camelot. Although social scientists were used by the British military command during the 'emergency' in Malaya in the 1950s (Deitchman 1976:116), their activities gave rise to no controversy. Professional responses in Britain to the changing environment for empirical inquiry have been equivocal and slower to appear. The British Sociological Association began to pay attention to ethical issues in 1966 and its current statement of ethical principles, dating from 1973, is currently under review. There is no corresponding statement for anthropologists in Britain. A conference on professional ethics for British psychologists was held in 1972. Unesco became concerned with the ethics of social science research in 1972 and commissioned an international survey of codes of professional ethics (Reynolds 1975:563).

The published codes are concerned with relations within the profession as well as with relations between scientists and others (e.g. Society for Applied Anthropology 1963). The committees on ethics set up by various professional associations are in practice more concerned with questions about appointments, tenure and scholarly attribution, relations between scientists and between them and their employers and students, than they are with relations between scientists and citizens and sponsors. Perhaps the formidable financial sanctions that sponsors can wield against wayward scientists explain why social scientists have not shown much anxiety of conscience about whether they are behaving correctly towards their sponsors. Citizens, unless constituted as an organized body, lack such powerful sanctions, and although all the codes enshrine the importance of citizens' interests, they seldom provide any machinery whereby an aggrieved citizen can claim redress from a scientist (Donnison et al. n.d.: 41–4). Thus the committees deal with questions of internal professional ethics which social science shares with the humanities and natural science, rather than with questions that are distinctive to social science (cf. American Sociological Association, Committee on professional ethics 1971; Coser 1971). Even associations that are divided among themselves about whether professional status is to be sought or shunned seem to experience the same phenomenon. The codes are also internal in that the only sanctions enforceable under them are directed by the associations at their own members. They are therefore likely to be less effective as a means of controlling the research activities of scientists than the vetting committees that have been established in some American universities with the aim of ensuring, among other things, that the rights of citizens in research projects are properly respected, as mentioned in Chapter 5. Recently, comments made in print by a British sociologist about some of his colleagues, reflecting adversely on their intellectual integrity, attracted attention in the public press under headlines such as 'Red sails on the campus' (Crick 1977). The attempt to refer the matter to the appropriate professional ethics committee highlighted the intra-professional orientation of these committees as well as their lack of power (*Times* 1977).

Individual scientists can employ sanctions of a kind against colleagues even in the absence of a binding code, by refusing to cooperate or by hindering professional preferment. A scientist may appeal to the community of scientists to censure a colleague and may indeed do so on behalf of citizens whose interests are thought to have been overridden unjustifiably, as in the recent controversy about what ought to happen to the Ik of Uganda (Barth 1974; Wilson, P. J. et al. 1975).

Yet as universities and professional associations become more scrupulous about how inquiries should be made, a greater proportion of social science research is carried out by commercial organizations, the so-called 'contract houses' which undertake social inquiries for profit rather than in search of enlightenment

162

and which are less concerned with ethical issues (Starr 1977). For this reason alone, it seems likely that sectional efforts to increase ethical awareness in social inquiry will sooner or later be supplemented by legislation.

Most of the ethical codes attempt to define both the status of social scientists as professionals vis-à-vis one another and the responsibilities of social scientists to the wider society. Their formulation and adoption has therefore been opposed in several associations by those scientists who object to professionalism, either in any form at all or in the form proposed by the code (cf. Dorn and Long 1974), as well as by those who do not want to make concessions to the interests of non-scientists (e.g. Sinick 1954; Gergen 1973), or who argue, particularly with anthropology in mind, that the circumstances in which research is carried out are so varied that no code would be flexible enough to cater for them all; or who simply proclaim that 'Decent mature people do not need to be told how to conduct themselves' (Hall 1952:430; cf. Denzin 1970:333). Blok (1973) argues that the existence of a code undermines individual ethical responsibility, though it might equally well be said that it increases individual awareness, even if not all members accept all its provisions. In some associations heterogeneous opposition of this kind has been strong enough to delay or prevent the adoption of a code. But a code is a defensive device, for pressure from sponsors, gatekeepers and citizens can to some extent be met by pointing to a professional code. A code adopted voluntarily lessens the danger that a code less satisfactory to scientists may be imposed on them by legislation. As Burridge (1973:231) says of anthropologists, they 'will not be able to draw up their codes by themselves. The role of the double-agent answerable only to himself, always implicit, has been exposed and made explicit.'

While the codes drawn up by professional associations have tended to consist mainly of statements of ahistorical, context-free, moral principles, sponsors who have made explicit their policies about providing support for research have sometimes mixed general principles of policy with more specifically ethical requirements. Soon after Project Camelot had been cancelled, the

163

Public Health Service of the United States, which provides funds for research in social science as well as in medicine, reviewed the ethical conditions to be met by scientists it sponsored (Brayfield 1967; United States, Office of the Surgeon General 1967; cf. United States, Office of Science and Technology 1967; Frankel 1972). As mentioned in Chapter 4, sponsors concerned with social science research in Latin America have adopted policies to ensure that expatriate social scientists collaborate with local research institutions, that local students are trained and that collaboration between expatriate and local scientists on research projects is encouraged (Portes 1975:132–5). The Russell Sage Foundation has stated ethical guidelines to be followed by those it supports (National Academy 1972:xv).

Some social scientists, while welcoming the increased recognition of citizens' interests achieved by these new procedures and by the establishment of university vetting committees, mentioned above, are nevertheless critical of the model of inquiry on which they are based. The research act is characterized in these arrangements, as it often is in fact in medical and natural science, as a transaction between two strangers, a powerful scientist and a powerless subject, rather than as a negotiated process between more equally matched parties, as in social science. For this reason, some of the requirements to be met by the social scientist planning an inquiry are held to be inappropriate and obstructive. For example, Wax (1977:326) argues that nothing is gained and much lost by insisting that an anthropologist should secure the written and informed consent of the citizens before he begins to study them. To attempt to do so while anthropologist and citizens are still strangers to each other could jeopardize the very possibility of carrying out the inquiry.

Citizens have been much slower than scientists and sponsors in formalizing their perceptions of the proper ethical basis for social inquiry. Most citizens experience social inquiries about themselves only sporadically. Those groups that have been subjected to continual inquiry, such as small but accessible ethnic minority communities, have reacted more often as suspicious or hostile gatekeepers, as described in Chapter 4, rather than as ethically sensitive citizens. Nevertheless one association of Indian chiefs in British Columbia was reported in 1974 to be drawing up a set of 'ethical guidelines', by means of which Indian bands can ensure responsible behaviour by anthropologists, linguists and others who wish to study the bands and their culture (Efrat and Mitchell 1974:406).

Formal codes of professional ethics are intended to specify what rights and obligations the different parties involved in teaching and research in social science have over and to one another. Paying attention to the interests of all the parties involved in an inquiry entails first deciding who these parties are and then specifying their rights and duties. Sometimes this may not be difficult or controversial, but at other times this may entail judgements that are manifestly value-laden. Likewise, in a specific research context, the definition of rights proposed by the scientist may differ widely from the context-free definition provided by a professional code. A striking example of how the values held by the scientist enter into his definition of the legitimate interests of others is given by a set of proposals made by two sociologists, one of them a Jesuit priest, writing in 1953. They emphasize the obligations the sociologist has to his sponsor, the gatekeepers, the citizens, his colleagues and the general public. They limit the rights to privacy, respect and secrecy which most individuals possess, and which the scientist must heed, to membership of the Western moral community, and argue that those individuals who have placed themselves outside this moral community have surrendered the protection of its norms. Such people include, they say, 'men like Hitler and Stalin, organized groups like "Murder Incorporated", the Ku Klux Klan, and some others'. In writing about such people, the scientist need have little inhibition in his report. On the other hand, ' "unpopular" racial, religious and political groups, prostitutes, homosexuals, drug addicts, and the psychologically ill, the poor and powerless' remain members of the moral community and though 'the needs of society may require a limitation of their rights by the courts or by the social scientist in his reporting', this limitation must be as little as possible (Fichter and Kolb 1953:549).

Who should know what?

While some writers have denied that pariah groups in society have rights that the scientist should respect, others have argued that those persons who hold public office should, in their public actions, be denied the protections enjoyed by other citizens (Rainwater and Pittman 1967:365). This argument is based on the distinction between public and private aspects of social life (cf. Shils 1959:130), to which different norms apply. Thus Galliher (1973) argues that 'when actors become involved in government and business or other organizations where they are accountable to the public, no right of privacy applies to conduct in such roles'. Here the scientist is not seeking any special dispensation in the interests of research but merely seeking to take advantage of the obligations placed on all holders of public office towards the public at large. The Scandinavian doctrine that official documents are open for all to see unless there is some specific reason for withholding them reflects this view, as does the United States Freedom of Information Act. Clearly it is much easier for a scientist to conduct inquiries in the public domain under these conditions than in a country like Britain where 'open government' still seems as far away as ever. The extent to which governmental processes are public varies as much as do other cultural distinctions between what is private and what is public.

Readers of the Kinsey report may remember the description of the elaborate precautions the research team took to ensure the confidentiality of their data: interview notes taken only in code, files housed in locked cabinets and so on (Kinsey et al. 1948:44–7). In recent years citizens have expressed fears not that personal reports would be accidentally left lying in unlocked drawers but that information about themselves would be supplied to a computer and kept in store indefinitely, potentially available to any curious scientist or bureaucrat. Rule (1973:37) shows how far we still are from living in what he calls a 'total surveillance society'; many of his readers would surely say that he shows that we in Britain are far too near. But his description of large-scale data collection in Britain and America by governmental and corporate bodies makes it clear that the threat of total surveillance comes mainly from governmental agencies and large commercial organizations rather than from the activities of

166

social scientists. Sociologists and others are rightly concerned with the conflicting requirements of confidentiality, privacy and availability that impinge on social science data banks. Yet these data banks constitute only a very small part of the centralized and partially computerized hoard of social data, and the scientist's ability to indulge in data-dredging is usually quite small compared to the bureaucrat's. In any case, as McNamee (1976) says with reference to threats to privacy, 'Let's not get sidetracked away from the real danger by blaming computers. It's people who need watching.'

In discussing data banks, we may follow Dunn (1967) in distinguishing between statistical information systems and intelligence systems. Dunn argues that, in the United States, intelligence systems, providing data about individuals, are already well developed. Statistical information systems, on the other hand, make use of information about the 'public face' of the individual (age, sex, race, occupation and the like), rather than his 'private face' (medical records, criminal records, psychological test results and similar information), and are built up by aggregating data relating to many individuals, rather than by juxtaposing many kinds of data about specified individuals. Systematic record-keeping is ubiquitous in industrialized societies (cf. National Academy 1972), but Dunn argues that it will be two or three decades before the United States can establish a comprehensive statistical information system, and that it will be wholly beneficial, particularly given the obsession with the protection of personal privacy which has characterized federal statisticians. In these terms, the interests of social scientists are in developing statistical information systems rather than intelligence systems. Malinowksi (1938:83), writing enthusiastically about the inauguration of Mass-Observation in Britain, said that 'A nationwide intelligence service, if it be really intelligent and made to cover community and subject matter alike, would become a real service to the nation.' Speaking in today's terms, I think he had some kind of quantitative and qualitative information system in mind rather than an intelligence system. Social scientists are however interested in the private as well as the public face of the individual, as Dunn puts it, even when they are making universalistic rather than context-centred kinds of inquiry (Kruglanski 1975:105). The ethical hazards of social science data banks are generated by the aggregations, and potential disaggregation, of private data as well as by the juxtaposition of private and public data about individual citizens.

Just as some economists see a danger in the infinitely fast circulation of money that might come from a fully computerized credit-card economy, so some politicians and political scientists see a universal interactive computerized system of instant mass opinion polls as inherently destructive of rational government (Kelman 1968:23; Eulau 1970; Tuchman and Coffin 1971; Gotlieb and Borodin 1973:220–21). Most of the objections to massive data banks are however aimed not at the macroscopic effects that they might engender but at their implications for individual citizens. The presumed ability of computerized information retrieval systems to provide their masters instantly with comprehensive dossiers on any citizen, and to alert them automatically to any new act of deviance or defiance, this is what most citizens tend to fear, not that society will choke on a surfeit of information. In the United States these fears led to the cancellation of ambitious plans for an omniscient National Data Center (Martin and Norman 1973:321–43).

The adoption of professional codes of ethics and the utilization of sophisticated electronic equipment for data handling are two aspects of the professionalization of social science that have manifested themselves in the last twenty-five years or so. Computerized data banks increase the potential power of scientific discovery but also increase the potential dangers in data collection and storage, forcing the scientist to be more careful with his information than he might have been earlier. Codes purport to offer him guidelines as to what he should do about his responsibilities to others, but their advice is unspecific and they do little to affect the balance of power between him and the other parties to the process of inquiry. In the last chapter we shall look at attempts to link research with social action and to alter the distribution of power in other ways.

9 Commitment, privacy and the pluralist society

In an essay protesting against the support, active or passive, given by many anthropologists to the United States' effort in Vietnam, Gough (1968:148) claims that one of the weaknesses of anthropology is that 'in the accumulation of factual detail and of limited hypotheses we have gradually lost sight of the initial question of the Enlightenment: How can the science of man help men to live more fully and creatively and expand their dignity, self-direction, and freedom?' During the last two decades the hopes of the Enlightenment have increasingly been called into question. Inequalities between nations and individuals in their attainment of dignity, self-direction and freedom have become more noticeable, less acceptable and more intractable. At the same time, scientists have come to appreciate more fully how great are the difficulties in developing a science of man capable of realizing these hopes.

In trying to come closer to the goal of a better world, scientists and citizens have pushed and pulled in many different directions. Scientists have been urged to commit themselves to political and social action, to query their support for the existing order and also to take fuller account of the diverse set of interests that constitute that order. The state has intervened to direct the activities of scientists, and to protect citizens from scientists as well as from the activities of the state. Scientists have become more aware of the social conditions necessary for the pursuit of science, and of the constraints within which alone there is the possibility of their efforts contributing to human welfare.

Although most of the discussion about what connexion there should be between research and action has taken place between scientists, gatekeepers and sponsors, some citizens have articu-

169

lated their views on the matter. Citizens who have become habituated to social inquiry divorced from action now seek some direct benefit from their participation. Thus, with reference to North American Indians, Deloria (1969:94) says, 'We should not be objects of observation for those who do nothing to help us.' If anthropologists contributed to the tribal budget an amount matching the cost of the inquiry, they 'would thus become productive members of Indian society instead of ideological vultures'. Communities in newly independent countries may view freedom from being studied by expatriate scientists as an important concomitant of independence (Talyaga 1974; Brennan 1975).

A few scientists advocate an ostrich-like policy of refraining from social inquiry completely, since the only use to which it will be put is to increase oppression. More take the opposite stance and advocate action as a regular consequence of research. They argue that the scientist should recognize the inequalities that abound in the world and, instead of treating these as phenomena of merely scientific interest, should take constructive action to end them (cf. Forster 1973; Robinson, S. S 1973). Becker (1967:239, 245) adopts a standpoint near to this in arguing that, whether or not the scientist is politically committed, his research findings will be used politically by others. '. . . we cannot avoid taking sides, for reasons firmly based in social structure . . . Almost all the topics that sociologists study, at least those that have some relation to the real world around us, are seen by society as morality plays and we shall find ourselves, willy-nilly, taking part in those plays on one side or the other.'

The decision to become committed and help the oppressed may be justified on moral grounds, by appealing to the views of the scientist as citizen, but some writers have argued that the choice is justified on scientific grounds also. Only by viewing society and the social environment from the point of view of the underdog can the scientist gain a true understanding, for whereas the ruling class have an interest in hiding the truth, the oppressed have an interest in knowing and broadcasting it. This argument is, of course, similar to that put forward by some Marxists about the contrast between false consciousness and the true consciousness of the politically awakened working class. Whatever utility the notion of true consciousness may have as a philosophical and ideological concept, it seems to me unsound to equate the view from below with truth and the view from above with falsity. Though we may accept an exploitative model of society, we can still recognize that a sophisticated ruling class may have an interest in the discovery of the truth, and may be comparatively well equipped to attain it, even if it also has an interest in keeping this knowledge to itself. We may view the conflict-ridden social field as like a conventional battlefield, in which the most 'objective' assessment of the deployment of forces on one side is likely to be found in the intelligence headquarters of the other. An exploited group, however vividly it may be conscious of the immediate context of exploitation, may be unable to see beyond that context to reach an understanding of how exploitation is perpetuated and how it may be overcome.

The supporters of a link between research and action see no necessary incompatibility between the quest for scientific reliability and validity and active support for one side in the struggle. In any case, active support is more honest than apparent neutrality which may amount to silent support for the existing unfair order. Huizer (1975:68), in pointing out that participant observation leads naturally to participant intervention, argues that the scientist can still be true to his calling despite taking sides. As he puts it, 'Objectivity, as claimed by pure researchers, is not so much a question of detachment from what one studies, but rather the distance or detachment which the researcher can take from himself and his personal and cultural biases while he is in the field or writing his opus.' Commitment to action research, to the achievement of some practical objective as well as some understanding of the social process by which it was achieved, may open the door to fresh sources of information and at the same time provide a powerful incentive for making sure that the information is reliable.

A social scientist is a citizen with special skills. His citizenship gives him the right to participate in public affairs, and his special-

171

ization can provide him with the ability to intervene particularly effectively in various areas of public life; it can impose on him an obligation to intervene, if only to make his specialized knowledge more widely available (Peattie 1958:7). Some commentators argue that social scientists may sometimes have a duty to use their special skills even in contexts they find distasteful. For example, Goodenough (1976:21) notes that when some of his fellow anthropologists were asked to help in devising plans for who should survive and who should be sacrificed in face of insoluble food shortages in Bangladesh, they felt that on moral grounds they must refuse. Goodenough criticizes them, arguing that 'when an anthropologist refuses on ethical grounds to advise on how to set up procedures, he is opting for the greater human misery and social dislocation that result from their absence'. Yet despite this urging from active colleagues, many social scientists try to avoid becoming politically and ethically involved in their professional work, either by shunning the study of topics that are relevant to current social conflicts, or by studying some small chunk of social life from such a narrowly-circumscribed view that the implications of their findings for the wider conflict can be left unexplored. But in a situation of political conflict, a tactic designed to avoid participation is itself a political stance, though not necessarily a stance to be avoided. As Thomas Weaver (1973a:3) says, 'Failure to take a position – or the assumption of a neutral position by failing to face ethical problems – is a political action'.

These prescriptions for a politically active social science, with scientists campaigning in most cases on the side of the citizens, contrasts strongly with the earlier model of a value-free and politically neutral science and with the orthodox model of a science applied to the citizens on behalf of a benign sponsor. The new model has not displaced its predecessors and is unlikely ever to do so completely (cf. Hymes 1972; Appell 1973:14–18). For example, Berger (1976:258) derides the activities of scientists who support 'advocacy research' with the comment 'Occam's Razor gives way to Marcuse's Shovel'. The balance of power favours the earlier models, and they do not work all the time against the interests of relatively powerless citizens. The paternalistic attitude current in many colonial administrations, and adopted widely by anthropologists working in the field during the colonial period, often served the short-term interests of tribal peoples subject to pressures from traders, recruiters, expatriate settlers and others. Some anthropologists continue to hold this attitude in the post-colonial era. For example, in a book published for the first time as late as 1969, Foster (1969:53, 173) comments that 'the sense of responsibility that has characterized anthropological research from its earliest days [has] worked amazingly well', and says that the best way for an anthropologist to protect the interests of tribal citizens is 'to have a close working relationship with the members of the bureaucracy itself. In this way . . . he can maintain a degree of informal control which in most instances is sufficient to ensure that anthropology's ethical standards are maintained.' This recommendation presupposes that the administrative bureaucracy is essentially benign, that the citizens are powerless, and that the scientist is a member of the elite whose informal intervention in the bureaucratic process can be effective. Probably these conditions still sometimes apply; but only a foolish and naïve scientist would take them for granted.

Scientists may find it easier to detect paternalism in the attitudes of sponsors and gatekeepers, and to protest against it, than recognize it in themselves. Yet an assumption that the expert knows best is inherent in the concept of professionalism, and the methodology of social inquiry no longer allows a scientist easily to protect himself against the charge of elitism or paternalism by claiming that his professional expertise is confined to some clearly demarcated technical field. By stressing the scientist's obligation to take full account of the interests of the citizens, the codes of professional ethics encourage him not to confine his attention merely to what, if anything, the citizens say they want. The codes tend to stress the responsibilities laid on the scientist because of his ability, as a professional, to see more clearly than the citizens what the likely consequences of alternative courses of action are likely to be. If the citizens cannot see so clearly or so far, then the scientist may be enjoined by the code

173

to act in what he sees to be their best interest; we are then back in the position of the scientist knowing best what is good for the citizens. Hence Cochrane (1971:33–4) complains that 'Provided that I do no harm and believe that my actions will do some good, then so far as the Society of Applied Anthropology is concerned I may meet my colleagues with an easy conscience.' Thus even when working within what we may call a human model of social inquiry, the scientist is still faced with serious ethical issues. Enlightened by social science, the scientist acquires responsibilities but in discharging them he may conflict with the interests of citizens, as they see them. To do nothing about the use of his knowledge is to support silently a social order his knowledge should transform.

Most social research is normal or paradigm-based science, as Kuhn (1970:25) calls it, the standardized application of conventionally accepted techniques of inquiry. The absence of a single dominant theoretical paradigm does not hinder social science from being, much of the time, as conventional as the most orthodox version of natural science. This is probably inevitable, as is the tacit support for the status quo that this body of applied knowledge provides. But some social scientists are likely always to challenge the appropriateness of this support, and are particularly likely to protest when social science is called in to help in maintaining the status quo for others, as in Project Camelot and counter-insurgency research in Indochina. Where social research is linked to proposals for social action by the citizens themselves, the scientist is more likely to be called in to facilitate change than to shore up the existing order or to restore an order that has already been superseded. Because the structure of sponsorship and the sentiments of the majority of social scientists produce an enduring bias in favour of research directed towards maintaining or merely ameliorating the existing order, some advocate the adoption of an heuristic bias in favour of research into the possibilities of change (cf. Nikelly 1971). As Kelman (1968:33) puts it, 'social science must counteract its potential role in the dehumanization of society by taking an active role in the *humanization* of society' (his emphasis) (cf. Stavenhagen 1971:337).

174

In advocating change, values have to be made explicit, whereas values can more easily be taken for granted, or never made explicit, when studying the reproduction of the present state of affairs. The explication of values is essential when advocating changes for other people, changes which they themselves will have to implement. Most action-linked research carried out by social scientists has been of this kind, with scientists appearing on the scene from elsewhere rather than materializing from within the community. A well-known example of action research is the work carried out over many years on a hacienda at Vicos, in Peru, by social scientists from Cornell University using a technique labelled 'participant intervention'. Holmberg (1955:25) says that the scientists' aim was to transform the hacienda into a 'just, peaceable, morally and intellectually progressive community of responsible men and women. While, of course, no such value system can ever be justified scientifically, we – and many Vicosinos – believe these to be good and desirable.' Holmberg's statement is interesting, not only for the separation he makes between values and science, but also for the tacit admission that some Vicosinos do not see even the very vaguely specified aims of the scientists as good or desirable. We are here up against the classic dilemma of moral relativism, as applied to social action. We may wish to respect values held by other people which we do not accept ourselves; we refrain from forcing our scheme of values and our way of life on to them. We perceive them, compared to ourselves, as poor, exploited and powerless, and wish to help them. But action requires a much closer specification of desirable ends than does merely 'respect for the values of others' as a moral attitude. As Hamilton (1974:338) asks, 'To what extent is it ethical to protect the interests of poor informants but condemn the interests of rich ones?' At the least, action entails withstanding the opposition of those who do not want to become members of a 'just, peaceable, morally and intellectual progressive community', or of providing alternative opportunities for them. But suppose members of the poor, exploited and powerless community seek change, but resist the notion that women as well as men should become responsible

175

citizens in the new regime? Does our respect for indgenous values make us confine our efforts to the removal of external exploitation while leaving internal exploitation unchallenged? And what if our wish to help them leads us to suggest that their whole way of life should be radically changed, and that they should lose their collective identity altogether? Turnbull (1972) made this suggestion for the Ik of Uganda, who, in his view, had lost the ability to live as a society; 'They had lost family, friendship, hope, love.' He was criticized by several of his colleagues on various grounds, notably that he was behaving unethically in recommending the total destruction of a culture, and defended himself by arguing that there was no culture left to destroy (Barth 1974; Wilson, P. J., et al. 1975). Turnbull's suggestion is draconic, and the conditions of life among the Ik may have been extreme, but the controversy engendered by his book points to the dilemma that arises whenever a scientist makes a recommendation for action affecting powerless citizens for their own good, as he sees it, without negotiating with them. In facing up to these dilemmas the scientist may be helped by a code of professional ethics to arrive at a standpoint which he can justify to his colleagues and to the world at large. But the code can do no more than enable him the better to defend his position; the position he has to find for himself.

The scientist thus faces a continuing dilemma. He may object to acting merely as the amoral agent of a powerful sponsor, and insist on negotiating with the citizens, to discover what they really want. But the citizens are part of the existing order and, whether they are powerful or not, the scientist as a morally committed citizen may or may not be in sympathy with their views. He still has to decide whether his decision to negotiate with them is likely to lead to an outcome which, on balance, he as well as they would prefer. The same consideration applies to negotiations with gatekeepers and sponsors and with the public at large. Thus for example Fichter and Kolb (1953: 549–50) state that 'it is objectively true that there are moral evils and modes of action which place the perpetrator outside this (moral) community . . . and the scientist need have little inhibition in the report he provides about them ... If the duly appointed authorities of a community or of the larger society believe certain information to be vitally needed, there is a *prima facie* case for the scientist to reveal such information.' This advice has been interpreted as blatant support for the status quo (Friedrichs 1970: 193–4), though in fact the authors go on to stress that the scientist has to make up his own mind whether or not he should tell the authorities what he knows, and that he must be ready to face the consequences if he decides not to cooperate with them (cf. Rein 1976:90–91). But how should we interpret the decision by the Public Opinion Laboratory of the University of Washington in deciding to reject 'a contractual agreement for a political poll if its phraseology is unacceptable to one of the major parties' (Friedrichs 1970:117)? Is the Laboratory being scrupulous in paying attention to the interests of the groups directly involved, the Democratic and Republican parties, or is it blatantly supporting the status quo in allowing these two parties to determine the framework in which political debate shall be conducted?

Much the same dilemma arises when the process of inquiry itself may seem likely to consolidate some incipient and still contested change in the social world. A clear example is provided by the debate about what questions, if any, should be asked about race and ethnicity in the British 1981 census. Here the interests of social scientists and some sections of government are opposed to those of others, with the general public also divided. Asking questions about race gives racial categorization a salience that many social scientists, as citizens, wish to prevent, yet without information on race or ethnicity we have no reliable indicators of the extent to which this categorization is still significant in terms of housing, employment, education, inter-marriage and so on. Should we be optimistic ostriches and hope that when we lift our heads from the sand racial discrimination will have miraculously disappeared? Or should we ask citizens to align themselves racially, if only on a census form, so that we can take private and public policy decisions, at all levels, in the light of knowledge rather than of ignorance and guesses?

The race issue also illustrates the conflict between positivist

177

and subjectivist views, since, unlike most of the categories used in the census, race and ethnic classifications are categories about which there is consensus among neither scientists nor the general public. To ask an entirely open-ended question 'What race do you belong to?' would be sociologically interesting but likely to be administratively useless; coding for statistical tabulation would be difficult and unreliable, and many citizens would surely answer 'human'. Yet to provide a forced-choice question with alternatives that correspond to administrative categories is to invite refusals and aggressive replies. The compromise currently proposed (Mack 1978) is based at least in part on attempts to discover how citizens think of themselves but is of reduced administrative and scientific value, and its inclusion seems likely to jeopardize public acceptance of the use of compulsion in the census. Horace Mann's remark about the census becoming too inquisitorial, mentioned in Chapter 6, could be applied as easily to race as to religion. Yet separating inquiries into race and ethnicity from the census would reduce the value both of the census and of any separate voluntary inquiry. In this instance the desire to find out has to be tempered not so much by the likely consequences of what is finally discovered but by the effects engendered in the course of trying to find out.

In trying to give full attention to the rights and interests of all parties to the process of inquiry, there is a danger that empirical research becomes restricted to innocuous topics that challenge nobody, or that whatever research is done serves to reinforce the position of those already in power, whether they be sponsors or citizens, and hence to be relatively disadvantageous to powerless groups. On the other hand the law may provide even the weakest citizens with some protection against the power of the state, and against the predatory curiosity of the scientist, so that to some extent the ethical responsibility of the scientist is embodied in legislation. Hence political constraints on research become intertwined with ethical constraints, and there is no hard and fast dividing line between the rights of the individual citizen and the rights of the regime. Yet if social research is to be based on the Andersonian doctrine that 'no subject of investigation is held to be sacrosanct', then some distinction must be made. As Kelman (1972:1013) puts it,

The challenge is to develop criteria and procedures that will make it possible to delegitimate research activities that are based on the systematic violation of the rights of subjects, without legitimizing the imposition of political controls on research.

I agree with him when he goes on to advocate the diversification of sponsors and the protection of their autonomy, the diversification of those who carry out research and the democratization of the 'research community', a broader participation in the research process, and an extension of the range of those who can utilize the findings, particularly so as to include the citizens themselves.

The citizens directly concerned with an inquiry have rights to privacy, while mankind at large has certainly an interest, if not a right, in knowledge. But what about groups in between? This question may not necessarily be important in nomothetic or universalistic research, but has to be faced whenever ideographic or context-specific inquiries are published, however disguised they may be. Reports that provide evidence that crime rates are rising or falling, or that truancy is higher or lower in single-sex schools, or that any other indicator of what has already been defined as a social issue is going up or down – these are certain to be used as ammunition by one side or the other, or by both, in ongoing public debates. Hence the scientist should be aware of the political context in which his report will be published and, as far as he can, present it in a form that is proof against instant distortion as well as designed to stand the test of time. He ought also to say where he stands in the debate, so that the reader can take this into account in assessing what he has to say.

The conscientious and ethically-aware scientist should not become so fully occupied in paying attention to the interests of others that he loses sight of his own. He has his career and reputation to think of, as well as his obligations to his colleagues and students, and he has to eat, but it is in relation to his commitment to the pursuit of knowledge that ethical issues mainly impinge. It is in this connexion that he has to balance most carefully his interests against those of the other parties involved. Provided he can protect the legitimate interests of the citizens who have confided in him, he has, in my view, an obligation to publish his findings, however unwelcome these may be. Governments, local authorities, commercial enterprises and voluntary associations vary enormously in the extent to which they want to, or are able to, prevent publication of findings that either reflect unfavourably on the public image they hope to maintain, or may, they fear, put them at a disadvantage relative to their rivals. Even members of unorganized aggregations like ethnic groups may feel threatened by the publication of reports showing that there are poor as well as rich among their ranks (cf. Patterson 1971). The sanctions available to ethnic groups may be limited but they certainly extend to non-cooperation with any future aspiring investigator. Organized bodies such as governments are much more powerfully placed to prevent publication, and there is a ubiquitous and structurally determined tendency for bureaucrats to hoard information rather than disseminate it. The scientist may have surrendered part of his freedom to publish in his negotiations with his sponsors and gatekeepers. Nevertheless, within these powerful constraints, he has in my view a clear commitment to make as much knowledge as widely available as he can (cf. Donnison et al. n.d.: 31–3). Science is a sham if its results are not open to challenge.

Scientists have the rights and responsibilities of citizenship in their own country, but when they carry out inquiries abroad they are guests. Their basis for intervention on their own account is weaker, and they have to recognize that the interests of their local professional colleagues may differ widely from their own. The comparatively weak autonomy of universities in Third World countries puts the local scientist in a position of occupational dependency on his own government to a much greater extent that is found in most Western countries. The salience of social change in the Third World, whether as slogan or fact, is conducive of attitudes of strong commitment for or against official policies, rather than the neutrality found widely among social scientists in industrialized countries. Whatever the extent and direction of his political commitment in his own country, the scientist working abroad may well hesitate to take an enthusiastic stand one way or the other in the local political arena, and hence may have difficulty in collaborating with deeply involved local social scientists (cf. Hymes 1972:52). Yet expatriate scientists who do attempt to intervene in local affairs can expect particularly hostile criticism from local colleagues whose views differ from their own (e.g. Saberwal 1968:13). In addition a scientist working in a foreign country who tries to link his research to social action is likely to run the risk only of being expelled if those in power dislike what he is doing, while he puts his local colleagues and the citizens themselves into much more serious danger (cf. Kielstra 1975).

Scientists in Third World countries are themselves members of the world of learning, and may welcome international recognition just as much as their colleagues in the industrial nations. Scientists in poor countries are even more dependent on institutional sponsorship than are those in rich countries. But a sponsor in country A who offers support to a scientist in country B will find his offer assessed not only in terms of the values and ambitions of the scientist but also with reference to the political relation between the two countries. A scientist X in A who wishes to collaborate with a local colleague Y in B in carrying out some inquiry may find that the sponsor with whom X has successfully negotiated for support is unacceptable to Y or to the government of B. This situation arose particularly in the sixties, when the CIA was indirectly providing significant support for research carried out abroad by American social scientists. Difficulties of this kind over sponsorship are likely to continue even if the CIA no longer supports research, and serve to illustrate how the range of interests that impinge on the process of research is even wider when members of more than one nation are involved.

If knowledge can be pursued only by reconciling a diversity of interests, how much leeway is there? How much does research in social science threaten to destroy privacy and how much does the protection of privacy threaten to block research? It would be

181

difficult to answer these questions quantitatively, but some kind of ordinal comparison is possible. The main danger to privacy does not lie in the activities of social scientists. Madgwick and Smythe (1974), in their account of *The invasion of privacy*, set out at length the ways in which the right to privacy of the typical citizen in Britain is being undermined by the police, the press, private detectives, credit agencies and the various dossier-collecting branches of government. They suggest legislation to reverse this trend. They scarcely mention the activities of scientists, either as a present danger or as a potential hazard to be legislated against. The only mention of market research in their book is in a comment by the head of a private detective agency, who says that one of his agents might use a genuine market researcher as a cover for his investigations (cf. Hewitt 1977). Likewise, Gotlieb and Borodin (1973:69) list nineteen different kinds of agencies currently engaged in collecting data about individuals in the United States, but do not bother to include social scientists in their list. Crispo (1975) is worried about the balance of power between citizens and those official and unofficial agencies who collect information about him, but makes no mention of the activities of social scientists. Miller (1971) is his *The assault on privacy* mentions intelligence and other psychological tests, but no other aspect of social science. Yet the fact that greater threats to freedom come from other quarters should not divert us from ensuring that social science does not add to the danger, and should encourage us to make use of social science to reduce it. Indeed, only by realizing how social research can be carried on with a maximum regard to the divergent interests of the parties involved can we hope to use its capabilities in working towards a freer society.

When legislation has been introduced to protect the privacy of citizens, it has been aimed at potential threats from official agencies and private corporations rather than from social scientists. In the United States local legislation restricting the conduct of house-to-house surveys began to worry polling organizations in the 1960s (Arnold 1964:120); some psychological testing by employers has been discontinued in conformity with legislation about fair employment practices (Miner 1974:49), while that country's Privacy Act of 1974 gives limited recognition to the citizen's right to be protected against the power of officials with access to data banks. Under this Act there are constraints on the kinds of information that agencies of the federal government may collect about individual citizens, and on the extent to which data of this kind may be transferred from one agency to another or otherwise disclosed. The agency collecting the information must inform the citizen under what authority it acts and for what purpose the information will be used. Discussions began in 1976 about extending the scope of the Act, with the possibility that some of its provisions might apply to data sets with personal identifiers collected by private bodies, either for commercial purposes or for scientific research. A study commission has advocated the prompt removal and destruction of personal identifiers as crucial for strengthening public trust in the confidentiality of data collected for research or statistical purposes (American Sociological Association 1977).

Scientists as well as citizens have sought to gain support for their interests from legislation. Suggestions have been made that research data should be treated in law as privileged information and not liable to be subpoenaed, and strong arguments have been made for exempting research data that are stored, with proper safeguards, in computerized form from the provisions for open access that have been advocated for commercial and official personal data banks (Gorsuch 1972; National Academy 1972:369; Boness and Cordes 1973). Although some jurisdictions provide journalists and others with limited privilege (King, F. W. 1970:984; Nejelski and Lerman 1971; American Anthropological Association 1976c), the tide of opinion seems to be running, at least in the United States, in favour of less secrecy and it seems unlikely that these suggestions will be adopted easily.

In Scandinavia, the process of legislative control of data collection has gone further, for in Sweden social survey data drawn from individuals may be collected for research and other purposes only under the supervision of a government agency (Datatilsynet) and after payment of a fee (Laver 1976:181). Legislation in this field has been proposed for Norway (Øyen 1976) and has been adopted in West Germany. Under the Swedish system, the government, in effect, becomes a gatekeeper in every social inquiry, and collects a fee which may be an appropriate charge for a commercial undertaking but which adds significantly to the cost of research. It also imposes a measure of censorship on the range of questions that may be asked of citizens. Thus the citizen may gain some protection but loses some of his right to negotiate. The American act, as originally implemented, was aimed at protecting the citizen against the executive arm of the federal government, while the Swedish legislation seems to appoint the government as the protector of the citizen against the credit-rating agency, the debt-collection corporation and, incidentally, the social scientist. The proposals for legislation made by a study group of the British Association for the Advancement of Science (1974) deal only with the research activities of natural, medical and social scientists. This group proposed that research data banks should be licensed by a statutory Data Bank Tribunal, and that data in the banks should be exempt from subpoenas and other judicial and administrative demands for identified personal information. It recommended that, particularly when the information is highly sensitive, the file linking the anonymous data with their personal identifiers should be kept outside the United Kingdom, in some country where it would not be subject to a subpoena from British courts. Another working party, set up by Social and Community Planning Research, recommended that there should be a Standing Commission, along the lines indicated by the Younger Committee on Privacy, but thought that legislation was neither necessary nor practicable (Donnison et al. n.d.: 46–56; Younger 1972:191).

The Organisation for Economic Co-operation and Development (OECD) began to consider data protection legislation internationally in 1974 and by now several countries are considering, or have brought into force, legislation to control the collection, storage and transmission of data concerning individual persons, whether computerized or not (Sieghart 1976:159–226). 'Data avoidance traffic', as it is called, has begun, the movement of personal data from one country to another to take advantage ot national differences in legal requirements (Pipe 1977). In the United Kingdom, following the publication of White Papers on computers and privacy (Home Office 1975a & b), the government established in 1976 a Data Protection Committee, with the task of advising on how a statutory Data Protection Authority might operate. At the time of writing (March 1978) its report was still awaited. Meanwhile, under the Consumer Credit Act 1974, the United Kingdom citizen has acquired since May 1977 the right to obtain, by paying a fee of 25p, a copy of the file held on him or her by any credit reference agency, and to protest if the information in it is false.

The United States legislation on privacy and data protection must be seen in conjunction with the federal Freedom of Information Act 1966 and other laws (Shils 1975; Ruebhausen and Brim 1965:1206–7). So long as promises of more open government, and of reforms in the Official Secrets Act, remain unfulfilled in Britain, the desirable scope of any legislation necessarily remains unclear (cf. Wraith 1977). The protection of privacy and the recognition of the citizen's right to know what others, including the government, have on record about him must go hand in hand (cf. Jones 1974:23). Indeed, both aspects of the maintenance of that permeable boundary between public and private are referred to in a Freedom of Information and Privacy Bill, introduced into Parliament by Tom Litterick in February 1977. Legislation, whatever form it takes, can not only provide desirable ways of altering the balance of power in the process of inquiry but can also impose constraints that are in nobody's interest. Experience in Scandinavia and America suggests that, so far as social research is concerned, the greater the awareness by social scientists of the issues involved in negotiated inquiries, the less the need for the formal constraints of legislation (Kelman 1968:206). Should legislation be necessary, if only because of the difficulty of separating the activities of scientists from those of official agencies and commercial enterprises, then again the more scientists are awake to the wider social and political implications of the research process, the better the chance that the legislation will be satisfactory.

Social science was born of the Enlightenment, we may say, and

Who should know what?

systematic social inquiry was a product of industrialization and imperialism in the nineteenth century. There is no reason for thinking that, once established, social research will continue to flourish whatever changes may come about in the structure of society. Evidence from the Soviet Union and China demonstrates how sensitive social science, both as theory and praxis, is to major changes in social structure (cf. Lane 1970; Shaw 1977; Wong 1975). It is possible to envisage a monolithic society in which social science might occupy a modest place in the apparatus of repression, in which negotiation between the scientist-bureaucrat and the citizen-subject would be merely an unnecessary sham. But since social inquiry as we know it today is based on the premiss that citizens are free to answer as they please, this repressive social science would be of quite a different kind. I cannot see how it could possibly contain anthropology, if, following Lévi-Strauss (1966:126), we characterize that discipline as the science of culture as seen from the outside. For, with the demise of classic colonialism, intercourse between societies, as between the segments of a pluralist society, can be only by negotiation. Willy-nilly the anthropologist has to adopt a stance of 'deep respect and concern for the people studied, responsiveness to their values, claims, and perspectives, trust in them, and commitment to the truth as it is determined'. Therefore, Berreman (1973c:178) concludes, 'The moral imperatives now coincide with anthropology's self-interest. Only recognition of this fact can prevent anthropology from becoming a discipline without a subject.' Palacio (1976:488) puts the matter more bluntly:

If anthropology . . . is to become acceptable to the peoples of the Third World, it has to participate in their liberation.

If anthropology is typically a discipline carried on where many of the values held by scientist and citizens are not shared, the other social sciences more often operate in contexts where the process of inquiry has been accepted as part of the ambient pluralist culture. This process brings together parties with divergent interests and with differences in power. In prescribing how the process should be carried on, methodologists seek to

overcome these divergences and differences, because they hold
either that the differences are morally wrong, or that the divergences constrict the possibilities of research, or that the
differences invalidate the results. Thus Kelman (1972:994–5)
seems to argue from the first and third of these positions in
saying that investigators are in a powerful position in relation
to their subjects, and must use their power legitimately. For
legitimacy, there must be norms shared by the profession and by
citizens; the norms must include rules that define the limits of
the investigator's power; and there must be a procedure for
complaining against abuses of power. These, he says, are not only
the characteristics that a system of inquiry ought to have, but
are also the characteristics it needs if it is to be perceived by
its members as functioning legitimately. These conditions can be
met only in a society in which the notion of a diversity of partly
conflicting and partly reinforcing interests is itself legitimated.

The idea of negotiation makes sense only when the parties
involved have different interests; it makes better sense when
they have some limited power over one another and when they are
not playing a zero-sum game, so that all can gain from a successful outcome to the bargaining. These conditions are met in what I
have called pluralist societies. Shils (1956:235) identifies pluralist
societies as those characterized by privacy and publicity, and
as we have seen many ethical issues turn on the conflict between
the need to know and the right to remain unknown. But the
adjective pluralist also implies a multiplicity of sources of power
and influence as well as a diversity of interests and a recognition
of the legitimacy of this diversity. Within a framework of this
kind negotiation is both necessary and possible. Privacy is
protected, but it may also be invaded peacefully, by agreement.
There are many kinds of sponsor, including the citizens themselves, and governmental sponsors do not all speak with the
same voice. Citizens are not forced to answer questions, and
because they answer freely, their answers are worth listening
to. Sponsors can seek out sympathetic scientists, while scientists
can select sponsors whose interests are compatible with their
own.

And gatekeepers? Maybe there would not be any in an ideal world. For the model I have sketched is clearly an ideal, but not necessarily how things ought to be and certainly not how things are. Here and now there is no cafeteria of sponsors, in which the scientist can take his pick, but only a restricted and impoverished set of governmental agencies, with private philanthropy dwindling. Many citizens exercise their rights by choosing to remain silent and, discouraged with the practical and philosophical difficulties of discovering what goes on in the real world, scientists divert their energies to the exegesis industry and other self-contemplating pursuits. The Enlightenment has ended and an age of despair has been announced (Hawthorn 1976). Fortunately despair arrives on the stage in a version that calls for more rather than less intellectual effort in applying our brains to understanding the human condition. As part of our survival kit in what is still a partly pluralist world we need not only empirical social science but also an awareness of the ethical issues that form an intrinsic part of its praxis.

References

Page numbers in square brackets at the end of each entry refer to this book.

ABBI, Behari Lal, and SABERWAL, Satish
1969   *Editors.* Urgent research in social anthropology: proceedings of a conference. Simla; Indian Institute of Advanced Study. x, 235 pp. *Transactions 10.* [*pp. 69*]

ABRAMS, Philip
1968   The origins of British sociology: 1834–1914. An essay with selected papers. Chicago; University of Chicago Press. x, 304 pp. [*p. 28*]

ACKROYD, Carol, and others
1977   The technology of political control. Harmondsworth; Penguin Books. 320 pp. [*p. 23*]

AHMED, Abdel Ghaffar M.
1973   Some remarks from the Third World on anthropology and colonialism. *In* Asad 1973: 259–70. [*p. 43*]

ALLEN, Michael Richard
1967   Male cults and secret initiations in Melanesia. Melbourne; Melbourne University Press. ix, 140 pp. [*p. 91*]

AMERICAN ANTHROPOLOGICAL ASSOCIATION
1968   Government releases guidelines for foreign area research. *Fellow newsletter* 9(5): 4–7. [*p. 120*]

1970   AAA: principles of professional responsibility. *Newsletter* 11(9). [*p. 156*]

1976a   Court rules anthropologist defamed by media reports of involvement in Thai research center. *Anthropology newsletter* 17(2): 3. [*p. 66*]

1976b   Candidates for Committee on ethics – 2 positions. *Anthropology newsletter* 17(5): 22–4. [*p. 161*]

1976c   Federal court rules on confidential status of academic research. *Anthropology newsletter* 17(8): 16. [*p. 183*]

AMERICAN PSYCHOLOGICAL ASSOCIATION
1952   Discussion on ethics. *American psychologist* 7: 425–55 [*p. 160*]

AMERICAN SOCIOLOGICAL ASSOCIATION
1977   Commission urges removal of identifiers. *ASA footnotes* 5(9): 1, 3. [*p. 183*]

AMERICAN SOCIOLOGICAL ASSOCIATION. Committee on professional ethics
1971   Statement. *American sociologist* 6: 57. [*p. 162*]

AMERICAN STATISTICAL ASSOCIATION
1974   Report of the ASA conference on surveys of human populations. *American statistician* 28: 30–34. [*pp. 55–6*]

AMRINE, Michael, and SANFORD, Fillmore Hargrave
1956   In the matter of juries, democracy, science, truth, senators, and bugs. *American psychologist* 11: 54–60. [*p. 127*]

APPELL, George Nathan
1971   Three cases dealing with dilemmas and ethical conflicts in anthropological inquiry. *Human organization* 30: 97–8. [*p. 161*]
1973   Basic issues in the dilemmas and ethical conflicts in anthropological inquiry. New York; MSS modular publications. 28 pp. *Module 19.* [*p. 172*]
1976   Teaching anthropological ethics: developing skills in ethical decision-making and the nature of moral education. *Anthropological quarterly* 49: 81–8. [*p. 22*]

ARMER, Michael, and GRIMSHAW, Allan Day
1973   *Editors.* Comparative social research: methodology problems and strategies. New York; Wiley. xxi, 473 pp.

ARNOLD, Rome G.
1964   The interview in jeopardy: a problem in public relations. *Public opinion quarterly* 28: 120–23. [*p. 182*]

ARONSON, Elliot, and CARLSMITH, James Merrill
1968   Experimentation in social psychology. *In* Lindzey and Aronson 1968: 1–79. [*pp. 91, 97*]

ARONSON, Elliot, and MILLS, Judson
1959   The effect of severity of initiation on liking for a group. *Journal of abnormal and social psychology* 59: 177–81. [*p. 91*]

ASAD, Talal
1973   *Editor.* Anthropology and the colonial encounter. London; Ithaca Press. 288 pp. [*p. 43*]

ASCH, Solomon Elliott
1956   Studies of independence and conformity: I. A minority of one against a unanimous majority. *Psychological monographs* 70(9). Whole number 416. 70 pp. [*p. 94*]

BACON, Francis
1861   Works. Vol. 7. Literary and professional works, vol. 2. London; Longman, etc. vi, 831 pp. [*p. 42*]

BARBER, Bernard, and others
1973   Research on human subjects: problems of social control in medical experimentation. New York; Russell Sage. viii, 263 pp. [*p. 18*]

BARITZ, Loren
1960   The servants of power: a history of the use of social science in American industry. Middletown, Conn.; Wesleyan University Press. xii, 273 pp. [*pp. 36, 83*]

BARNES, Harry Elmer
1966   An introduction to the history of sociology. Abridged ed. Chicago; University of Chicago Press. xi, 485 pp. [*p. 44*]

BARNES, John Arundel
1967   Some ethical problems in modern field work. *In* JONGMANS, Douwe Geert, and GUTKIND, Peter Claus Wolfgang, eds. Anthropologists in the field. Assen; Van Gorcum. Pp. 193–213. [*pp. 71, 112*]
1969   Politics, permits, and professional interests: the Rose case. *Australian quarterly* 41 (1): 17–31. [*p. 66*]
1977   The ethics of inquiry in social science: three lectures. Delhi; Oxford University Press. 67 pp. [*pp. 10–11, 83, 89, 112, 113, 116, 123, 125, 127–8*]

BARTH, Frederik
1974   On responsibility and humanity: calling a colleague to account. *Current anthropology* 15: 99–103. [*pp. 162, 176*]

BATALLA, Guillermo Bonfil
1966   Conservative thought in applied anthropology: a critique. *Human organization* 25: 89–92. [*p. 39*]

BAUMHART, Raymond C.
1961   How ethical are businessmen? *Harvard business review* 39: 6–19 [*p. 159*]

BEALS, Ralph Leon
1969   Politics of social research: an inquiry into the ethics and responsibilities of social scientists. Chicago; Aldine. vii, 228 pp. [*pp. 46, 48, 56, 71, 83*]

BECKER, Howard Paul, and BARNES, Harry Elmer
1952   Social thought from lore to science. 2nd ed. Washington, DC; Harren Press. 2 vols. [*p. 27*]

BECKER, Howard Saul
1967   Whose side are we on? *Social problems* 14: 239–47. [*p. 170*]

BELL, Earl Hoyt
1959   'Freedom and responsibility in research': comments. *Human organization* 18: 49. [*p. 142*]

BERG, Irwin August
1954   The use of human subjects in psychological research. *American psychologist* 9: 108–11. [*p. 160*]

BERGER, Peter Ludwig
1976   Pyramids of sacrifice: political ethics and social change. London; Allen Lane. 272 pp. [*p. 172*]

BERGER, Peter Ludwig, and LUCKMANN, Thomas
1966   The social construction of reality: a treatise in the sociology of knowledge. Garden City, NY; Doubleday. vii, 203 pp. [*p. 61*]

BERREMAN, Gerald Duane
1969   Academic colonialism: not so innocent abroad. *Nation* 209: 505–8. *Reprinted in* Weaver, T. 1973b: 152–6. [*pp. 58, 81, 85*]

1972   Hindus of the Himalayas: ethnography and change. 2nd ed. Berkeley; University of California Press. lviii, 440 pp. [*pp. 106, 108, 109, 137*]

1973a   The social responsibility of the anthropologist. *In* Weaver, T. 1973b: 8–10. [*p. 20*]

1973b   Contemporary anthropology and moral accountability. *In* Weaver, T. 1973b: 58–61. [*p. 24*]

1973c   Anthropology and moral accountability. *In* Weaver, T. 1973b: 178–9. [*p. 186*]

1976   Himachal: science, people and 'progress'. Keynote address, symposium on ecology and geology of the central Himalaya, Paris, 7–10 December (cited with permission). [*p. 149*]

BERREMAN, Gerald Duane, and others
1968   Social responsibilities symposium. *Current anthropology* 9: 391–435. [*p. 160*]

BERSCHEILD, Ellen, and others
1973   Anticipating informed consent: an empirical approach. *American psychologist* 28: 913–25. [*p. 94*]

BÉTEILLE, André
1975   The tribulations of fieldwork. *In* Béteille and Madan 1975: 99–113. [*p. 115*]

References

BÉTEILLE, André, and MADAN, Triloki Nath
1975   Editors. Encounter and experience: personal accounts of fieldwork. Delhi; Vikas. xi, 225 pp.

BETTELHEIM, Bruno
1943   Individual and mass behavior in extreme conditions. *Journal of abnormal and social psychology* 38: 417–52. [*p. 128*]

BICKMAN, Leonard, and HENCHY, Thomas
1972   Editors. Beyond the laboratory: field research in social psychology. New York; McGraw-Hill. xii, 340 pp. [*pp. 95, 98*]

BLAIR, Calvin Patton
1969   Social science research in Guatemala and the role of US personnel: 1950–1967. *In* Blair et al. 1969: 1 1–43. [*p. 57 58, 59*]

BLAIR, Calvin Patton, SCHAEDEL, Richard P., and STREET, James Harry
1969   Responsibilities of the foreign scholar to the local scholarly community: studies of US research in Guatemala, Chile and Paraguay. New York; Council on Educational Cooperation with Latin America. 112 pp.

BLAU, Peter Michael
1964   The research process in the study of the dynamics of bureaucracy. *In* Hammond 1964: 16–49. [*p. 105*]

BLAUNER, Robert, and WELLMAN, David
1973   Toward the decolonization of social research. *In* Ladner 1973: 310–30. [*pp. 55, 68*]

BLOK, Anton
1973   A note on ethics and power. *Human organization* 32: 95–107. [*p. 163*]

BOAS, Franz
1919   Scientists as spies. *Nation* 109: 797. *Reprinted in* Weaver, T. 1973b: 51–2. [*p. 128*]

BODMER, Walter Fred, and CAVALLI-SFORZA, Luigi Luca
1976   Genetics, evolution, and man. San Francisco; Freeman. xvii, 782 pp. [*p. 85*]

BONESS, Frederick H., and CORDES, John F.
1973   The researcher-subject relationship: the need for protection and a model statute. *Georgetown law journal* 62: 243–72. [*p. 183*]

BOTT, Elizabeth
1971   Family and social network. 2nd ed. London; Tavistock. xxx, 363 pp. [*p. 142*]

193

Who should know what?

BRAYFIELD, Arthur Hills
1967   Surgeon General of PHS clarifies directive on human experimentation. *American psychologist* 22: 241–4. [*p. 164*]
BRENNAN, Paul W.
1975   Reply to Kundapen Talyaga. *Research in Melanesia* 1 (3–4): 28–9. [*p. 170*]
BRIDGES, Esteban Lucas
1948   Uttermost part of the earth. London; Hodder and Stoughton. 558 pp. [*p. 33*]
BRIM, Orville Gilbert, jr
1965   American attitudes towards intelligence tests. *American psychologist* 20: 125–30. [*p. 153*]
BRITISH ASSOCIATION FOR THE ADVANCEMENT OF SCIENCE
1974   Does research threaten privacy or does privacy threaten research? Report of a study group. London; BAAS. 23 pp. *Publication 74/1*. [*p. 184*]
BRITISH SOCIOLOGICAL ASSOCIATION
1973   Statement of ethical principles and their applications to sociological practice. 5 pp. [*pp. 105, 161*]
BROEDER, Dale W.
1959   The University of Chicago jury project. *Nebraska law review* 38: 744–60. [*p. 127*]
1960   Silence and perjury before police officers: an examination of the criminal law risks. *Nebraska law review* 40: 63–103. [*p. 112*]
BRONFENBRENNER, Urie
1952   Principles of professional ethics: Cornell studies in social growth. *American psychologist* 7: 452–5. [*pp. 5, 160*]
BROWN, George Gordon, and HUTT, Alec McDonald Bruce
1935   Anthropology in action. London; Oxford University Press. xviii, 272 pp. [*p. 45*]
BROWN, Richard
1973   Anthropology and colonial rule: the case of Godfrey Wilson and the Rhodes-Livingstone Institute, Northern Rhodesia. *In* Asad 1973: 173–97. [*p. 39*]
BRUNT, Lodewijk
1974   Anthropological fieldwork in the Netherlands. *Current anthropology* 15: 311–14. [*p. 115*]
BURCHARD, Waldo Wadsworth
1958   Lawyers, political scientists, sociologists – and concealed microphones. *American sociological review* 23: 686–91. [*p. 127*]

194

BURRIDGE, Kenelm
1973   Encountering Aborigines: a case study: anthropology and the Australian Aboriginal. New York; Pergamon. xi, 260 pp. [*p. 163*]

CAMBRIDGE, Charles
1971   Observations on involvement. *Human organization* 30: 95–6. [*p. 54*]
CANNELL, Charles Frederick, and KAHN, Robert Louis
1968   Interviewing. *In* Lindzey and Aronson 1968: 526–95. [*p. 110*]
CAREY, Alex
1967   The Hawthorne studies: a radical criticism. *American sociological review* 32: 403–16. [*p. 41*]
CAUDILL, William
1958   The psychiatric hospital as a small society. Cambridge, Mass.; Harvard University Press. xxiii, 406 pp. [*p. 125*]
CAVALLI-SFORZA, Luigi Luca, and BODMER, Walter Fred
1971   The genetics of human populations. San Francisco; Freeman. xvii, 965 pp. [*p. 85*]
CHALLENOR, Herchelle Sullivan
1973   No longer at ease. Confrontation at the 12th annual African Studies Association meetings at Montreal. *In* Weaver, T. 1973b: 165–70. [*p. 67*]
CHAMBLISS, William
1975   On the paucity of original research on organized crime: a footnote to Galliher and Cain. *American sociologist* 10: 36–9. [*p. 113*]
CHAPPLE, Eliot Dismore
1951   [unsigned editorial] Ethics in applied anthropology. *Human organization* 10 (2): 4. [*p. 160*]
1952   [unsigned editorial] The applied anthropologist – informant or professional. *Human organization* 11 (2): 3–4. [*p. 160*]
CHILUNGU, Simeon W.
1976   Issues in the ethics of research method: an interpretation of the Anglo-American perspective. *Current anthropology* 17: 457–81. [*p. 160*]
CLEGG, Stewart
1975   Power, rule and domination. London; Routledge and Kegan Paul. viii, 208 pp. [*p. 109*]

CLINARD, Marshall Barron
1966   The sociologist's quest for respectability. *Sociological quarterly* 7: 399–412. [*p. 68*]

COCHRANE, Glynn
1971   Development anthropology. New York; Oxford University Press. 125 pp. [*p. 174*]

COLSON, Elizabeth
1976   Culture and progress. *American anthropologist* 78: 261–71. [*p. 104*]

COLSON, Elizabeth, and others
1976   Long-term research in social anthropology. *Current anthropology* 17: 494–6. [*p. 149*]

CONDOMINAS, Georges
1973   Ethics and comfort: an ethnographer's view of his profession. Annual report of the American Anthropological Association, 1972. Pp. 1–17. [*p. 155*]
1977   We have eaten the forest: the story of a Montagnard village in the central highlands of Vietnam. London; Allen Lane. xxii, 423 pp. [*p. 156*]

CONRAD, Herbert Spencer
1967   Clearance of questionnaires with respect to 'invasion of privacy', public sensitivities, ethical standards, etc. *American psychologist* 22: 356–9. [*p. 87*]

COOPER, Joel
1976   Deception and role playing: on telling the good guys from the bad guys. *American psychologist* 31: 605–10. [*p. 101*]

CORNELL PROGRAM IN SOCIAL PSYCHIATRY
1959–60 'On freedom and responsibility in research': memorandum on understanding concerning basic principles for publication of program research. *Human organization* 18: 147–8. [*pp. 147, 160*]

COSER, Lewis Alfred
1971   Report of the Committee on professional ethics. *American sociologist* 6: 353. [*p. 162*]

COX, Peter Richard
1976   Demography. 5th ed. Cambridge; Cambridge University Press. ix, 393 pp. [*p. 27*]

CRICK, Bernard
1977   Red sails on the campus. *Observer* (London). 25 September, p. 10. [*p. 162*]

References

CRISPO, John Herbert Gillespie
1975   The public right to know: accountability in the secretive society. Toronto; McGraw-Hill Ryerson. 395 pp. [*p. 182*]

CROCOMBE, Ronald Gordon
1976   Anthropology, anthropologists, and Pacific islanders. *Oceania* 47: 66–73. [*p. 71*]

DARWIN, Charles
1959   The voyage of the Beagle. London; Dent. xvi, 496 pp. [*pp. 33, 35*]

DAVIES, Martin, and KELLY, Elinor
1976   The social worker, the client and the social anthropologist. *British journal of social work* 6: 213–31. [*p. 118*]

DAVIS, Allison, GARDNER, Burleigh Bradford, and GARDNER, Mary R.
1965   Deep South: a social anthropological study of caste and class. Abridged ed. Chicago; University of Chicago Press. xix, 364 pp. [*p. 118*]

DEITCHMAN, Seymour J.
1976   The best-laid schemes: a tale of social research and bureaucracy. Cambridge, Mass.; MIT Press. xv, 483 pp. [*pp. 47, 48, 66, 81, 161*]

DELORIA, Vine, jr
1969   Custer died for your sins: an Indian manifesto. New York; Macmillan. 279 pp. [*pp. 68, 170*]

DENZIN, Norman Kent
1970   The research act in sociology: a theoretical introduction to sociological methods. Chicago; Aldine. xvii, 368 pp. [*p. 163*]

DICKSON, William John, and ROETHLISBERGER, Fritz Jules
1966   Counseling in an organization: a sequel to the Hawthorne researches. Boston; Harvard University, Graduate School of Business Administration. xviii, 480 pp. [*p. 40*]

DONNISON, David, and others
n.d.   Survey research and privacy. Report of a working party. London; Social and Community Planning Research. v, 56 pp. [*pp. 162, 180, 184*]

DORN, Dean Sherman, and LONG, Gary L.
1974   Brief remarks on the Association's code of ethics. *American sociologist* 9: 31–5. [*p. 163*]

197

Who should know what?

DOUGLAS, Jack Daniel
1976   Investigative social research: individual and team field research. Beverly Hills; Sage. xv, 229 pp. [*pp. 22, 116, 122*]

DUNN, Edgar Streeter
1967   The idea of a national data center and the issue of personal privacy. *American statistician* 21 (1): 21–7. [*p. 167*]

EASTHOPE, Gary
1974   A history of social research methods. London; Longman. x, 164 pp. [*p. 31*]

EDEN, Frederick Morton
1797   The state of the poor: or a history of the labouring classes in England. London. 3 vols. [*p. 28*]

EFRAT, Barbara, and MITCHELL, Marjorie
1974   The Indian and the social scientist: contemporary contractual arrangements on the Pacific northwest coast. *Human organization* 33: 405–7. [*p. 165*]

ELESH, David
1972   The Manchester Statistical Society: a case study of discontinuity in the history of empirical social research. *Journal of the history of the behavioral sciences* 8: 280–301, 407–17. [*p. 28*]

ELWIN, Verrier
1964   The tribal world of Verrier Elwin. Bombay; Oxford University Press. xii, 356 pp. [*p. 39*]

ERIKSON, Kai T.
1967   A comment on disguised observation in sociology. *Social problems* 14: 366–73. [*p. 123*]

EULAU, Heinz
1970   Some potential effects of the information utility on political decision-makers and the role of the representative. *In* SACKMAN, Harold, and NIE, Norman Hugh, eds. The information utility and social choice. Montvale, NJ; AFIPS Press. Pp. 187–99. [*p. 168*]

EVAN, William Martin
1960–61 Conflict and the emergence of norms: the 'Springdale' case. *Human organization* 19: 172–3. [*p. 160*]

EVANS-PRITCHARD, Edward Evan
1937   Witchcraft, oracles and magic among the Azande. Oxford; Clarendon Press. xxvi, 558 pp. [*pp. 39–40*]
1946   Applied anthropology. *Africa* 16: 92–8. [*p. 43*]

198

FENTON, William Nelson
1972   Return to the longhouse. *In* Kimball and Watson 1972: 102–18. [*p. 56*]

FESTINGER, Leon
1953   Laboratory experiments. *In* Festinger and Katz 1953: 136–72. [*p. 97*]

FESTINGER, Leon, and CARLSMITH, James Merrill
1959   Cognitive consequences of forced compliance. *Journal of abnormal and social psychology* 58: 203–10. [*p. 95*]

FESTINGER, Leon, and KATZ, Daniel
1953   *Editors.* Research methods in the behavioral sciences. New York; Holt. xi, 660 pp.

FICHTER, Joseph Henry, and KOLB, William L.
1953   Ethical limitations on sociological reporting. *American sociological review* 18: 544–50. [*pp. 165, 176*]

FILSTEAD, William Joseph
1970   Introduction. *In* FILSTEAD, W. J., ed. Readings in qualitative methodology. Chicago; Markham. Pp. 1–11. [*p. 26*]

FIRTH, Raymond William
1956   Human types. Rev. ed. London; Nelson. vi, 7–224 pp. [*p. 37*]
1972   The sceptical anthropologist? Social anthropology and Marxist views on society. *Proceedings of the British Academy* 58: 177–213. [*p. 31*]

FLUGEL, John Carl, and WEST, Donald James
1964   A hundred years of psychology 1833–1933. London; Duckworth. 394 pp. [*p. 34*]

FORM, William Humbert
1973   Field problems in comparative research: the politics of distrust. *In* Armer and Grimshaw 1973: 83–117. [*pp. 76, 106*]

FORSTER, Peter
1973   Empiricism and imperialism: a review of the New Left critique of social anthropology. *In* Asad 1973: 23–38. [*p. 170*]

FORSYTHE, Dennis
1973   Radical sociology and Blacks. *In* Ladner 1973: 213–33. [*p. 68*]

FOSTER, George McClelland
1953   Use of anthropological methods and data in planning and operation. *Public health reports* 68: 841–57. [*p. 49*]
1969   Applied anthropology. Boston; Little, Brown. xiv, 238 pp. [*pp. 45, 67, 160, 173*]

FRANKEL, Mark S.
1972   The Public health service guidelines governing research in-
         volving human subjects: an analysis of the policy-making
         process. Washington, DC; George Washington University.
         iii, 64 pp. *Program of policy studies in science and technology.*
         Monograph 10. [*p. 164*]

FRAZER, James George
1911–15 The golden bough. 3rd ed. London; Macmillan. 12 vols.
         [*p. 32*]

FRIEDRICHS, Robert Winslow
1970   A sociology of sociology. New York; Free Press. xxiii, 429
         pp. [*p. 177*]

FULFORD, Roger
1957   Votes for women: the story of a struggle. London; Faber.
         343 pp. [*p. 91*]

GALLAHER, Art, jr
1964   Plainville: the twice-studied town. *In* VIDICH, Arthur
         Joseph, and others, eds. Reflections on community studies.
         New York; Wiley. Pp. 285–303. [*pp. 138, 146*]

GALLIHER, John F.
1973   The protection of human subjects: a re-examination of the
         professional code of ethics. *American sociologist* 8: 93–100.
         [*p. 166*]

GALTUNG, Johan
1967   Scientific colonialism. *Transition* (Kampala) 6 (5): 11–15.
         [*p. 57*]

GEDDES, William Robert
1975   [Contribution to] More thoughts on the Ik and anthropology.
         Current anthropology 16: 348–52. [*p. 66*]

GERGEN, Kenneth Jay
1973   The codification of research ethics: views of a doubting
         Thomas. *American psychologist* 28: 907–12. [*p. 163*]

GIBBONS, Don Cary
1975   Unidentified research sites and fictitious names. *American*
         sociologist 10: 32–6. [*p. 140*]

GIDDENS, Anthony
1976   New rules of sociological method. London; Hutchinson.
         192 pp. [*p. 70*]

GLASS, David Victor
1973   Numbering the people. Farnborough; Saxon House. 205 pp.
         [*p. 90*]

GLAZER, Myron
1972   The research adventure: promise and problems of field work. New York: Random House. xviii, 203 pp. [*p. 85*]

GLICK, Paula Brown
1970   Academics and research. *Mankind* 7: 311. [*p. 83*]

GLUCKMAN, Max
1940   Analysis of a social situation in modern Zululand. *Bantu studies* 14: 1–30, 147–74. [*p. 38*]

GOFFMAN, Erving
1969   The presentation of self in everyday life. London; Allen Lane. xi, 228 pp. [*p. 106*]

GOLANN, Stuart Eugene
1970   Code and conduct: on the ethical program. *American psychologist* 25: 206–8. [*p. 160*]

GOLDSTEIN, Arnold Paul, HELLER, Kenneth, and SECHREST, Lee Burton
1966   Psychotherapy and the psychology of behavior change. New York; Wiley. ix, 472 pp. [*p. 63*]

GOODENOUGH, Ward Hunt
1976   Intercultural expertise and public policy. *In* SANDAY, Peggy Reeves, ed. Anthropology and the public interest: fieldwork and theory. New York; Academic Press. Pp. 15–23. [*p. 172*]

GORSUCH, Richard Lee
1972   An APA-sponsored law to protect psychologists and subjects from unwarranted use of research data. *American psychologist* 27: 667–8. [*p. 183*]

GOTLIEB, Calvin Carl, and BORODIN, Allan
1973   Social issues in computing. New York; Academic Press. xv, 284 pp. [*pp. 159, 168, 182*]

GOUGH, Kathleen
1968   World revolution and the science of man. *In* ROSZAK, Theodore, ed. The dissenting academy. New York; Pantheon Books. Pp. 135–58. [*p. 169*]

GOULD, Harold A.
1973   Contribution to discussions. In ARMER, Michael, and GRIMSHAW, Allan Day, eds. Comparative social research. New York; Wiley. Passim. [*p. 56*]

GOULDNER, Alvin Ward
1965a   Enter Plato: classical Greece and the origins of social theory. New York; Basic Books. ix, 407 pp. [*p. 27*]
1965b   Explorations in applied social science. *In* GOULDNER,

A. W., and MILLER, Seymour Michael, eds. Applied sociology. New York; Free Press. Pp. 5–22. [*p. 102*]

1970   The coming crisis of western sociology. New York; Basic Books, xv, 528 pp. [*pp. 29, 31, 39*]

GRAYSON, Donald K.

1969   Human life vs science. *American Anthropological Association newsletter* 10 (6). *Reprinted in* Weaver, T. 1973b: 32–3. [*p. 75*]

GREER, Frederick Loyal

1977   More on Camelot. *American sociologist* 12: 53. [*p. 48*]

GUNDAKER, Guy

1922   Campaign of the International Association of Rotary Clubs for the writing of codes of standards of practice for each business and profession. *Annals of the American Academy of Political and Social Science* 101: 228–36. [*p. 159*]

HADDON, Alfred Cort

1901   Head-hunters black, white, and brown. London; Methuen. xxiv, 426 pp. [*pp. 33, 35*]

1935   General ethnography. Cambridge; Cambridge University Press. xvi, 421 pp. *Reports of the Cambridge anthropological expedition to Torres Straits, vol. 1.* [*p. 33*]

HALL, Calvin Springer

1952   Crooks, codes, and cant. *American psychologist* 7: 430–31. [*p. 163*]

HAMILTON, Annette

1971   Review: Gould, Yiawara. *Mankind* 8: 156–7. [*p. 157*]

1974   Review: Stevens, Aborigines in the Northern Territory cattle industry. *Man* 10: 337–8. [*p. 175*]

HAMMOND, Phillip Everett

1964   *Editor.* Sociologists at work: essays on the craft of social research. New York; Basic Books. xi, 401 pp.

HANEY, Craig, BANKS, Curtis, and ZIMBARDO, Philip George

1973   Interpersonal dynamics in a simulated prison. *International journal of criminology and penology* 1: 69–97. [*pp. 92, 129*]

HANSARD

1813   The parliamentary history of England, . . . Vol. XIV. AD 1747–1753. London. 1432 cols. [*p. 90*]

HARRIS, Albert J.

1952   New York adopts a code of ethics. *American psychologist* 7: 447–52. [*p. 160*]

HARRISSON, Tom
1961   Britain revisited. London; Gollancz. 285 pp. [*p. 51*]

HAU'OFA, Epeli
1975   Anthropology and Pacific islanders. *Oceania* 45: 283–9. [*p. 71*]

HAWTHORN, Geoffrey Patrick
1976   Enlightenment and despair: a history of sociology. Cambridge; Cambridge University Press. 295 pp. [*p. 188*]

HAYEK, Friedrich August von
1952   The counter-revolution in science: studies on the abuse of reason. Glencoe, Ill.; Free Press. 255 pp. [*p. 62*]

HAYTER, Teresa
1971   Aid as imperialism. Harmondsworth; Penguin Books. 222 pp. [*p. 45*]

HELD, Gerrit Jan
1953   Applied anthropology in government: the Netherlands. *In* INTERNATIONAL SYMPOSIUM ON ANTHROPOLOGY. Anthropology today. Chicago; University of Chicago Press. Pp. 866–79. [*pp. 36, 45*]

HEWITT, Patricia
1977   Privacy: the information gatherers. London; National Council for Civil Liberties. 98 pp. [*pp. 90, 182*]

HIATT, Lester Richard
1969   Editorial. *Mankind* 7: 1–2. [*p. 83*]
1970   Editor's reply. *Mankind* 7: 312. [*p. 83*]

HICKS, George L.
1977   Informant anonymity and scientific accuracy: the problem of pseudonyms. *Human organization* 36: 214–20. [*p. 144*]

HILGER, Mary Inez
1954   An ethnographic field method. *In* SPENCER, Robert Francis, ed. Method and perspective in anthropology. Minneapolis; University of Minnesota Press. Pp. 25–42. [*p. 38*]

HOBBS, Nicholas
1948   The development of a code of ethical standards for psychology. *American psychologist* 3: 80–84. [*p. 159*]
1968   Ethics: ethical issues in the social sciences. *In* SILLS, David Lawrence, ed. International encyclopedia of the social sciences. Vol. 5. New York; Macmillan and Free Press. Pp. 160–67. [*pp. 159, 160*]

HOFLING, Charles Kreimer, and others
1966   An experimental study in nurse-physician relationships.

Journal of nervous and mental disease 143: 171–80. [*p. 101*]

HOGBIN, Herbert Ian
1957   Anthropology as public service and Malinowski's contribution to it. *In* FIRTH, Raymond, ed. Man and culture. London; Routledge and Kegan Paul. Pp. 245–64. [*p. 45*]

HOLLEMAN, Johan Frederik
1958   African interlude. Capetown; Nasionale Boekhandel. 269 pp. [*p. 38*]

HOLMBERG, Allan Richard
1955   Participant observation in the field. *Human organisation* 14(1): 23–6 [*p. 175*]

HOMANS, George Caspar
1949   The strategy of industrial sociology. *American journal of sociology* 54: 330–37. [*pp. 26, 101*]

HOME OFFICE
1975a   Computers and privacy. London; HMSO. 13 pp. Cmnd. 6353. [*p. 185*]
1975b   Computers: safeguards for privacy. London; HMSO. 48 pp. Cmnd. 6354. [*p. 185*]

HOROWITZ, Irving Louis
1967   *Editor.* The rise and fall of Project Camelot. Cambridge, Mass.; MIT Press. xii, 385 pp. [*p. 46*]
1973   *Trans*action magazine: a decade of critical social science journalism. *International social science journal* 25: 169–89. [*p. 46*]

HUGHES, Everett Cherrington
1956   The improper study of man. *In* WHITE, Lynn, ed. Frontiers of knowledge in the study of man. New York; Harper. Pp. 79–93. [*p. 117*]

HUIZER, Gerrit
1975   The a-social role of social scientists in underdeveloped countries: some ethical considerations. *In* Kloos and Claessen 1975: 63–72. [*pp. 114, 171*]

HUMPHERYS, Anne
1971   Introduction. *In* MAYHEW, Henry. Voices of the poor: selections from the *Morning Chronicle*. London; Frank Cass. Pp. ix–xx. [*pp. 29, 31*]

HUMPHREYS, Laud
1975   Tearoom trade: impersonal sex in public places. Enlarged ed. Chicago; Aldine. xviii, 238 pp. [*pp. 74, 113, 139*]

HYMES, Dell Hathaway
1972   *Editor*. Reinventing anthropology. New York; Pantheon Books. vi, 470 pp. [*pp. 172, 181*]

INTERNATIONAL COMMISSION OF JURISTS
1972   The legal protection of privacy: a comparative survey of ten countries. *International social sciences journal* 24: 417–583. [*p. 112*]

JANES, Robert William
1961   A note on the phases of the community role of the participant observer. *American sociological review* 26: 446–50. [*p. 78*]

JAQUES, Elliott
1951   The changing culture of a factory. London; Tavistock. xvii, 341 pp. [*pp. 89, 142, 143*]

JONES, Mervyn
1974   *Editor*. Privacy. Newton Abbot; David and Charles. 230 pp. [*p. 185*]

JOPLING, David G., GAGE, Stephen J., and SCHOEMAN, Milton Edward Franklin
1973   Forecasting public resistance to technology: the example of nuclear reactor siting. *In* BRIGHT, James Rieser, and SCHOEMAN, M. E. F., eds. A guide to practical technological forecasting. Englewood Cliffs, NJ; Prentice-Hall. Pp. 53–66. [*p. 50*]

JORGENSEN, Joseph Gilbert, and others
1971   Toward an ethics for anthropologists. *Current anthropology* 12: 321–56. [*p. 160*]

JOSEPHSON, Eric
1970   Resistance to community surveys. *Social problems* 18: 117–29. [*p. 55*]

JUNKER, Buford Helmholz
1960   Fieldwork; an introduction to the social sciences. Chicago; University of Chicago Press. xvii, 209 pp. [*pp. 104, 112, 121*]

KAMIN, Leon Judah
1977   The science and politics of IQ. Harmondsworth; Penguin Books. 252 pp. [*p. 43*]

KATZ, Daniel
1953   Field studies. *In* Festinger and Katz 1953: 56–97. [*p. 109*]

KATZ, Jay
1972   Experimentation with human beings. New York; Russell
        Sage Foundation. xlix, 1159 pp. [*pp. 74, 105, 127*]

KEESING, Roger Martin
1975   Anthropology in Melanesia: retrospect and prospect. *Re-
        search in Melanesia* 1(1): 32–9. [*p. 57*]

KELMAN, Herbert Chanoch
1967   The human use of human beings. *Psychological bulletin* 67:
        1–11. [*p. 95*]
1968   A time to speak: on human values and social research. San
        Francisco; Jossey-Bass. xvii, 349 pp. [*pp. 48, 80, 128, 153,
        168, 174, 185*]
1972   The rights of the subject in social research: an analysis in
        terms of relative power and legitimacy. *American psychologist*
        27: 989–1016. [*pp. 24, 93, 99, 114, 179, 187*]

KIELSTRA, Nico
1975   Is useful action research possible? Mimeograph, 10 pp. (cited
        with permission). [*p. 181*]

KIMBALL, Solon Toothaker, and WATSON, James Bennett
1972   *Editors.* Crossing cultural boundaries: the anthropological
        experience. San Francisco; Chandler. xxi, 306 pp.

KING, Arnold J., and SPECTOR, Aaron J.
1963   Ethical and legal aspects of survey research. *American psycho-
        logist* 18: 204–8. [*p. 146*]

KING, Francis Walter
1970   Anonymous versus identifiable questionnaires in drug usage
        surveys. *American psychologist* 25: 982–5. [*p. 183*]

KINSEY, Alfred Charles, POMEROY, Wardell Baxter, and MARTIN,
Clyde Eugene
1948   Sexual behavior in the human male. Philadelphia; Saunders.
        xv, 804 pp. [*p. 166*]

KLARE, Michael T.
1972   War without end: American planning for the next Vietnams.
        New York; Knopf. xx, 464, xviii pp. [*pp. 46, 66*]

KLAW, Spencer
1970   The Faustian bargain. *In* BROWN, Martin, ed. The social
        responsibility of the scientist. New York; Free Press. Pp. 3–
        15. [*p. 79*]

KLOOS, Peter, and CLAESSEN, Henri J. M.
1975   *Editors.* Current anthropology in the Netherlands. Rotter-
        dam; Anthropological branch of the Netherlands Sociological
        and Anthropological Society. 184 pp.

KROUT, Maurice Haim
1954   Comments on 'The use of human subjects in psychological research'. *American psychologist* 9: 589. [*p. 97*]

KRUGLANSKI, Arie W.
1975   The human subject in the psychology experiment: fact and artifact. *Advances in social psychology* 8: 101–47. [*pp. 102, 168*]

KUHN, Thomas Samuel
1970   The structure of scientific revolutions. 2nd ed. Chicago; University of Chicago Press. xii, 210 pp. [*p. 174*]

KUPER, Adam
1973   Anthropologists and anthropology: the British school 1922–1972. London; Allen Lane. 256 pp. [*p. 43*]

LADNER, Joyce A.
1973   *Editor*. The death of white sociology. New York; Random House. xxxiii, 476 pp.

Lancet
1977   Involved in dying. *Lancet* 1977 (i): 736 [*p. 125*]

LANDIS, Carney
1927   National differences in conversations. *Journal of abnormal and social psychology* 21: 354–7. [*p. 121*]

LANDSBERGER, Henry Adolf
1958   Hawthorne revisited. Ithaca, NY; Cornell University, New York State School of Industrial and Labor Relations. vii, 119 pp. [*p. 40*]

LANE, David Stuart
1970   Ideology and sociology in the USSR. *British journal of sociology* 21: 43–51. [*p. 186*]

LAVER, Murray
1976   An introduction to the uses of computers. Cambridge; Cambridge University Press. viii, 232 pp. [*p. 183*]

LECLERC, Gérard
1972   Anthropologie et colonialisme: essai sur l'histoire de l'africanisme. Paris; Fayard. 256 pp. [*pp. 33, 43*]

LEIRIS, Michel
1950   L'ethnographie devant le colonialisme. *Temps modernes* 6: 357–74. [*p. 38*]

LEVI, Leone
1885   What is the social condition of the working classes in 1884 as compared with 1857, . . . *Transactions of the National Association for the Promotion of Social Science* 1884: 588–605. [*p. 30*]

Lévi-Strauss, Claude
1966   Anthropology: its achievements and future. *Current anthropology* 7: 124–7 [*pp. 75, 186*]

Lewis, Oscar
1961   The children of Sánchez: autobiography of a Mexican family. New York; Random House. 499 pp. [*p. 71*]

Lienhardt, Godfrey
1964   Social anthropology. London; Oxford University Press. xi, 216 pp. [*p. 33*]

Likert, Rensis, and Lippitt, Ronald
1953   The utlization of social science. *In* Festinger and Katz 1953: 583–646. [*p. 81*]

Lindzey, Gardner, and Aronson, Elliot
1968   *Editors.* The handbook of social psychology. 2nd ed. Vol. II. Research methods. Reading, Mass.; Addison-Wesley. xv, 819 pp.

Lowe, George E.
1966   The Camelot affair. *Bulletin of the atomic scientists* 22 (5): 44–8. [*p. 46*]

Lurie, Nancy Oestreich
1972   Two dollars. *In* Kimball and Watson 1972: 151–63. [*p. 34*]

Lynd, Robert Staughton
1939   Knowledge for what? The place of social science in American culture. Princeton; Princeton University Press. x, 268 pp. [*pp. 10, 62*]

Lynd, Robert Staughton, and Lynd, Helen Merrell
1929   Middletown. New York; Harcourt Brace. xi, 550 pp. [*pp. 54, 111, 136, 137, 138*]

McGrew, John M.
1967   How 'open' are multiple-dwelling units? *Journal of social psychology* 72: 223–6. [*p. 98*]

McGuire, Ralph J.
1972   The psychologist and the data bank. *In* Rowe, Beverley Charles, ed. Privacy, computers and you. Manchester; National Computing Centre. Pp. 77–81. [*p. 153*]

Mack, Joanna
1978   A question of race. *New society* 43: 8–9. [*p. 178*]

McNamee, P. A.
1976   Teachers' secrets. *New society* 37: 602. [*p. 167*]

References

MADAN, Triloki Nath
1965   Family and kinship: a study of the Pandits of rural Kashmir. Bombay; Asia Publishing House. xix, 259 [*p. 146*]
1975   On living intimately with strangers. *In* Béteille and Madan 1975: 131–56. [*p. 147*]
MADGE, Charles, and HARRISSON, Tom
1937   Mass-observation. London; Frederick Muller. 64 pp. [*p. 51*]
1938   *Editors*. First year's work 1937–38 by Mass observation. London; Lindsay Drummond. 121 pp. [*p. 128*]
MADGWICK, Donald, and SMYTHE, Tony
1974   The invasion of privacy. London; Pitman. ix, 197 pp. [*pp. 90, 182*]
MAFEJE, Archie
1971   The ideology of 'tribalism'. *Journal of modern African studies* 9: 253–61. [*p. 68*]
MALINOWSKI, Bronislaw
1938   A nation-wide intelligence service. *In* Madge and Harrisson 1938: 81–121. [*pp. 63, 167*]
MANN, Horace
1855   On the statistical position of religious bodies in England and Wales. *Journal of the statistical society* 18: 141–59. [*p. 90*]
MANNERS, Robert Alan
1956   Functionalism, realpolitik and anthropology in under-developed areas. *América indígena* 16: 7–33. [*p. 46*]
MARCH, James Gardner, and SIMON, Herbert Alexander
1958   Organizations. New York; Wiley. xi, 262 pp. [*p. 103*]
MARSH, Cathie
1978   Opinion polls – social science or political manoeuvre? *In* EVANS, J., IRVINE, J., and MILES, Ian, eds. Demystifying social statistics. London; Pluto Press. [*p. 120*]
MARTIN, James Thomas, and NORMAN, Adrian Roger Dudley
1973   The computerized society: an appraisal of the impact of computers on society over the next fifteen years. Harmondsworth; Penguin Books. xi, 608 pp. [*p. 168*]
MAYHEW, Henry
1851   London labour and the London poor. London. 2 vols. [*p. 29*]
MEAD, Margaret
1953   *Editor*. Cultural patterns and technical change. Paris; Unesco. 348 pp. [*p. 45*]
1966   The changing culture of an Indian tribe. New York; Capricorn. xxiiii, 19–313 pp. [*pp. 126, 136, 137, 148*]

209

1969   Research with human beings: a model derived from anthropological field practice. *Daedalus* 98: 361–86. [*p. 149*]

1972   Fieldwork in high cultures. *In* Kimball and Watson 1972: 120–32. [*p. 80*]

MEAD, Sidney M.

1976   [Our readers write] *Current anthropology* 17: 778. [*p. 59*]

MENGES, Robert J.

1973   Openness and honesty versus coercion and deception in psychological research. *American psychologist* 28: 1030. [*p. 93*]

MILGRAM, Stanley

1974   Obedience to authority: an experimental view. New York; Harper and Row. xvii, 224 pp. [*pp. 95, 96*]

MILLER, Arthur Greenberg

1972a   Role playing: an alternative to deception? A review of the evidence. *American psychologist* 27: 623–36. [*p. 101*]

1972b   *Editor*. The social psychology of psychological research. New York; Free Press. ix, 454 pp. [*p. 95*]

MILLER, Arthur Raphael

1971   The assault on privacy: computers, data banks, and dossiers. Ann Arbor; University of Michigan Press. xiv, 333 pp. [*p. 182*]

MILLER, Seymour Michael

1952   The participant observer and 'over-rapport'. *American sociological review* 17: 97–9. [*p. 116*]

MILLS, Charles Wright

1963   Power, politics and people. New York; Oxford University Press. 657 pp. [*p. 5*]

MINER, John B.

1974   Psychological testing and fair employment practices: a testing program that does not discriminate. *Personnel psychology* 27: 49–62. [*p. 183*]

MISRA, Bhabagrahi

1973   Verrier Elwin; a pioneer Indian anthropologist. London; Asia Publishing House. xii, 162 pp. [*p. 39*]

MITCHELL, Geoffrey Duncan

1968   A hundred years of sociology. London; Duckworth. xiii, 310 pp. [*p. 51*]

MIXON, Don

1974   If you won't deceive, what can you do? *In* ARMISTEAD,

Nigel, ed. Reconstructing social psychology. Harmondsworth; Penguin Books. Pp. 72–85. [*p. 100*]

MORENO, Jacob L.
1953   Who shall survive? Foundations of sociometry, group psychotherapy and sociodrama. Rev. ed. Beacon, NY; Beacon House. cxiv, 763 pp. [*p. 100*]

MURPHY, Gardner, and KOVACH, Joseph Kocsard
1972   Historical introduction to modern psychology. 3rd ed. New York; Harcourt Brace Jovanovich. xv, 526 pp. [*p. 34*]

MURRAY, W. B., and BUCKINGHAM, R. W.
1976   Implications of participant observation in medical studies. *Canadian Medical Association journal* 115: 1187–90. [*p. 126*]

NADEL, Siegfried Frederick
1953   Anthropology and modern life. Canberra; Australian National University. 22 pp. [*p. 66*]

NASH, June
1975   Nationalism and fieldwork. *In* SIEGEL, Bernard Joseph, et al., eds. Annual review of anthropology. Vol. 4. Palo Alto; Annual reviews. Pp. 225–45. [*p. 62*]

NATIONAL ACADEMY OF SCIENCES, Washington, DC. Project on computer databanks
1972   Databanks in a free society: computers, record-keeping, and privacy. Report by Alan F. Westin and Michael A. Baker. New York; Quadrangle Books. xxi, 522 pp. [*pp. 164, 167, 183*]

NEJELSKI, Paul, and LERMAN, Lindsey Miller
1971   A researcher-subject testimonial privilege: what to do before the subpoena arrives. *Wisconsin law review* 1971: 1085–148. [*p. 183*]

NEWCOMB, Theodore Mead
1953   The interdependence of social-psychological theory and methods: a brief overview. *In* Festinger and Katz 1953: 1–12. [*p. 74*]

NIKELLY, Arthur George
1971   Ethical issues in research on student protest. *American psychologist* 26: 475–8. [*p. 174*]

NOOTER, Gert
1975   Ethics and the acquisition policy of anthropological museums. *In* Kloos and Claessen 1975: 156–64. [*p. 65*]

Nursing times
1971   Rcn approves of census use for Briggs' ex-nurses study.
        Nursing times 67: 1104. [*p. 90*]

OBERSCHALL, Anthony
1972   *Editor*. The establishment of empirical sociology: studies in
        continuity, discontinuity, and institutionalization. New York;
        Harper and Row. xvi, 256 pp. [*pp. 27, 36, 62*]
ODUM, Howard Washington
1951   American sociology: the story of sociology in the United
        States through 1950. New York; Longmans Green. vii, 501
        pp. [*p. 62*]
OLSON, Mancur Lloyd
1971   The logic of collective action: public goals and the theory of
        groups. Rev. ed. New York; Schocken Books. viii, 184 pp.
        [*p. 50*]
ORLANS, Harold
1967   Ethical problems in the relations of research sponsors and
        investigators. *In* Sjoberg 1967b: 3–24. [*p. 81*]
1973   Contracting for knowledge: values and limitations of social
        science research. San Francisco; Jossey-Bass. xvi, 286 pp.
        [*p. 160*]
OXAAL, Ivar, BARNETT, Tony, and BOOTH, David
1975   *Editors*. Beyond the sociology of development: economy and
        society in Latin America and Africa. London; Routledge and
        Kegan Paul. xi, 295 pp. [*p. 45*]

PALACIO, Joseph O.
1976   Anthropology in Belize. *Current anthropology* 17: 485–90.
        [*p. 186*]
PATRICK, James
1973   A Glasgow gang observed. London; Eyre Methuen. 256 pp.
        [*p. 141*]
PATTERSON, James
1971   Problems in urban ethnic research. *Human organization* 30:
        99–100. [*p. 180*]
PEATTIE, Lisa Redfield
1958   Interventionism and applied science in anthropology. *Human
        organization* 17(1): 4–8. [*p. 172*]

PENNOCK, James Roland, and CHAPMAN, John William
1971   *Editors*. Privacy. New York; Atherton Press. xx, 255 pp.
        Nomos 13.
PETTIFER, H. J.
1885   [Contribution to] Condition of the working classes. Discussion. *Transactions of the National Association for the Promotion of Social Science* 1884: 635–6. [*p. 30*]
PETTY, William
1970   The political anatomy of Ireland . . . Shannon; Irish University Press. viii, 205, 24 pp. [1st ed. 1691] [*p. 27*]
PHILLIPS, Pearson
1976   How the BM could lose its loot. *Observer* 9642: 6. (23 May) [*p. 65*]
PICKERING, William Stuart Frederick
1967   The religious census of 1851 – a useless experiment? *British journal of sociology* 18: 382–407. [*p. 90*]
PILIAVIN, Irving M., RODIN, Judith, and PILIAVIN, Jane Allyn
1969   Good Samaritanism: an underground phenomenon? *Journal of personality and social psychology* 13: 289–99. [*p. 99*]
PIPE, G. Russell
1977   At sea over private data banks. *New scientist* 73: 86–7. [*p. 185*]
PLATT, Jennifer
1976   Realities of social research: an empirical study of British sociologists. London; Chatto and Windus. 223 pp. [*p. 140*]
POLSKY, Ned
1971   Hustlers, beats and others. Harmondsworth; Penguin Books. 217 pp. [*p. 112*]
POOL, Ithiel de Sola
1967   The necessity for social scientists doing research for government. *In* Horowitz 1967: 267–80. [*p. 119*]
PORTER, Jack Nusan
1977   Letter to the editor. *American sociologist* 12: 203. [*p. 113*]
PORTES, Alejandro
1973   Perception of the US sociologist and its impact on cross-national research. *In* Armer and Grimshaw 1973: 149–69 [*pp. 57, 100, 105*]
1974   Trends in international research cooperation: the Latin American case. Mimeographed. 28 pp. (cited with permission). [*p. 79*]

1975   Trends in international research cooperation: the Latin American case. *American sociologist* 10: 131–40. [*pp. 57, 58, 60, 164*]

RAINWATER, Lee, and PITTMAN, David J.
1967   Ethical problems in studying a politically sensitive and deviant community. *Social problems* 14: 357–66. [*p. 166*]

REIN, Martin
1976   Social science and public policy. Harmondsworth; Penguin Books. 272 pp. [*pp. 82, 177*]

REYNOLDS, Paul Davidson
1972   On the protection of human subjects and social science. *International social science journal* 24: 693–719. [*pp. 23, 84, 122*]
1975   Value dilemmas in the professional conduct of social science. *International social science journal* 27: 563–611. [*p. 161*]

RIESMAN, David, and WATSON, Jeanne
1964   The sociability project: a chronicle of frustration and achievement. *In* Hammond 1964: 235–321. [*pp. 78, 103*]

ROBERTS, John Milton, and GREGOR, Thomas
1971   Privacy: a cultural view. *In* Pennock and Chapman 1971: 199–225. [*p. 112*]

ROBINSON, Alma
1976   The seized treasures of Asante. *New Society* 38: 69–71. [*p. 65*]

ROBINSON, Scott S.
1973   The declaration of Barbados: for the liberation of the Indians. *Current anthropology* 14: 267–70. [*p. 170*]

ROCHFORD, Gerard
1974   Violating the principle of informed consent. *Bulletin of the British Psychological Society* 27: 485–92. [*p. 95*]

ROETHLISBERGER, Fritz Jukes, and DICKSON, William John
1939   Management and the worker. Cambridge, Mass.; Harvard University Press. xxiv, 615 pp. [*p. 40*]

ROSENHAN, David L.
1973   On being sane in insane places. *Science* 179: 250–58. [*p. 124*]

ROSENTHAL, Robert, and JACOBSON, Lenore
1968   Pygmalion in the classroom: teacher expectation and pupils' intellectual development. New York; Holt, Rinehart and Winston. xiii, 240 pp. [*p. 153*]

ROTH, Julius Alfred
1959   Dangerous and difficult enterprise? *American sociological review* 24: 398. [*p. 121*]

ROY, Donald F.
1952   Quota restriction and goldbricking in a machine shop. *American journal of sociology* 57: 427–42. [*p. 121*]
1953   Work satisfaction and social reward in quota achievement: an analysis of piecework incentive. *American sociological review* 18: 507–14. [*p. 121*]
1954   Efficiency and 'The fix': informal intergroup relations in a piecework machine shop. *American journal of sociology* 60: 255–66. [*p. 121*]
1965   The role of the researcher in the study of social conflict: a theory of protective distortion of response. *Human organization* 24: 262–71. [*p. 115*]

RUEBHAUSEN, Oscar M., and BRIM, Orville Gilbert, jr
1965   Privacy and behavioral research. *Columbia law review* 65: 1184–211. [*pp. 73, 127, 185*]

RULE, James Bernard
1973   Private lives and public surveillance. London; Allen Lane. 382 pp. [*p. 166*]

RYŃKIEWICH, Michael Allen, and SPRADLEY, James Phillip
1976   *Editors.* Ethics and anthropology: dilemmas in fieldwork. New York; Wiley. xi, 186 pp. [*p. 161*]

SABERWAL, Satish
1968   The problem. *Seminar* 112: 12–13. *Reprinted in* Weaver, T. 1973b: 174–7. [*pp. 57, 59, 181*]

SAKSENA, Ram Narain
1967   Sociology in India. *In* UNNITHAN, Thottamon Kantankesavan Narayanan, et al., eds. Sociology for India. New Delhi; Prentice-Hall of India. Pp. 61–70. [*pp. 67–8*]

SARAN, Awadh Kishore
1958   India. *In* ROUCEK, Joseph Slabey, ed. Contemporary sociology. New York; Philosophical Library. Pp. 1013–34. [*p. 68*]

SAVIN, Harris Benjamin
1973a   Professors and psychological researchers: conflicting values in conflicting roles. *Cognition* 2: 147–9. [*p. 130*]
1973b   Ethics for gods and men. *Cognition* 2: 257. [*p. 130*]

SCHULTZ, Duane Philip
1969   The human subject in psychological research. *Psychological bulletin* 72: 214–28. [*pp. 24, 92, 95, 102*]

SHALLICE, T.
1972   The Ulster depth interrogation techniques and their relation

to sensory deprivation research. *Cognition* 1: 385–405.
[*p. 83*]

SHAW, Kenneth
1977   The dilemma of the Soviet sociologist. *New society* 40: 392–3.
[*p. 186*]

SHILS, Edward Albert
1956   The torment of secrecy: the background and consequences
of American security policies. Glencoe, Ill.; Free Press. 238
pp. [*p. 187*]
1959   Social inquiry and the autonomy of the individual. *In*
LERNER, Daniel, ed. The human meaning of the social
sciences. New York; Meridian Books. Pp. 114–57. [*pp. 97,
166*]
1967   Privacy and power. *In* POOL, Ithiel de Sola, ed. Contemporary
political science: toward empirical theory. New York;
McGraw-Hill. Pp. 228–76. [*p. 69*]
1975   The confidentiality and anonymity of assessment. *Minerva*
13: 135–51. [*p. 185*]

SHULMAN, Arthur David, and BERMAN, Harry J.
1974   On Berscheid et al. *American psychologist* 29: 473–4.
[*p. 94*]

SIEGHART, Paul
1976   Privacy and computers. London; Latimer New Dimensions.
viii, 228 pp. [*p. 184*]

SIMMEL, Arnold
1968   Privacy. *In* SILLS, David Lawrence, ed. International encyclopedia of the social sciences. Vol. 12. New York; Macmillan
and Free Press. Pp. 480–87. [*p. 112*]

SINCLAIR, John
1791–1799 *Editor*. The statistical account of Scotland. Edinburgh. 21
vols. [*p. 28*]

SINGH, Yogendra
1968   Sociological issues. *Seminar* 112: 25–9. [*p. 57*]

SINICK, Daniel
1954   Comments on 'The use of human subjects in psychological
research'. *American psychologist* 9: 589. [*p. 163*]

SISSONS, Mary
1971   The psychology of social class. *In* OPEN UNIVERSITY.
Understanding society: a foundation course. Units 14–18:
Money, wealth and class. Bletchley; Open University Press.
Pp. 111–31. [*p. 99*]

SJOBERG, Gideon
1967a   Project Camelot: selected reactions and personal reflections. *In* Sjoberg 1967b: 141–61. [*p. 46*]
1967b   *Editor.* Ethics, politics, and social research. Cambridge, Mass.; Schenkman. xvii, 358 pp.
1975   Politics, ethics and evaluation research. *In* GUTTENTAG, Marcia, and STRUENING, Elmer L., eds. Handbook of evaluation research. Vol. 2. Beverly Hills; Sage. Pp. 29–51. [*p. 82*]

SJOBERG, Gideon, and NETT, Roger
1968   A methodology for social research. New York; Harper and Row. x, 355 pp. [*p. 20*]

SMITH, Herman W.
1975   Strategies of social research: the methodological imagination. Englewood Cliffs, NJ; Prentice-Hall. xxi, 423 pp. [*p. 20*]

SOCIETY FOR APPLIED ANTHROPOLOGY
1963   Statement on ethics. *Human organization* 22: 237. [*p. 161*]

SOLOMON ISLANDS. Ministry of Education and Cultural Affairs
1976   Information for research workers in the Solomon Islands. *Current anthropology* 17: 163–4. [*p. 59*]

SPIRO, Herbert J.
1971   Privacy in comparative perspective. *In* Pennock and Chapman 1971: 121–48. [*p. 112*]

STAPLES, Robert
1973   What is Black sociology? Toward a sociology of Black liberation. *In* Ladner 1973: 161–72. [*p. 69*]

STARR, Paul D.
1977   Social science for sale. *New society* 41: 652–4. [*pp. 82, 163*]

STAVENHAGEN, Rodolfo
1971   Decolonializing applied social sciences. *Human organization* 30: 333–57. [*p. 174*]

STOCKING, George Ward, jr
1968   Race, culture, and evolution: essays in the history of anthropology. New York; Free Press. xix, 380 pp. [*p. 128*]

STRATHERN, Andrew
1974   Editorial: visiting research workers and students. *Man in New Guinea* 6 (3): 4–5. [*p. 71*]

STREET, James Harry
1969   Social science research in Paraguay: current status and future opportunities. *In* Blair et al. 1969: 81–101. [*p. 156*]

SULLIVAN, David S., and DEIKER, Thomas E.
1973   Subject-experimenter perceptions of ethical issues in human research. *American psychologist* 28: 587–91. [*p. 20*]

TAJFEL, Henri
1977   Social psychology and social reality. *New society* 39: 653–4. [*p. 101*]

TALYAGA, Kundapen
1974   Should we allow research workers into the Enga District? *Man in New Guinea* 6 (4): 17. [*p. 170*]

THOMPSON, David Michael
1967   The 1851 religious census: problems and possibilities. *Victorian studies* 11: 87–97. [*p. 90*]
1972   Nonconformity in the nineteenth century. London; Routledge and Kegan Paul. xiv, 281 pp. [*p. 90*]

THOMPSON, Edward Palmer
1967   The political education of Henry Mayhew. *Victorian studies* 11: 41–62. [*p. 29*]

Times
1977   Ethics hearing over Marxism charges. *Times* (London) 5 October, p. 4. [*p. 162*]

TUCHMAN, Sam, and COFFIN, Thomas E.
1971   The influence of election night television broadcasts in a close election. *Public opinion quarterly* 35: 315–26. [*p. 168*]

TURNBULL, Colin Macmillan
1972   The mountain people. New York; Simon and Schuster. 309 pp. [*p. 176*]

UBEROI, Jitendra Pal Singh
1968   Science and swaraj. *Contributions to Indian sociology* n.s. 2: 119–23. [*p. 57*]

UNITED STATES, Office of Science and Technology
1967   Privacy and behavioral research. Washington, DC; Government Printing Office, v, 30 pp. [*p. 164*]

UNITED STATES, Office of the Surgeon General
1967   Surgeon General's directives on human experimentation. *American psychologist* 22: 350–55. [*p. 164*]

UNIVERSITY OF PAPUA NEW GUINEA
1975   Procedures for the affiliation of foreign research workers in Papua New Guinea. *Research in Melanesia* 1 (3–4): 16–17. [*pp. 59–60*]

VAN DEN BERGHE, Pierre Louis
1964   Caneville: the social structure of a South African town. Middletown, Conn.; Wesleyan University Press. x, 276 pp. [*p. 152*]
1967   Research in South Africa: the story of my experiences with tyranny. *In* Sjoberg 1967b: 183–97. [*p. 151*]
1973   The Montreal affair: revolution or racism. *In* Weaver, T. 1973b: 171–2. [*p. 67*]
VARGUS, Brian S.
1971   On sociological exploitation: why the guinea pig sometimes bites. *Social problems* 19: 238–48. [*p. 87*]
VARMA, Baidya Nath
1967   Contributions of qualitative research for macroscopic quantitative data. *Annals of the New York Academy of Sciences* 136: 523–46. [*p. 116*]
VAUGHAN, Ted Ray
1967   Governmental intervention in social research: political and ethical dimensions in the Wichita jury recordings. *In* Sjoberg 1967b: 50–77. [*p. 127*]
VIDICH, Arthur Joseph, and BENSMAN, Joseph
1954   The validity of field data. *Human organization* 13 (1): 20–27. [*p. 54*]
1968   Small town in mass society. Rev. ed. Princeton, NJ; Princeton University Press. xxviii, 493 pp. [*pp. 71, 136*]
VINACKE, William Edgar
1954   Deceiving experimental subjects. *American psychologist* 9: 155. [*p. 93*]

WALLIS, Roy
1976   The road to total freedom: a sociological analysis of Scientology. London; Heinemann. xiv, 282 pp. [*p. 143*]
1977   The moral career of a research project. *In* BELL, Colin, and NEWBY, Howard, eds. Doing sociological research. London; Allen and Unwin. Pp. 149–69. [*p. 143*]
WALSH, John
1971   National Academy of Sciences – awkward moments at the meeting. *Science* 172: 539–41. [*p. 85*]
WARD, Lester Frank
1906   Applied sociology: a treatise on the conscious improvement of society by society. Boston; Ginn. xviii, 384 pp. [*p. 44*]

WARNER, Malcolm, and STONE, Michael
1970   The data bank society: organizations, computers and social freedom. London; Allen and Unwin. 244 pp. [*pp. 56, 112*]

WARNER, William Lloyd, and DAVIS, Allison
1939   A comparative study of American caste. *In* THOMPSON, Edgar Tristram, ed. Race relations and the race problem. Durham, NC; Duke University Press. Pp. 219–45. [*p. 118*]

WARWICK, Donald P.
1975   Tearoom trade: means and ends in social research. *In* Humphreys 1975: 191–212. [*p. 123*]

WATERMAN, Alan S.
1974   The civil liberties of the participants in psychological research. *American psychologist* 29: 470–71. [*p. 94*]

WAX, Murray L.
1977   On fieldworkers and those exposed to fieldwork: federal regulations and moral issues. *Human organization* 36: 321–8. [*p. 164*]

WAX, Rosalie Hankey
1952   Field methods and techniques: reciprocity as a field technique. *Human organization* 11 (3): 34–7. [*p. 55*]
1971   Doing fieldwork: warnings and advice. Chicago; University of Chicago Press. x, 395 pp. [*p. 29*]

WEAVER, Sally Mae
1971   A challenge to anthropological inquiry. *Human organization* 30: 99–100. [*p. 72*]

WEAVER, Thomas
1973a   Toward an anthropological statement of relevance. *In* Weaver, T. 1973b: 1–4. [*p. 172*]
1973b   *Editor.* To see ourselves: anthropology and modern social issues. Glenview; Scott Foresman. 485 pp.

WEBB, Eugene John, and others
1966   Unobtrusive measures: nonreactive research in the social sciences. Chicago; Rand McNally. xii, 225 pp. [*p. 121*]

WEEKS, Sheldon
1975   Margaret Mead revisited. *Research in Melanesia* 1 (3–4): 30–35. [*p. 71*]

WEICK, Karl E.
1968   Systematic observational methods. *In* Lindzey and Aronson 1968: 357–451. [*p. 121*]

WEST, James
1945   Plainville, U.S.A. New York; Columbia University Press.
          xviii, 238 pp. [*p. 141*]
WESTERN, John Stuart
1975   Investigators, subjects and social research. *Australian and
          New Zealand journal of sociology* 11 (3): 2–9. [*p. 137*]
WESTIN, Alan Furman, and BAKER, Michael A.
1974   Data banks in a free society. *See* NATIONAL ACADEMY OF
          SCIENCES.
WHYTE, William Foote
1941   Corner boys: a study of clique behavior. *American journal of
          sociology* 46: 647–64. [*p. 107*]
1955   Street corner society: the social structure of an Italian slum.
          2nd ed. Chicago; University of Chicago Press. xx, 364 pp.
          [*p. 113*]
1959   Man and organization: three problems in human relations in
          industry. Homewood, Ill.; Irwin. vii, 104 pp. [*p. 151*]
WILLIAMS, James G. L., and OUREN, Louis H.
1976   Experimenting on humans. *Bulletin of the British Psycholo-
          gical Society* 29: 334–8. [*p. 160*]
WILSON, Godfrey Baldwin
1941 & 1942 An essay on the economics of detribalization in Northern
          Rhodesia. Livingstone; Rhodes-Livingstone Institute. 2 parts.
          [*p. 39*]
WILSON, Peter Joseph, and others
1975   More thoughts on the Ik and anthropology. *Current anthro-
          pology* 16: 343–58. [*pp. 162, 176*]
WOLF, Eleanor Paperno
1964   Some questions about community self-surveys: when ama-
          teurs conduct research. *Human organization* 23: 85–9.
          [*p. 51*]
WONG SIU-LUN
1975   Social enquiries in the People's Republic of China. *Sociology*
          9: 459–76. [*p. 186*]
WORCESTER, Robert M.
1972   Corporate image research. *In* WORCESTER, R. M., ed. Con-
          sumer market research handbook. London; McGraw-Hill.
          Pp. 505–18. [*p. 50*]
WRAITH, Ronald
1977   Open government: the British interpretation. London; Royal
          Institute of Public Administration. 74 pp. [*p. 185*]

YOUNG, Michael Willis
1975   History or nothing? *Research in Melanesia* 1 (1): 50–59. [*p. 65*]
YOUNGER, Kenneth
1972   *Chairman.* Report of the committee on privacy. London; HMSO. xi, 350 pp. Cmnd. 5012. [*p. 184*]

ZANNA, Mark Peter, and others
1975   Pygmalion and Galatea: the interactive effect of teacher and student expectancies. *Journal of experimental social psychology* 11: 279–87. [*p. 154*]
ZEISEL, Hans
1971   Toward a history of sociography. *In* JAHODA, Marie, and others. Marienthal: the sociography of an unemployed community. Chicago; Aldine. Pp. 99–125. [*p. 27*]
ZIMBARDO, Philip George
1973   On the ethics of intervention in human psychological research: with special reference to the Stanford prison experiment. *Cognition* 2: 243–56. [*pp. 129, 130, 132*]
ZIMBARDO, Philip George, and others
1973   The mind is a formidable jailer: a Pirandellian prison. *New York times magazine* 8 April, Section 6: 38–60. [*pp. 92, 129*]

ØYEN, Ørjar
1976   Social research and the development of privacy: a review of the Norwegian development. *Acta sociologica* 19: 249–62. [*p. 184*]

Index

Page references to citations are shown under the author's name in the list of References, at the end of each item, and are not repeated in this Index

DATE DUE

FEB 4 1986		
APR 13 1986		
MAY 1 2 1995		